MISUNDERSTANDING NEWS AUDIENCES

Misunderstanding News Audiences interrogates the prevailing myths around the impact of the Internet and social media on news consumption and democracy. The book draws on a broad range of comparative research into audience engagement with news, across different geographic regions, to provide insight into the experience of news audiences in the twenty-first century.

From its inception, it was imagined that the Internet would benignly transform the nature of news media and its consumers. There were predictions that it would, for example, break up news oligarchies, improve plurality and diversity through news personalisation, create genuine social solidarity online, and increase political awareness and participation among citizens. However, this book finds that, while mainstream news media is still the major source of news, the new media environment appears to lead to greater polarisation between news junkies and news avoiders, and to greater political polarisation. The authors also argue that the dominant role of the USA in the field of news audience research has created myths about a global news audience, which obscures the importance of national context as a major explanation for news exposure differences.

Misunderstanding News Audiences presents an important analysis of findings from recent audience studies and, in doing so, encourages readers to re-evaluate popular beliefs about the influence of the Internet on news consumption and democracy in the West.

Eiri Elvestad is Associate Professor of Sociology at the University College of Southeast Norway. She is the author of two books, including one concerned with Norwegian adolescents' relationship to news, and she has written several articles in international journals about the changing media environment and news exposure.

Angela Phillips is Professor of Journalism at Goldsmiths, University of London, UK. She worked as a journalist for print and online publications, as well as in broadcasting, before focusing on academic research in ethical working practices and news audiences. Her last book was *Journalism in Context* (2015).

COMMUNICATION AND SOCIETY

Series Editor: James Curran

This series encompasses the broad field of media and cultural studies. Its main concerns are the media and the public sphere: on whether the media empower or fail to empower popular forces in society; media organisations and public policy; the political and social consequences of media campaigns; and the role of media entertainment, ranging from potboilers and the human-interest story to rock music and TV sport.

For a complete list of titles in this series, please see: https://www.routledge.com/series/SE0130

MISUNDERSTANDING NEWS AUDIENCES

Seven Myths of the Social Media Era

Eiri Elvestad and Angela Phillips

Routledge
Taylor & Francis Group

LONDON AND NEW YORK

First published 2018
by Routledge
2 Park Square, Milton Park, Abingdon, Oxon OX14 4RN

and by Routledge
711 Third Avenue, New York, NY 10017

Routledge is an imprint of the Taylor & Francis Group, an informa business

British Library Cataloguing in Publication Data
A catalogue record for this book is available from the British Library

Library of Congress Cataloging in Publication Data
Names: Elvestad, Eiri, author. | Phillips, Angela, author.
Title: Misunderstanding news audiences : seven myths of the social media era / Eiri Elvestad and Angela Phillips.
Description: New York : Routledge : Abingdon, Oxon, 2018. | Includes bibliographical references and index.Identifiers: LCCN 2017047028 | ISBN 9781138215184 (hardback : alk. paper) | ISBN 9781138215191 (pbk. : alk. paper) | ISBN 9781315444369 (ebook)
Subjects: LCSH: News audiences--History--21st century. | Journalism--History--21st century. | Journalism--Technological innovations. | Social media.
Classification: LCC PN4784.N48 E48 2018 | DDC 302.23--dc23
LC record available at https://lccn.loc.gov/2017047028

ISBN: 978-1-138-21518-4 (hbk)
ISBN: 978-1-138-21519-1 (pbk)
ISBN: 978-1-315-44436-9 (ebk)

Typeset in Bembo
by Taylor & Francis Books

CONTENTS

FIGURES

ACKNOWLEDGEMENTS

We owe thanks to many people but first of all to Mira Feuerstein who initiated our research project into students' use of news in 2013 and brought us together. Thank you also to Aeron Davis, Olivia Solon, Natalie Fenton, Terry Kirby and Arild Danielsen for reading early drafts, and to the anonymous reviewers who read the proposal and the whole manuscript and gave useful comments. And finally to Mike and Even for listening, discussing, passing on links, reading drafts and everything else. This book has been a true collaboration. Like all good collaborations it has been by turns infuriating and enlightening and we have been for each other perhaps the most exacting critics of all. We both look forward to working together in the future.

1

INTRODUCTION

News audiences, and the myths of the social media era

We started out to produce a book that would de-bunk some of the prevailing myths about the Internet and its impact on news audiences. By the time we finished, we found ourselves engaged in drawing together the empirical and intellectual underpinning of one of the most important debates of our time, as concerns that had been circulating in the academic community, about the impact of personalised information systems on democracy, were catapulted into the mainstream by a series of elections across Europe and the USA.

Our initial concern had been to explore a gap in the literature. While there was a great deal of research on the use of different platforms to find news, there seemed to be little information about what news was being found there, where it came from and who was producing it. We started our own research (with Mira Feuerstein) into students' use of news in three national contexts (Elvestad, Phillips, & Feuerstein, 2017). This was a small study, using mixed methods, carried out in 2014.[1] Our intention was to examine the ways in which students access news, what news sources they trusted, what sources they tended to use, and whether and under what circumstances they interacted with news. Alongside surveys we carried out in-depth interviews with students who were selected to produce a varied sample in terms of study programme, gender, age, and ethnicity. We refer to the in-depth interviews with the 12 Norwegian and 12 UK students in the study in this book as "our interviews". We are of course aware that this is a small sample but where we find these interviews help to provide insight into news audiences and democracy in the social media era, we have included them.

Our study raised many questions, which we went on to address through a far-reaching review of secondary literature (articles, books, reports etc.) and data from the increasing range of research in the field of news audiences. While we were working, it became clear that our research was just a small stitch in an ever-growing tapestry of work following changes in the way in which people were accessing, circulating and using news. This new research, adding to some older work that foreshadowed the changes, was clearly overturning many of the utopian assumptions that had been made about the impact of the Internet on news and democracy.

From its inception, a mythical assumption of the benignly transformative and democratic nature of the Internet, drawn from its origins as a collaborative tool, had permeated discussion of its possible impact on news audiences and democracy. From that foundational misconception, many other myths had developed about the collapse of trust in "mainstream" news; the development of new forms of news information un-corrupted by power; and the emergence of a more collaborative form of journalism, powered by a democratically engaged, globally aware audience. In practice, as we can now see, the Internet has been shaped by globalisation and the power of free market economics into a means by which a handful of companies have achieved world dominance, autocratic governments have increased their powers of surveillance, and communication options for anti-democratic organisations have been enabled outside the normative structures of the mainstream.

This is not to suggest that the Internet as a technology does not have democratic potential. At the heart of every myth there lies a kernel of truth, but that kernel has been layered beneath distortions and misunderstandings which have had far-reaching and often totally unexpected consequences. This book will use the evidence provided by audience studies to reflect on these misunderstandings and to demonstrate how the impact of untrammelled market pressures, allied to technical change, has affected the way in which people find out about information that is important to them, and what that means for the way in which they understand themselves, the society in which they live, their place in the global order and how they then engage as deliberative citizens.

The advent of new systems for circulating news and information via the Internet and on social media inevitably changed old habits of news engagement and, as a result, it has been accompanied by a wealth of speculation and a growing research literature. However, the speculation has too often been entirely disconnected from the research, allowing for the development of narratives that assumed a new world in which old media hierarchies are disappearing and audiences have become "prosumers" (Tapscott, 1998; Toffler, 1970) actively involved in the production, distribution and consumption of news.

Many of these assumptions pre-dated or ignored research findings that might have thrown light on developments. Where research has been used, it is often US research, much of it produced by media companies, which maps uneasily onto different media and political systems. Yet too often lessons learned are assumed to be directly transferable. While US research has much to tell the rest of the world about what might happen elsewhere, it needs to be interrogated carefully, not taken as a blueprint. Comparative research, which takes national differences into account, often tells a different story about the interaction between policy, democracy and the media.

Models of democracy

In this book we look carefully at the research on news audiences. We focus mainly on democracies but we recognise that they are not all the same. Different normative models of democracy have different expectations of citizen engagement (e.g. Ferree, Gamson, Gerhards & Rucht, 2002) as well as different media systems (Hallin & Mancini, 2004). If we are to truly understand the impact of new media forms on citizen involvement and deliberation, then we need to look at them as media ecologies in which technology plays one part alongside public policy and legal frameworks.

We divide models of democracy very broadly into liberal (competitive or rational choice) like that in the USA, and participatory and deliberative, such as that in Northern European countries.[2] These normative models of democracy expect participation from citizens on different levels, require different models of media and therefore have different approaches to the role of law making and regulation. In the US competitive model of democracy, the central mechanism for securing the primacy of common good is through competitive elections, while for countries with a participatory model of democracy, citizens' participation in public life, both outside and within political parties, is also important (Strömbäck, 2005).

These two models of democracy also have different normative expectations of citizens' political knowledge and engagement. The competitive model expects citizens to have "clear opinions of societal problems; knowledge of who has had power; knowledge about the record of the office holders; knowledge about party platforms and promises" (Strömbäck, 2005, p. 337). On the other hand, the participatory model has normative expectations of citizens who are more trustful and cooperative, are more interested in politics, have a high degree of knowledge about how to influence public life, clear opinions of societal problems and the relevant factual information to form opinions about them (Strömbäck, 2005, p. 337).

In most of Europe, proportional, multi-party systems of representation allow voters to choose the candidate that most closely represents their views. Coalition government is the norm and debate and compromise is built into systems that require constant negotiation with partners. In the Nordic countries, for example, there is an expectation that the media will contribute to citizen participation in political processes in between elections. In these countries there is more media regulation aimed at encouraging citizens to participate in the political process. In the US model of democracy, critical decisions about the choice of candidates take place within the two major parties and it is through the system of party primaries that presidential candidates emerge, offering a winner-takes-all choice to the electorate and little opportunity for impact on political decisions between elections. Here, media regulation for citizen involvement is largely absent, the information needs of citizens are left to the market, and citizen participation tends to be seen as a choice rather than an obligation or duty.

Media systems also differ. As Hallin and Mancini (2004) observed, Southern European media organisation is quite unlike that of Nordic countries even though they mostly have systems of proportional representation. In Southern Europe, the "polarised pluralist" system is based on political parallelism and media represent differing political positions from which they argue a case rather than report it. In the Nordic countries, a "democratic corporatist" media system (Hallin & Mancini, 2004) combines a degree of political parallelism with professionalisation reminiscent of US print media, alongside public service broadcasting. The UK has a competitive model of democracy, in common with the USA, but a hybrid media system in which the press is openly partisan and unregulated whereas broadcasting (both public and private) is bound by rules of impartiality.

In spite of these differences, all of these democratic systems rely on the idea of an informed citizen. The competitive, or rational choice, democracy model implies that citizens need to have enough information to be able to decide between competing elites in elections, but they do not necessarily have to follow the political processes closely in between elections. The "burglar alarm" (Zaller, 2003) function will be enough to keep them informed about emergency matters. This model presupposes an electorate that is happy to leave governing to political parties and sees little role for citizens in shaping public policy.

In participative or deliberative models, the role of media in spreading information assumes that citizens need to be alert to the actions of government; that public pressure from citizens has a meaningful role to play in shaping policy; and that there needs to be systems both for circulating information and for public deliberation in order to facilitate this process. Habermas (1989) describes such a system as a "public sphere" in which citizens can come together to deliberate without coercion, and the news media provide the means by which information can be spread, so that such deliberation can take place. In this model:

> Democratic public discourse does not depend on pre-existing harmony or similarity among citizens but rather on the ability to create meaningful discourses across lines of difference.
>
> *(Calhoun, 1988, p. 220)*

Habermas noted that a true public sphere could only come into being if the full range of differing views are actually accessible to all, a state of grace that he found unlikely in a capitalist economy, in which news media are dominated by sectional interests and elites are intertwined with media interests. His original paper has been criticised from a number of positions for its failure to recognise the complexity of media systems and the dynamic between the centre and periphery (Peters, 1993); for being too pessimistic about the possibilities of regulation (Benson, 2009); and for conceptualising such a sphere in too rigid a fashion so that it ignores the potential impact of radical campaigning and social movements on the structures he describes (Fraser, 1990). Nevertheless, in spite of these critiques and of his reformulation of this model, the idea of a plural and diverse system of news provision, free from government interference, provides a benchmark for the empirical investigation of news media within a democracy (Benson, 2004).

Plurality and diversity

In order to critique any system using these measures it is necessary to define what is meant by plurality and diversity, terms that are generally used rather loosely with little attention to the conditions in which either can actually emerge. Des Freedman (2008) describes "plurality" as relating to media structures that enable a variety of views whereas "diversity", he suggests, relates to the content of the media and refers to the variety of people who speak and the expression of a variety of opinions (p. 72). The liberal assumption has been that, provided there is plurality in the media market, diversity should follow. Generally speaking, liberal scholars and policy makers have used this conception of plurality as a benchmark against which to measure the democratic health of media systems.

However, market forces have historically tended to operate against plurality. After the introduction of new media technologies there is often a brief flowering of pluralism (Phillips, 2018), but market leaders have tended to become monopoly or near-monopoly providers and to dominate the market (Bourdieu, 1998; Bourdieu, 2005; McChesney & Nichols, 2011). The move towards consolidation and market dominance happened slowly in the print media so the use of market regulation has been less interventionist, particularly in the UK and the USA. It happened very quickly in the case of the telegraph, radio and television (Carey, 1983; Flichy, 1999; McChesney & Nichols, 2011; Wu, 2010), and the differing examples of state action taken to address monopoly formation informs the kinds of action which could be considered today when contemplating the speedy adoption of the Internet as a news channel.

In Europe, the response to the growth of a telegraph monopoly was to nationalise. In the USA, a self-regulating monopoly was formed. Similarly, with the advent of broadcasting, nationalisation and then regulatory intervention to enforce "fairness" became the norm across European democracies. Whether in public or private hands, broadcasters were either enjoined to be neutral or "balanced" in the expression of political views, or broadcasting licences were used to ensure a balance of viewpoints. These values are enshrined in article 11 of the European Union Charter of Fundamental Rights that guarantees: "the freedom and *pluralism* of the media".

Typically, the establishment of plurality involved legislation against monopoly formation and, in broadcasting, regulation for fairness in representation and impartiality in delivery. In some cases it also involves subsidies to encourage alternative providers. In Belgium, legislation ensures that different language communities are represented. In Holland, different religious and social groups are guaranteed representation on broadcast media. In France, subsidy ensures that marginal political voices are heard; and in Italy, public broadcasting channels are divided among the dominant political parties (Hallin & Mancini, 2004).

The American Constitution is silent on the question of plurality; it merely prohibits: "infringing on the freedom of the press". Nevertheless, in 1949, in the aftermath of the Second World War, the Federal Communications Commission of the United States introduced a Fairness Doctrine to ensure that broadcast licensees covered political issues even-handedly; but this came under fire from conservatives as an attack on press freedom and was finally revoked in 1987 at the advent of cable television. The argument was that cable removed the problem of scarcity (Patterson, 2000). If there were now hundreds of channels to choose from, market forces should be able to ensure that viewers could select the programmes that they wanted from a wide variety of providers. This change to the system meant that the USA moved decisively away from any attempt to manage plurality and as such, it provides a media model that is quite distinct from those in most other democracies and a means of comparing change between more managed systems and free market systems. This difference is critical for understanding news consumption as it now is but also for imagining a different future, if, for example, Europe chooses to impose regulation on new media systems as it has done in the past.

For liberal media theorists, who see choice-making as inherently empowering and audiences as: "rational and purposeful agents who work, individually and collectively, to choose among available options to best meet their perceived personal and social needs" (Meyrowitz, 2008, p. 649), the Internet appears to be an excellent means of enabling rational choice and thereby increasing plurality via demand. Any downsides in the distribution of information and benefits are merely the price to be paid for individual freedom. Indeed, the existence of the Internet pretty much ended the debate in the USA about how to ensure plurality and diversity because both concepts depend on a market that provides untrammelled opportunity and choice. Since access to the Internet is cheap, the argument goes, the old concern that: "Freedom of the press is only guaranteed to those who own one" (Liebling, 1960), no longer applies. So the Internet was hailed as a networked public sphere (Benkler, 2006) in which everyone would be able to edit their own news (Negroponte, 1995, p. 153).

At times, this liberal approach seems indistinguishable from that of radical cultural theorists who suggest that, although the mass media will inevitably reflect the views of the elite, networked audiences can subvert such messages and create alternative readings which undermine power elites (Fiske, 1992; Jenkins, 2006). By this account, the Internet, by empowering the audience and increasing involvement in news-making and reporting, has increased plurality and diversity. Lance Bennett (2008) suggests that the options available online have produced a new kind of participative or "actualising" citizenship in place of the older form of "dutiful" citizenship (see also Bennett, Wells, & Allison, 2009). As a result, it is argued, the messages of the elite are capable of being diluted or overturned or at the very least the voices of underrepresented groups are heard more loudly (Hind, 2010). It could be argued that the rise of right-wing populism and the fragmentation of liberal centrist politics is evidence of this change.

All these approaches however are questioned by critical scholars for their failure to fully recognise that the power of ownership will inevitably distort the range of views that it is possible to hear. For critical scholars, concerned with participative or deliberative democracy, the argument that plurality by itself provides diversity of opinion has not been demonstrated. They point to the ways in which the power of global corporations has already undermined the original egalitarian promise of the Internet and found new ways to dominate the news narrative (Curran et al., 2013; McChesney, 2014).

This is because the design and operation of search engines favours the biggest players (Hindman, 2009). So free markets continue to distort choice by favouring the popular over the serious; information flows are distorted and power elites are still in control online. In other words, it doesn't matter how much information is out there, if, for the individual, choice is still limited. Diversity of opportunity to publish may not increase the diversity of information received; indeed, social media may well be reducing choice in some instances. All of these debates also need to be seen in the context of media systems that differ from one country to another and fluctuating levels of trust in the more traditional news media.

Plan of the book

In each chapter we take on one of the prevailing myths about the Internet and news audiences. In Chapter 2 "Personalisation is Democratisation", we consider whether the personalisation of news choices has improved the diversity of news. While those who share more arcane interests gain a great deal from the participative and distributed nature of the Internet, when it comes to news, it is the biggest media players, or those with sufficient understanding of the technology to manipulate the results, that get to the top of the search engines and users tend to go to the most popular options for their news updates. By squeezing out the middle-sized players Hindman (2009) argues, the Internet reduces the diversity of information available for the average person and also tends to divide people into groups of media haves and have-nots (Prior, 2007), while those who are engaged with news become increasingly politically polarised (Pariser, 2011; Sunstein, 2009).

As we discuss in Chapter 3 "We Are All Journalists Now", the idea of networked citizen journalists participating in an idealised public sphere has not come to pass. Indeed, Internet technologies have undermined the means by which news organisations pay for reporting and has reduced the number of news-gathering organisations while, at the same time, possibilities for commenting on the news are dispersed and diluted and only the most popular rise to the top.

> In a host of areas, from political news to blogging to issue advocacy... online speech follows winners-take-all patterns. Paradoxically the extreme "openness" of the Internet has fuelled the creation of new political elites
>
> *(Hindman, 2009, p. 4)*

These new political elites still include most of the old established mass media companies, but as we explain in Chapter 4 "The Wisdom of Crowds?", they also include the new technology billionaires who can now buy influence via interventions in the ownership, or increasingly, in the control, of news distribution. Robert Mercer, CEO of hedge fund Renaissance Technologies, used his money and his technological know-how to back right-wing political candidates in the USA and to bank-roll media such as the *Breitbart News Network*. Whereas Amazon CEO, Jeff Bezos, put his money and technical support into the liberal-leaning *Washington Post*.

This algorithmic favouring of an elite was noted by Clay Shirky, who pointed out in a blog about "power law distributions" that the most popular sites stay at the top of the search returns, where they are always easier to find than new sites, thereby ensuring that their popularity is continually reinforced in comparison to newer entrants. He was however unperturbed by this finding:

> Given the ubiquity of power law distributions, asking whether there is inequality in the weblog world (or indeed almost any social system) is the wrong question, since the answer will always be yes. The question to ask is: "Is the inequality fair?"
>
> *(Shirky, 2003)*

The separation of "fairness" and "equality" goes to the heart of the differences in approach between those who favour the market as a mechanism for democracy and those who see regulation of the market as a necessary pre-condition for democracy. The rise of the Internet and the concentration of power in the hands of a small number of media giants means that American free market assumptions can now be exported across the world, where in the past the operation of political systems and media systems allowed for greater intervention at national level.

In Chapter 5 "Globalisation", we consider the belief that the Internet would make us all global citizens. In fact, we find that for most people, news is rarely international; it is local or national. As the range of available information has grown, there is little evidence that individuals have a more global news diet. In this context, in Chapter 6 "Communities Online are Replacing Communities Offline", we examine the assumption that the mass media play a role in either integrating societies or fragmenting them. Early predictions assumed that the ability to make contact with like-minded people online would undo some of the concerns raised by Robert Putnam in his book, *Bowling Alone* (2000), that mass media, in particular television, was undermining civic life. The research is not conclusive but the most recent findings suggest that the Internet is producing greater polarisation so that although it creates more group bonding, which engages people in civic action, it may be undermining the bridging activity that links citizens across barriers of difference.

The impact of differing systems, we argue, is fundamental to the trust that audiences invest in their news media and in Chapter 7 "The End of Trust in Mainstream Media", we look at comparative studies of trust and find that mainstream, bridging media are still the most trusted sources of news information, when compared with native online or social media sources (Newman, Fletcher, Kalogeropoulos, & Nielsen, 2017).[3] We are conscious that studies of trust are complicated by the lack of any agreed definition of media trust but, broadly speaking, in those countries with public broadcasting and media regulation, there are higher levels of trust and lower use of social media as the main means for distributing news. There are also better-informed audiences (Aalberg & Curran, 2012). Trust in media tends to be higher in those countries where there is also trust in other institutions, so it is not easy to discover which (if either) is the causal factor, but, given plummeting levels of trust in bridging media, in a number of countries, we examine the factors used by audiences themselves to assess trust.

Finally, in Chapter 8 "The Net Generation will Revolutionise the Way we Relate to News", we look to the future through the lens of generational research on media consumption and ask whether studies looking at the behaviour of young "digital natives" will tell us anything about how news consumption is likely to develop in the future. We conclude that on the whole, news consumption will continue to change over a lifetime, that the consumption patterns of the youngest news consumers are probably not the best predictors of the future, and that assumptions about the existence of a generation of "digital natives" that differ markedly from older generations is misconceived and potentially dangerous in its failure to recognise that differences within generations are as important as those between them.

Perhaps the most important thing that we draw from this work is a concern about the role of governance and law in the development of news media. Citizens in most democratic nation states have, until now, had some degree of democratic control over plurality in television and newspapers, but they have none over the means by which growing numbers of citizens access news online and via social media. The experience of news audiences will, in the future, depend as much on the way in which the clash of ideologies between liberal and participatory democracy plays out, as it will on any further changes in the technology itself. It is against this background that we will be examining prevailing myths and accumulating evidence on news audiences.

Notes

1 Survey data from a sample of 944 students from Israel, Norway and the UK, and in-depth interviews with 37 students within these three countries (Elvestad, Phillips, & Feuerstein, 2017).
2 Others have used different names to describe different models. Ferree, Gamson, Gerhards, and Rucht (2002) use the theory of representative liberal democracy and the theory of participating liberal democracy to describe what Rasch (2004) calls the models of competitive and participatory democracy, respectively.
3 Only in Greece do more people trust social media (Newman, Fletcher, Kalogeropoulos, & Nielsen, 2017).

References

Aalberg, T., & Curran, J. (2012). *How media inform democracy: A comparative approach*. London, England: Routledge.

Benkler, Y. (2006). *The wealth of networks: How social production transforms markets and freedom*. New Haven, CT; London, England: Yale University Press.

Bennett, W. L. (2008). Changing citizenship in the digital age. In W. L. Bennett (Ed.), *Civic life online: Learning how digital media can engage youth*. The John D. and Catherine T. MacArthur Foundation Series on Digital Media and Learning (pp. 1–24). Cambridge, MA: MIT Press.

Bennett, W. L., Wells, C., & Allison, R. (2009). Young citizens and civic learning: Two paradigms of citizenship in the digital age. *Citizenship Studies*, 13(2), 105–120. doi:10.1080/13621020902731116

Benson, R. (2004). Bringing the sociology of media back in. *Political Communication*, 21(3), 275–292.

Benson, R. (2009). Shaping the public sphere: Habermas and beyond. *The American Sociologist*, 40(3), 175–197.

Bourdieu, P. (1998). *On television*. New York, NY: New Press.

Bourdieu, P. (2005). The political field, the social science field, and the journalistic field. In R. Benson & E. Neveu (Eds.), *Bourdieu and the journalistic field* (pp. 29–47). Cambridge, England: Polity Press.

Calhoun, C. (1988). Populist politics, communication media and large scale societal integration. *Sociological Theory*, 6(3), 219–241.

Carey, J. W. (1983). Technology and ideology: The case of the telegraph. In J. W. Carey (Ed.), *Communication as culture: Essays on media and society* (pp. 155–177). London, England: Routledge.

Curran, J., Coen, S., Aalberg, T., Hayashi, K., Jones, P. K., Splendore, S., … Tiffen, R. (2013). Internet revolution revisited: A comparative study of online news. *Media, Culture & Society*, 35(7), 880–897. doi:10.1177/0163443713499393

Curran, J., Fenton, N., & Freedman, D. (2012). *Misunderstanding the internet*. London, England: Routledge.

Elvestad, E., Phillips, A., & Feuerstein, M. (2017). Can trust in traditional news media explain cross-national differences in news exposure of young people online? *Digital Journalism* (published online June 16, 2017). doi:10.1080/21670811.2017.1332484

Ferree, M. M., Gamson, W. A., Gerhards, J., & Rucht, D. (2002). Four models of the public sphere in modern democracies. *Theory and Society*, 31(3), 289–324.

Fiske, J. (1992). Popularity and the politics of information. In P. Dahlgren & C. Sparks (Eds.), *Journalism and popular culture* (pp. 45–63). London, England: Sage Publications.

Flichy, P. (1999). The wireless age: Radio broadcasting. In H. Mackay & T. O'Sullivan (Eds.), *The media reader: Continuity and transformation* (pp. 73–90). London, England: Sage Publications.

Fraser, N. (1990). Rethinking the public sphere: A contribution to the critique of actually existing democracy. *Social Text*, 25(26), 56–80.

Freedman, D. (2008). *The politics of media policy*. Cambridge, England: Polity.

Habermas, J. (1989). *The structural transformation of the public sphere: An inquiry into a category of bourgeois society*. Cambridge, England: Polity Press.

Hallin, D. C., & Mancini, P. (2004). *Comparing media systems: Three models of media and politics*. Cambridge, England: Cambridge University Press.

Hind, D. (2010). *The return of the public*. London, England; New York, NY: Verso.

Hindman, M. (2009). *The myth of internet democracy*. Princeton, NJ: Princeton University Press.

Jenkins, H. (2006). *Convergence culture: Where old and new media collide*. New York, NY: New York University Press.

Liebling, A. J. (1960, May 14). *The Wayward Press*: Do you belong in journalism. *The New Yorker Magazine*. Retrieved May 7, 2017 from www.newyorker.com/magazine/1960/05/14/do-you-belong-in-journalism

McChesney, R. (2014). *Digital disconnect: How capitalism is turning the internet against democracy.* New York, NY: New York Press.

McChesney, R., & Nichols, J. (2011). *The death and life of American journalism: The media revolution that will begin the world again.* Philadelphia, PA: Nation Books.

Meyrowitz, J. (2008). Power, pleasure, patterns: Intersecting narratives of media influence. *Journal of Communication, 58*(4), 641–663.

Negroponte, N. (1995). *Being digital.* London, England: Hodder & Stoughton.

Newman, N., Fletcher, R., Kalogeropoulos, D., & Nielsen, R. K. (2017). *Reuters Institute digital news report 2017.* Retrieved July 3, 2017 from https://reutersinstitute.politics.ox.ac.uk/sites/default/files/Digital%20News%20Report%202017%20web_0.pdf?utm_source=digitalnewsreport.org&utm_medium=referral

Pariser, E. (2011). *The filter bubble: What the internet is hiding from you.* London, England: Penguin.

Patterson T. E. (2000). The United States: News in a Free-Market Society. In R. Gunther and A. Mughan (Eds.), *Democracy and the Media: A Comparative Perspective.* Cambridge: Cambridge University Press.

Peters, J. D. (1993). Distrust of representation: Habermas on the public sphere. *Media, Culture & Society, 15*(4), 541–571.

Phillips, A. (2018). The technology of journalism. In T. P. Vos (Ed.), *Handbooks of communication science: Journalism* (Vol. 19). Berlin, Germany; New York, NY: Mouton de Gruyter.

Prior, M. (2007). *Post-broadcast democracy: How media choice increases inequality in political involvement and polarizes elections.* New York, NY: Cambridge University Press.

Putnam, R. D. (2000). *Bowling alone.* New York, NY: Simon & Schuster Paperbacks.

Rasch, B. E. (2004). Innledning [Introduction]. In I. K. Midgaard & B. E. Rasch (Eds.), *Demokrati: Vilkår og virkninger* [Democracy: Terms and effects] (pp. 11–20). Bergen, Norway: Fagbokforlaget.

Shirky, C. (2003). Power laws, weblogs, and inequality. *Clay Shirky's Writings About the Internet, Economics & Culture, Media & Community.* Open Source. Retrieved July 12, 2016 from www.shirky.com/writings/powerlaw_weblog.html

Strömbäck, J. (2005). In search of a standard: Four models of democracy and their normative implications for journalism. *Journalism Studies, 6*(3), 331–345. doi:10.1080/14616700500131950

Sunstein, C. R. (2009). *Republic.com 2.0.* Princeton, NJ: Princeton University Press.

Tapscott, D. (1998). *Growing up digital: The rise of the net generation.* New York, NY: McGraw Hill.

Toffler, A. (1970). *Future shock.* New York, NY: Bantam.

Wu, T. (2010). *The master switch: The rise and fall of information empires.* New York, NY: Knopf.

Zaller, J. (2003). A new standard of news quality: Burglar alarms for the monitorial citizen. *Political Communication, 20*(2), 109–130. doi:10.1080/10584600390211136

2

PERSONALISATION IS DEMOCRATISATION

Myth: news personalisation will improve plurality, diversity and ultimately democracy

Many people welcomed the World Wide Web and its capacity for personalising the delivery of news as a step towards a more democratic public sphere in which enlightened individuals would choose to engage with a range of news sources, tailored to their own requirements, thus undermining the agenda-setting power of news editors and news organisations. Nicholas Negroponte exemplified this view. Writing in 1995 he imagined the *Daily Me*:

> a future in which your interface agent can read every newswire and newspaper and catch every TV and radio broadcast on the planet, and then construct a personalised summary. This kind of newspaper is printed in an edition of one.
>
> *(Negroponte, 1995, p. 153)*

He saw this as an unalloyed benefit to democracy and was convinced that the distributive effects of the Internet and the impact of personal choice would usher in an era of true media pluralism:

> The monolithic empires of mass media are dissolving into an array of cottage industries... Media barons of today will be grasping to hold onto their centralized empires tomorrow... The combined forces of technology and human nature will ultimately take a stronger hand in plurality than any laws Congress can invent.
>
> *(Negroponte, 1995, pp. 57–58)*

The concern that US mass media had become overly centralised and that the owners (media barons) had far too much power to shape political life was not new. It was echoed by numerous media academics, including Herman and Chomsky, whose book *Manufacturing Consent* (1988) proposed that the mass media: "are effective and powerful ideological institutions that carry out a system-supportive propaganda function" (1988, p. 306) and more recently by Herman and McChesney (1997) who entitled their book *The Global Media: The New Missionaries of Corporate Capitalism*.

Negroponte saw the Internet as a means of challenging corporate power, not by challenging the market, but by creating a better market, capable of improving plurality, diversifying political messages and thereby undermining the elite control of mainstream news organisations. Personalised news is now with us. Increasingly news can be filtered to individual choice but how much has Negroponte's dream really come to pass? Can the market really deliver a more democratic media space?

For those who see the individual as the best editor of her own news content there is little argument that the Internet delivers a rich diversity of information and provides for debate, discussion and counter-narratives. However recent empirical research demonstrates a downside. Increasing numbers of people, particularly in the USA, are using their abundance of choice to watch more entertainment and to screen out news and current affairs altogether (Prior, 2007; Purcell, 2013), while others are watching news that increasingly confirms their own pre-existing prejudices, creating polarisation in place of democratic exchange of views. We may have greater choice, but if we use it mainly to search for entertainment media content we could end up "amusing ourselves to death" (Postman, 1986) on the one hand, or creating echo chambers (Jamieson & Cappella, 2010; Sunstein, 2009) or bubbles of agreement and extremism on the other (Pariser, 2011).

This chapter will explore the impact of personalisation on the kind of news that individuals receive. Does personalisation loosen the grip of the elite on channels of communication, does it simply reproduce existing patterns of social inequality or does it have a more far-reaching effect in fragmenting the very possibility of a shared public space in which society can formulate common aims (Fuchs, 2015, p. 325; Karppinen, 2013)?

Regulation, disengagement and democracy

There have always been news junkies and news avoiders. Some citizens have always been better informed than those who, for example, might only have read a newspaper for the sports news or the crime. With the advent of television, news consumption spread to a wider audience because of what has been described as the "trapping effect" of television (Blumler, 1970; Schoenbach & Lauf, 2002). By this they were referring to the way in which viewers, with only a small number of television channels to choose from, would encounter news during an evening's viewing even if they were not very interested in it. Newspapers were still important and people still discussed what they saw with others, but large numbers of people were being informed, directly, about what was considered by news editors to be important in the world (Aalberg & Curran, 2012, p. 193).

Given the small number of channels in the earlier decades of television, and the high cost of television production, those who controlled the channels had the capacity to wield huge influence and, because of this, democratic countries introduced ways of ensuring that news coverage was balanced and allowed access for people with differing political views. European countries established publicly funded broadcasters as did other countries including Canada, Australia and India. Channels were either shared out between differing political tendencies (for example in Italy) or regulated to ensure that they provided balanced coverage (for example in the UK). In the USA, licences were provided for privately owned channels, but content was governed by the "Fairness Doctrine", which ensured that coverage was shared out between the major political parties (Hallin & Mancini, 2004).

The introduction of cable television in the 1980s changed the equation because audiences now had a larger number of channels to choose from and this is the point at which the number of people who avoided news started increasing in the USA (Duca & Saving, 2012; Prior, 2007). In his book, *Post-Broadcast Democracy*, Prior (2007) analyses news audience data in the USA. He found that amongst those using mainstream traditional news platforms, in particular network television, there was little difference in news knowledge between individuals. Pretty much everyone knew about major issues in the news whether they were very interested or not very interested in news. Those using cable television and the Internet, however, were increasingly able to personalise their own viewing around entertainment and avoid news altogether. This meant that although, on average, news exposure, knowledge and turnout remained stable, there had been important differences in the variation of news exposure. Those who chose to use the Internet and cable television could disengage completely from news and many of them did so. In this group, those who were not interested in news had very little news knowledge and were less likely to vote. In Prior's research, this finding held true irrespective of class and educational background.

> News junkies get more news, and entertainment fans and 'switchers' get less news than before. The variance in news exposure has increased, as has the variance in political knowledge and turnout.
>
> *(Prior, 2007, p. 160).*

In Europe (later than in the USA), there is also a trend of increasing numbers of people who disconnect themselves from news and current affairs and spend more time watching entertainment programmes on TV (Aalberg, Blekesaune, & Elvestad, 2013; Blekesaune, Elvestad, & Aalberg, 2012). However, whereas in the USA 19 per cent had not accessed news in any form on the previous day (Pew, 2008), in Europe there were fewer news avoiders and there were also major differences across the European countries. In the Nordic countries, and in the Northern European countries of Austria, Germany and the Netherlands, only 1–2 per cent of citizens did not watch news on TV, listen to news on radio or read news in newspapers, while 15 per cent of Greek citizens avoided news from these news sources (Blekesaune, Elvestad, & Aalberg, 2012, p. 118).

In the Netherlands, Wonneberger, Schoenbach, and van Meurs (2012) found that instead of abstaining or escaping from the TV news, the time spent watching news increased from 1988 to 2010. In the Netherlands, short news bulletins are provided regularly, at the same time, across all channels, so people are less motivated to tune away from news, even if they are not particularly interested. Those who are interested in more serious programmes tend to see these news bulletins as a supplement to traditional public affairs formats so they do not detract from audiences watching more in-depth programmes (Wonneberger, Schoenbach, & van Meurs, 2012).

The difference in the numbers of people disengaging from news seems to be related to the availability of publicly funded news channels. In a comparative study using data from the USA and five European countries, the difference in political knowledge between the news avoiders and the news seekers is much smaller where there is strong, publicly funded television, than it is in countries with a highly commercialised media system, like in the USA (Aalberg & Curran, 2012).

The more commercial provision in the USA also added to the division of audience understanding along class lines. News consumption and news knowledge amongst those educated to degree level was as high in the USA as in the Nordic and Northern European countries. However, amongst those with only a high school education, there was a big discrepancy in news knowledge in the USA and very little difference in news knowledge in the Nordic and Northern European countries. In the USA, those with only a high school education were considerably less likely to be aware of news-related information.

It has been suggested that the increasing use of the Internet as a major conduit for news consumption could increase news avoidance, even in countries where publicly funded television has, until recently, maintained a sense of a common national narrative (Strömbäck, Djerf-Pierre, & Shehata, 2013). However, if we look at the online news consumption across countries, there are differences. In the UK, for example, the BBC still has a unifying function, on- and offline, with the lion's share of news audiences across the political spectrum (Newman, Fletcher, Kalogeropoulos, & Nielsen, 2017). On the other hand, in the USA, which has high levels of news avoidance, and no major publically funded broadcaster, the news sources that dominated offline have lost audience share to online sources. The countries that used to have a low share of news avoiders are also less polarised in their choice of news sources even when they move online. In many of these countries, the traditional news brands offline are still the main news sources online. It seems that the degree of fragmentation or polarisation amongst citizens offline is mirrored by news exposure online (Newman, Fletcher, Levy, & Nielsen, 2016).

To illustrate this, we show how citizens in four quite different media regimes are exposed to different media brands (Reuters digital report, Newman et al., 2016). Figure 2.1 shows the share of citizens in Norway, Japan, the USA and the UK who used the four top news brands offline at least weekly, while Figure 2.2 shows the four most used news brands online. By looking at Figure 2.1, we see how the exposure to the offline news brands differs across countries; in two countries (Norway and Japan) there are four strong news brands, while one country (USA) has no news brands being followed by more than 33 per cent of the population.

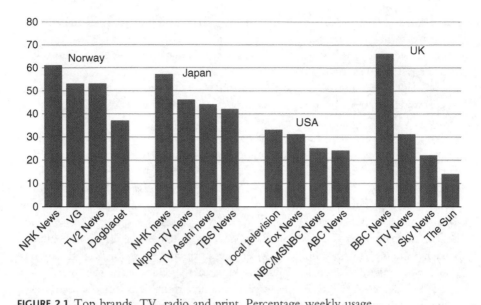

FIGURE 2.1 Top brands, TV, radio and print. Percentage weekly usage (Source: Reuters digital report/Newman et al., 2016)

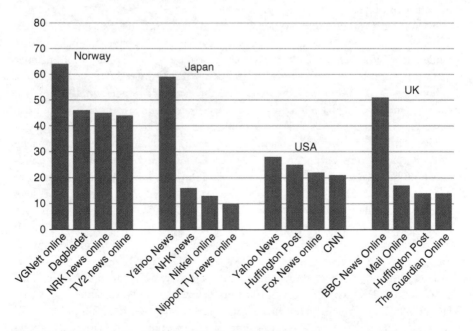

FIGURE 2.2 Top brands, online. Percentage weekly usage (Source: Reuters digital report/Newman et al., 2016)

The last country (the UK) has one major news brand, which is the national public broadcaster that 66 per cent of the population use for news exposure weekly, while the other news media have a much lower reach.

Figure 2.2 shows that for three of the countries (Norway, the USA and the UK) there is a similar pattern online. But there are some differences. In the Norwegian sample, the top four news brands offline are also the top news brands online. The national newspapers have a stronger position online than the public service and commercial broadcaster. This must be understood as a consequence of the strong position of newspapers in Norway and their early start with online news. The online position in the USA is similar to the offline pattern: none of the news sources reach a majority of the population, and the fragmented/polarised news exposure is transferred online. In the UK, the BBC is the dominant brand offline and online, but the next most frequently used news brands online are not similar to the number 2, 3 and 4 news brands offline. The majority follow the BBC news weekly, but the rest of the news exposure is more fragmented/polarised. In Japan, the main difference between the online and offline news exposure is that the Japanese use fewer online services for news. This is because the major newspapers there have not invested in online news products. The main source for news online in Japan is the news aggregator Yahoo News.

Countries with a strong public service broadcaster are less fragmented/polarised in their news exposure because in these countries, the majority of the population still follow their public service news.

A small study for the Reuters Institute attempted to find reasons for why people tune out from news. The most likely reasons offered were that respondents had "something more interesting to do" or that "news tends to upset or depress me" or that it "isn't relevant to me". The younger the respondent, the more likely they were to find other things to do. The major national difference was that those from the UK, Americans, and Spaniards are likely to avoid news because it makes them upset or angry whereas Danish consumers very rarely find that news makes them angry (Schrøder & Blach-Ørsten, 2016). These national differences also correlate with differences in trust. A Eurobarometer poll in 2016 found that amongst the European countries, trust in the media was by a very large margin higher in Denmark than in either the UK or Spain (EBU, 2016).

News polarisation/political polarisation

The new media environment, with greater news personalisation, doesn't only create more news avoiders who now can spend their time on entertainment. With more choices, and more opportunities for personalised news diets, there is a concern that news exposure is becoming more niche and ideologically polarised (Van Aelst et al., 2017). Some would argue that political polarisation is not a new trend. Audiences tend to avoid "cognitive dissonance" and seek out messages that confirm their own world-view (Festinger, 1957/1964). Research during a US election campaign in 1940 found that Democrats were more likely to pay attention to the

Democratic campaign, and Republicans to the Republican campaign (Lazarsfeld, Berelson, & Gaudet, 1944). Chaffee and McLeod (1973) also found that those who discussed political campaigns more often were more likely to seek out partisan information.

Indeed, even when most people were watching similar narratives on television, they were not interpreting them in the same way. David Morley interviewed different groups of people watching the same news magazine programme, *Nationwide*, in the early 1980s and found that viewers would interpret news in the context of their own knowledge (Morley, 1980). They might see the same story but they would "read" it differently. Morley identified three different ways of interpreting, which roughly corresponded with the degree of prior knowledge of the subject under discussion. Those with little prior knowledge would accept the "dominant narrative" as provided by the broadcaster; those with some knowledge that might contradict this version of events would arrive at a "negotiated reading", accepting some points but with reservations; those whose experience told them that the version of events offered was unreasonable would form an "oppositional reading". This research opened up a new way of considering plurality and diversity that recognised the audience's power to resist information that does not chime with their own experience.

When people watch mainstream news bulletins and share roughly the same version of events, even those with strongly divergent opinions are still aware of what mainstream assumptions actually are, even if they disagree with them or have alternative explanations. This common experience started to change in the USA in 1987 when the Fairness Doctrine, which regulated television news, was repealed and US broadcasting was freed to be partisan. To begin with the impact was confined to radio, with a series of highly partisan, conservative talk shows (Jamieson & Cappella, 2010). It was followed in 1996 by changes to the Telecommunications Act, allowing more cable news channels and a greater degree of cross-ownership of channels. That was the year in which Fox News launched as the first avowedly conservative television channel. The competition that followed the increase in the number of channels meant that staff numbers on cable channels were slashed to cut costs and Fox, as a new entrant, depended on attitude more than news-gathering to build its audience (Hmielowski, Beam, & Hutchens, 2015).

Fox was initially only available in 20 per cent of towns so researchers were able to compare Fox towns with towns that were Fox free. Between 1996 and 2000, towns with Fox News, with its avowedly conservative bias, had increased the proportion of Republican voters by between 0.4 and 0.7 in vote share while increasing voter turnout, irrespective of the national voting patterns (DellaVigna & Kaplan, 2007). The change was small but given the closeness of US elections, significant. Follow-up research from Hmielowski et al. (2015) found that in the period between 1996 and 2008, the levels of political polarisation started to rise sharply. As Americans started watching more polarised television news, their opinions started to harden and they were less likely to be tolerant of the views of others.

According to US data presented in the book *Echo Chamber*, Jamieson and Cappella (2010) argue that the shift was the result of a long-term campaign to establish a conservative media eco-system to challenge what right-wing Republicans saw as a liberal consensus in US news media. Where the previously dominant US news channels had maintained a degree of neutrality in reporting political events, the Fox channel was deeply partisan, framing news from a conservative point of view while accusing the more established news media of liberal bias (Jamieson & Cappella, 2010). The addition of social media (in particular, Facebook) as a platform for news consumption didn't create a right-wing echo chamber but it did provide the means by which these messages could more easily be shared with similar people, thus strengthening the echo chamber effect and protecting them from cross-cutting information (information that they do not initially agree with).

When the audience is broken up into small groups of like-minded people, the very forces that cause resistance in the mass market, broadcast, television audience are likely to lead to the formation of groups around shared readings (Hall, 1973; Lelkes, Sood, & Iyengar, 2015; Morley, 1980). This reduces audience exposure to views that they disagree with. As a body of research has shown, groups of people sharing information that reinforces their pre-existing views will resist alternative explanations, move to a more polarised position when challenged and be less tolerant of difference (Janis, 1982; Mutz, 2002; Nyhan & Reifler, 2010; Stroud, 2007; Stroud, 2010; Sunstein, 2009). In their review of research on the trends in political information environments and their implications on democracy, Van Aelst et al. (2017, p. 13) found that:

> all findings available to date suggest that, by and large, citizens with extreme views are more likely to show polarization after exposure to media messages compared to citizens with less extreme views. Exposure to, or demand for, partisan media may therefore increase polarization, but typically only for certain groups of people.

Stroud (2010) tested this theory using US election survey data and found that, as expected, those who chose a partisan news diet became more extreme in their views as the campaign progressed. Later research found that 18 per cent of social media users have blocked or unfriended or hidden someone for political reasons (Rainie & Smith, 2012).

> Countless editions of the *Daily Me* can produce serious problems of mutual suspicion, unjustified rage, and social fragmentation – and [that] these problems will result from the reliable logic of social interactions.
>
> *(Sunstein, 2007)*

When only a small percentage of already politically involved individuals were engaged in online news creation, distribution and consumption, this tendency to form groups of like-minded people, as Prior (2007) notes, had relatively little direct effect on broader consumption patterns. Most people still received most of their news via the traditional platforms and were therefore routinely exposed to "cross-cutting" information which challenged their world-view or exposed them to unexpected information. Early research about the impact of the Internet and social media suggested that access to such a wealth of information would ensure that most people had access to a wider variety of material than ever before and that this would increase tolerance. Research by Yardi and Boyd suggested that, even though citizens are more likely to read tweets from like-minded people, they also engaged with people with whom they disagree (Yardi & Boyd, 2010).

More recently, however, a growing body of research on polarisation and social media from the USA tends to confirm the concerns of Sunstein (2009) and Pariser (2011) of increasing divisions along ideological lines. Yoo and Gil de Zúñiga (2014, p. 33) found that Twitter and Facebook "amplify or reinforce inequality of political engagement". Flaxman, Goel, and Rao (2016, p. 318) report that: "articles found via social media or web-search engines are indeed associated with higher ideological segregation than those an individual reads by directly visiting news sites".

Himelboim, McCreery, and Smith (2013, p. 169) found that hyperlinking patterns show that conservative messages in the USA were more likely than liberal messages to include a link to grassroots websites, mainly blogs. Websites of traditional media were more popular amongst messages coded as liberal oriented. A study for the *Columbia Journalism Review* (Benkler, Faris, Roberts, & Zuckerman, 2017) confirmed this, finding an almost total division of attention amongst those using social media: people who shared links with *Breitbart*, the right-wing news website, were unlikely to share information from any of the mainstream news outlets. Those who read the more partisan left-wing or liberal news sites were still engaging with the traditional sources. The only news outlet to maintain a balance of left and right shares was the *Wall Street Journal*.

Most of this research on the rise of political polarisation comes from the USA and its important to note that the work may not be replicated in different countries with differing national media environments and political systems. Research from the Reuters Institute (Fletcher, 2017) has analysed the level of political polarisation in the use of news brands across a number of countries and has produced an "online polarisation score" for 22 countries, which broadly describes the degree to which audiences read broadly similar or highly polarised news material. They found that polarisation was most entrenched in the USA where, as Benkler et al. (2017) also found, people who self-describe as on the political right consume a completely different news diet from those who self-describe as politically liberal or on the left. The Northern European, Democratic Corporatist countries (Hallin & Mancini, 2004), with public broadcasters and well-respected news organisations, had low levels of polarisation.

In most Southern European countries (Portugal is the exception), serious newspapers have party political ties (political parallelism), and polarisation is the norm for the media system (cf. Hallin & Mancini, 2004). However, even in these countries, the level of political polarisation is not as complete as it appears to be in the USA (Fletcher, 2017). In the Reuters Institute study, the UK is clustered with the more highly polarised Southern European countries, with high levels of press polarisation balanced by the role of the BBC, which tends to be consumed by people across the political spectrum.

The impact of polarisation is arguably different in different systems. When media polarisation goes hand in hand with multi-party elections, those who are voting do so in expectation that their representatives will hammer out compromises once in coalition with other parties. In the Netherlands, for example, 28 parties entered the 2017 elections and people could therefore vote in accordance with quite small differences in opinion in the knowledge that a coalition would be built after the votes had been counted. In these countries, social media may still have an impact in raising the profile of extreme political actors, but the voting system is less sensitive to the actions of a vocal minority. Therefore, although European commentators focused on the rising fortunes of the right-wing candidate, Geert Wilders, who did indeed increase his vote share, the voting system, arguably, did not magnify his influence as it might have done in a different system.

Polarisation in a competitive democracy such as the USA or the UK can create a situation in which a relatively small number of highly involved voters can have a disproportionate effect on voting outcomes and gain a disproportionate amount of power relative to their actual base. The first-past-the-post electoral system hands power to a relatively small number of marginal areas, where a swing of just a few percentage points may not only clinch the election locally, but may put a party in power on the basis of a minority of the popular vote.

Arguably, therefore, we are seeing in the USA the effect of a relatively small number of highly politically engaged people in a country with a competitive, first-past-the-post electoral system, who were able to have a disproportionate impact in a very polarised system. That small percentage may well grow as more people turn towards their own tailored version of news. So we could see the spread of a series of bubble cultures, unconnected by the normative stream of national broadcast news. While this would represent a shift in the hegemonic control of the traditional mainstream, it seems likely to be replaced, or at least augmented, by a new kind of media hegemony, operated through personalised targeting of voters on the basis of their personal search data.

The way we choose to communicate with like-minded people provides opportunities for authoritarian regimes that want to control and monitor political or ideological groups of citizens in society. But it also provides opportunities for those in democracies who want to tailor political messages for different groups of people in order to encourage them to vote a certain way. The data company Cambridge Analytica worked for Donald Trump in the presidential election campaigns and also provided advice to the Leave.UK campaign in the UK. In a press release on November 9, 2016, Cambridge Analytica confirmed: "We are thrilled that our revolutionary approach to data-driven communication has played such an integral part in President-elect Trump's extraordinary win" (PR Newswire and Cambridge Analytica, 2016).

There is as yet no evidence that data-driven political advertising is as effective as this company wants us to believe it is. After all, the same company failed to get

Ted Cruz selected as Republican candidate. However, the use of data for political targeting raises many questions. We have no control over the way in which data generated from the sources we use for information is used. Nor do we control the data about us generated from what we "like", "dislike" and comment on in social media. Everything we do online is providing data to others who may profit from it either economically or politically and, unlike printed or broadcast media, we have as yet to devise a means of monitoring or regulating the use of data and social media for the purposes of political propaganda.

Who is editing your feed?

While those countries with high trust in their news media and well-funded public service broadcasters have so far been spared the impact of a completely polarised system of news media, any increase in the use of social media as an access point for news could begin to change the landscape. Now that the *Daily Me* is available, not only to the small percentage of avid news selectors, or even to the larger percentage of those who are deeply politically engaged, but to all, the question of where news comes from, who selects it, and how it is accessed, has taken on greater urgency. The means of sorting and filtering news streams can now be set automatically, not by individuals themselves but by computers that monitor user behaviour and serve up news information, guided by a mixture of influences including shopping habits, clicks and friendship groups. So concerns about the impact of "social sorting" have moved up the research agenda and provided impetus for studies looking at how audiences use personalisation.

Most of the early research into "collaborative filtering" examined systems in which people selected their own sources of news. Zuiderveen Borgesius et al. (2016) describe this as "self-selected personalisation", whereas Beam (2014) describes these as "user-customised recommender systems", which is the term we prefer. There has been less systematic research on what Zuiderveen Borgesius et al. (2016) describe as "pre-selected personalisation" in which the choices are organised by algorithmic methods based on data use. Beam (2014) describes these systems as "personalised recommender systems".

A user-customised system, such as Tumblr, or Twitter (before the reorganisation of the Twitter interface in 2016), allows the user to link to a variety of possibly incompatible information sources, which are presented more or less in the order in which they are generated. A computer-generated pre-selected system like Facebook, on the other hand, does the thinking for the user and chooses material based on previous preferences and the preferences of associates linked through social media.

In an experimental setting, Beam (2014) examined choices made by people using one or other of these systems and concluded that, where explicit user customisation has been used, there is significantly higher counter-attitudinal news exposure. In other words, people who choose their own news feeds were also more likely to select general interest news sources which would expose them to a greater variety of topics and opinions (Beam, 2014; Beam & Kosicki, 2014). Where the feed automatically "personalises", there is less exposure to alternative opinions. Beam also found that computer-generated pre-selected personalisation had "a negative effect on knowledge" (Beam, 2014, p. 1036).

This research seems to suggest that, where individual users are explicitly choosing their news sources, they are more open to other opinions. In other words, it appears to contradict Sunstein's (2009) concern that people are deliberately wrapping themselves into cocoons or "filter bubbles". Those who deliberately choose news that conforms to their own beliefs may be no different from those who choose newspapers according to their political leanings. They are already politically aligned and they read material that confirms their own beliefs. On the plus side, the easy access to a range of material also leads to a deeper engagement (Mutz, 2002). On the minus side, those who turn away from mainstream media are less likely to encounter views that challenge their beliefs or information that they have not deliberately sought out.

Using data from the 2004 National Annenberg Election Survey, Stroud was able to trace the relationship between partisan media exposure and political polarisation over time. She concluded that "partisan selective exposure is related to higher polarisation and that the consumption of uncongenial media is related to lower polarisation" (Stroud, 2010, p. 569). In other words, she found that people are influenced by the media they engage with. Where they come into contact with mostly partisan news they will move to a more extreme position. Where they engage with alternative viewpoints they tend to be less polarised in their views.

The impact of social media on news

The data Stroud used looked at all media outlets including online. At that time, most respondents would have been making their own selection of news products. However, increasingly people are not fully customising their feeds themselves; they are using systems that are partly generated by algorithm and partly by social network. This change means that it is no longer only the politically involved whose information is pre-selected. Those who are less engaged with news also have their news exposure tailored. A 2016 study by the Pew Research Center in the USA found that:

> The less newsy are more likely to say friends and family are important pathways to news: 69% of those who follow news less often say friends and family are important, compared with 57% of those who follow news all or most of the time. Additionally, women are more likely than men to say friends and family are important, young adults are more likely than older adults, and blacks are more likely than whites to say this.
>
> *(Mitchell, Gottfried, Barthel, & Shearer, 2016a, p. 2)*

They may believe that they are reading a wide variety of material but the platform that they use is pre-selecting stories that match with their previous choices and the choices of their friends. Therefore, it is increasingly likely that a previously uncommitted person, who is friends on Facebook with a committed supporter of an extreme organisation, will soon start seeing more of those stories on their feed. Experiments by Mutz (2002) found that, for people without a great deal of news interest, exposure to a variety of viewpoints was likely to foster a greater sense of tolerance of other people's views. In a world of filter bubbles curated by friends and family, they may well never encounter alternative views.

Researchers in Europe (Valeriani & Vaccari, 2016) found that "accidental exposure" to information was reported by 16% of Germans in the sample, 33% of Italians and 27.7% of British respondents, and that those with little interest in politics were marginally more likely than those with a prior political interest to respond to such inadvertent exposure by, for example, signing an online petition. This seems to suggest that politically uncommitted people, who stumble across material passed on by people in their social circles, are to some extent influenced. At times when engagement increases (for example, in the lead-up to an election), uncommitted people, who are less likely to inform themselves via a mixture of different platforms, may be disproportionately influenced by what they see on social media because they are less likely to be getting any of their news from a more mainstream source or to hear alternative views (Lelkes, Sood, & Iyengar, 2015).

In response to concerns about "filter bubbles", Facebook commissioned its own research using a large sample of politically committed Facebook users (Bakshy, Messing, & Adamic, 2015) and found that it is indeed friendship groups, more than algorithms, that drives selection in an individual's news stream. It is mostly the people who you link with, and what you click on, that drives your selection. While this appears to counteract fears of a computerised filter bubble, it would be disingenuous to find this reassuring for a number of reasons. Firstly, the Bakshy sample is skewed – it only looks at people who self-identify as politically committed so it cannot be used to look at the behaviour of everyone else. Secondly, the research confirms the fact that the key issue in a news feed is placement. People are more likely, by a very high margin, to click on stories at the top of their news feed and that is dictated by the algorithm, which in turn is guided by your past behaviour and the behaviour of those you link to. Your more prolific and apparently more "popular" friends will always be more visible than those who rarely post (Gillespie, 2014). It is Facebook that decides which of the stories in your feed you are most likely to click on.

Both this and other research have found an apparently confounding additional effect: people using social media to access news tend to use a wider variety of sources and to come into more contact with cross-cutting material (Flaxman et al., 2016; Newman et al., 2017). This has often been used as evidence that social media is in fact increasing cross-cutting news consumption (Barberá, Jost, Nagler, Tucker, & Bonneau, 2015) but research from Nahon and Hemsley (2014) finds a rather more disconcerting reason for this cross-linking to material that comes from a different ideological position. People are posting examples of material that will "strengthen previously held stances" (Nahon & Hemsley, 2014, p. 17). In other words, they are using material to negatively reframe the views they dislike (Newman et al., 2016, p. 102). This behaviour is particularly prevalent on Twitter where people deliberately follow those whose views they dislike in order to attack them (Buckels, Trapnell, & Paulhus, 2014). Although most of these studies are from the USA, Newman et al. (2016, p. 102) found that respondents across a number of other countries, including Finland and Korea, were just as likely to share material that they disapprove of as they were to share material they agree with.

The power of groups

We have established that social networks link people via friendship and family groups and that algorithms tend to prioritise people who post more regularly and people who are "more popular" in a particular network. In combination that means that if someone is not particularly proactive about politics, but has a friend who is very politically active and a prolific poster, it is likely that they will see what that person posts. Indeed, that might be the only thing they see that links them to the world of politics.

Social scientists began to do systematic observations of group formation and network ties in the 1920s and 1930s (Hubbard, 1929 in McPherson, Smith-Lovin, & Cook, 2001). Social media have increased the interest in group formation and networks and their consequences for plurality, diversity and democracy. The principle of homophily,[1] or "birds of a feather flock together", limits people's world and has consequences for the information they receive and their opinions (Christakis and Fowler, 2009; McPherson et al., 2001). If you vote, your friend, and your friends' friends are more likely to vote too (Christakis & Fowler, 2009).

There is considerable research indicating that groups have a powerful social effect on their members. When people find themselves in the company of people with differing views, they tend to moderate their own views or keep quiet. This is referred to as "the Spiral of Silence" (Noelle-Neumann, 1974). Social media tends to exacerbate this effect. People are considerably less likely to venture alternative views online than they would amongst friends or around a family dinner table (Jang, Lee, & Park, 2014).

Conversely, if people believe that everyone agrees with them, they are more likely to state their views. The more partisan they are, the more likely they are to be resistant to corrections of "facts" that they believe to be true. Indeed, Nyhan and Reifler (2010) found that presenting ideologically committed people with facts that contradict their beliefs actually reinforced their beliefs rather than undermining them. This means that, in the sheltered space of an online group, the dominant members of that group tend to reinforce each other's opinion and the volume of like-minded posts being shared will rise, as will the likelihood of political activity. Research also shows that the greater the exposure to one-sided media, the more people believe that public opinion is on their side and that in turn leads to increased confidence and increased political participation (Dvir-Gvirsman, Garrett, & Tsfati, 2015). Slater (2007) refers to this as the creation of "reinforcing spirals".

In the debate leading up to the election of Trump, most mainstream news organisations were convinced that he could not possibly win. His supporters, on the other hand, were convinced that they would win. The divergence of opinion was reinforced by the almost total polarisation of news consumption (Benkler et al., 2017), which ensured that Trump supporters were consistently exposed to material that suggested Trump could win, that Hillary was "a crook" and that the traditional mainstream media were in the pockets of the liberal establishment and therefore not to be trusted. They were rarely, if ever, exposed to negative coverage of Trump that had not already been filtered by his supporters. Democrats, on the other hand, were exposed to mainstream media that, while very critical of Trump, was also critical of Clinton. A study of mainstream news found that 64 per cent of news reports about Clinton where critical of her (Patterson, 2016). Thus, it could be argued that while Trump supporters were encouraged to be on the winning side and to turn out and vote, a large number of Democrats stayed at home, unconvinced about their own candidate.

The influentials

The position in a group or a social network is not without importance. Those who are observers, rather than participants, may find that their online environment is skewed towards the beliefs of the most active members. These passive news consumers, who are not particularly interested in news, are increasingly passing over the job of news filtering to the individuals that Robert Merton (1949) identified as "local or cosmopolitan influentials". Merton found that people evaluated people in their communities according to their information skills. Local influentials were better informed about local matters (and read more local newspapers), while cosmopolitans were better informed about the wider society (and read more national and international news). Lazarsfeld et al. (1944/1952) also noted that, during the 1940 election campaign, voters were far more influenced by people in their own social circles, who interpreted news events, than they were by the news media itself. Lazarsfeld and Katz went on to study this "two-step flow" in further research which looked at the influentials and found that they were people within social groups who tended to be interested in and more easily influenced by the news media than their associates and who acted as intermediaries for other group members (Katz & Lazarsfeld, 1955). They also noted how social pressure within the group ensured conformity in the interpretation of news messages. When people change their opinions they "will be likely to change them in the direction of the group norm" (Katz & Lazarsfeld, 1955, p. 66).

The two-step flow model seems to have particular relevance in social media where "influentials" have an important role in diffusing information through social networks. Research from the Media Insight Project in the USA found that trust in information shared online is more strongly influenced by the identity of the sharer than the identity of the source (Media Insight Project, 2017). So the question of who shares information matters a great deal. A Norwegian study of influentials found that they were significantly more likely than other people to follow political parties and politicians with the clear intention of using their information to influence others (Karlsen, 2015). Social media allows "influentials" to assemble information and pass it around their networks. The "reinforcing spiral" effect ensures that people who disagree with the dominant voice remain silent because to intervene risks being attacked. But also, "birds of a feather flock together" so they become more like each other, which is the principle of homophily (McPherson et al., 2001). More recent research from Princeton finds that people are also less likely to check the facts of what they are reading if they think someone else is watching them (Jun, Meng, & Johar, 2017).

Taken together this suggests that social media combine the algorithmic "winners-take-all" patterns found by Hindman (2009) with the social fragmentation feared by Sunstein (2009), Tufekci (2015) and Jamieson and Cappella (2010). Just as Hindman demonstrated, the combination ensures that only the most popular item in any particular niche group is likely to be "shared" when it is a computer, rather than a human being, that is doing the sharing. This means that it is the strongest opinions that take precedence, pushing out those who are interested in reasoned debate.

The consequences of a "choice"-based news system

While it is reasonable to conclude that the "monolithic empires of mass media" have indeed been eroded by the viral system of the Internet, the effects on democracy have been mixed. The market approach to news provision has been excellent for intensifying political interest amongst like-minded people. The changing behaviour of those who are interested in news shows that the Internet allows them to be more engaged and to influence others via social networks. For those who are less interested in news, the impact seems to be the opposite: they are less engaged and more easily influenced.

Curran et al. (2014), reviewing the literature, contend that the news media are capable of both enabling democracy and obstructing it and that the kind of news media and the system in which it operates are critical. Generally speaking, news matters for democracy but the news media don't always work in the interests of democracy. A number of studies have shown higher rates of news knowledge and public participation in countries with public service television (Aalberg & Curran, 2012; Aarts & Semetko, 2003; Curran et al., 2014; Strömbäck & Shehata, 2010). Where news information is distributed as a secondary goal to generating profit, it is less likely to engage people in political debate or political action – indeed, it can hasten disengagement. Where news is provided as a public service, it has a greater capacity for encouraging engagement and there also appears to be greater discernment in recognising news that is authoritative. In an Oxford University study of news during elections, US users were found to be just as likely to share what researchers called "junk news" as they were to share professional news content. Sharing of junk news was significantly less likely in France, Germany and the UK (all countries with independent public service broadcasters) and sharing of professional news content was substantially higher (Kaminska, Gallacher, Kollany, Yasseri, & Howard, 2017).

Social media and Internet sorting systems such as Google are often seen as having a public service role, but the role they actually occupy is intensely commercial. They use their pre-eminent position as conduits of information on a global scale to maximise their own commercial success. This is hardly surprising. They are public companies dedicated to providing a return on investment for shareholders. In so doing they need to maintain user trust and, to the extent that it is necessary to do that, they attempt to maintain the role of neutral information conduits. However, these conduits are not neutral; they are the site of intense competition by media entities that seek to maximise their own audiences, taking advantage of the affordances of the Internet and social media to increase their contact with potential audiences in order to draw revenue.

In this feverishly competitive media market, individual research results have been used to support any number of different theories. Some have seen the intensification of news and political involvement as evidence that the Internet and social media are drawing more people into political debate and a great deal of research energy has been used to refute suggestions that social media creates "filter bubbles". Messing and Westwood (2014) found that people are more likely to click on material that has been endorsed (trending stories) than to stick within partisan boundaries. They read this as evidence that social media "reduces partisan selective exposure". Barberá et al. (2015) analysed Twitter and observed that "liberals are significantly more likely than conservatives to participate in cross-ideological dissemination of political and non-political information" (p. 1540). They saw this as evidence that filter bubbles were not forming. Bakshy et al. (2015) concluded that algorithms are not creating filter bubbles because: "individuals' choices played a stronger role in limiting exposure to cross-cutting content". They saw this as evidence that filter bubbles may be formed but that the platforms are not to blame.

But when all the evidence is looked at together, the big themes are clear. Greater choice in news provision leads users to adopt heuristic cues in order to make decisions about what to consume. One of the key cues will be headlines indicating issues that interest them but an equally important cue will be "trending" bars that flag up the popularity of the subject (Messing & Westwood, 2014) and the "implied endorsement" of a link to a site or a story in their news feed. This initial set of choices is then intensified by algorithms that cut out information considered less interesting to that particular individual and prioritise (by pushing them higher up the news feed) stories that are likely to be considered important. This has the effect of narrowing news choices for those who are more interested and filtering out news stories for those who are less interested.

Those who are less interested in news tend to be: younger, less well educated and more likely to be female (Grabe & Kamhawi, 2006; Knobloch-Westerwick & Alter, 2007; Poindexter, Meraz & Weiss, 2008). We know also that women are considerably more likely than men to use social media to find news (Newman et al., 2016). The net results will be that women, who are less interested in hard news than their male counterparts, will see less hard news and more "pro-social" shareable news stories. People with lower levels of education are also likely to see less political news (Aalberg & Curran, 2012; Prior, 2007) and, when they do see political stories, they will often have been shared by intermediaries who are more extreme in their attitudes; they are also more likely to be influenced by such material if they are not regular, mainstream news consumers (Stroud, 2010, p. 569).

A shared news narrative is important for democracy, not in order to produce a docile populous, but to ensure that people hear the same version of what is being said. That doesn't mean that they will necessarily agree with what they hear. The fact that messages are transmitted indiscriminately ensures that they link together groups of people who may not be natural allies and would not have been capable of making contact through the bubble culture of the Internet. The media coverage of the 2016 contest for the London Mayoral elections demonstrates this. The news media, led by the *Evening Standard* newspaper, which is distributed free on the public transport system in London and seen by over a million people every day, generated stories that attempted to link Labour candidate Sadiq Khan with Islamic extremism (Media Reform Coalition, 2016). Local television news followed the *Evening Standard*'s agenda and also gave publicity to these sensational messages – albeit with rejoinders from Khan. The impact of this vicious campaign was to bring Londoners out in particularly high numbers to vote for Khan in a complete rejection of the *Evening Standard* and the candidate that it had backed.

It is the linking function of a shared news narrative that disappears when large numbers of people get their news via social media. While the mainstream media still exist to provide the task of linking, social media have an important role to play in rallying alternative views and intensifying the involvement of those who are more directly involved with campaigning. When social media start to replace mainstream media they are likely to create fissures between differing polarised groups and to produce news deserts in between. This may well be the point at which, as Karl Karppinen suggests, "healthy diversity turns into unhealthy dissonance" (Karppinen, 2013, p. 7).

Note

1 Homophily is the principle that a contact between similar people occurs at a higher rate than amongst dissimilar people. The pervasive fact of homophily means that cultural, behavioural, genetic, or material information that flows through networks will tend to be localised. Homophily implies that distance in terms of social characteristics translates into network distance; the number of relationships also implies that any social entity that depends to a substantial degree on networks for its transmission will tend to be localised in social space and will obey certain fundamental dynamics as it interacts with other social entities in an ecology of social forms (McPherson et al., 2001, p. 416).

References

Aalberg, T., & Curran, J. (2012). *How media inform democracy: A comparative approach*. London, England: Routledge.

Aalberg, T., Blekesaune, A., & Elvestad, E. (2013). Media choice and informed democracy. *The International Journal of Press/Politics*, 18(3), 281–303. doi:10.1177/1940161213485990

Aarts, K., & Semetko, H. A. (2003). The divided electorate: Media use and political involvement. *Journal of Politics*, 65(3), 759–784. doi:10.1111/1468-2508.00211

Bakshy, E., Messing, S., & Adamic, L. A. (2015). Exposure to ideologically diverse news and opinion on Facebook. *Science*, 348(6239), 1130–1132. doi:10.1126/science.aaa1160

Barberá, P., Jost, J. T., Nagler, J., Tucker, J. A., & Bonneau, R. (2015). Tweeting from left to right: Is online political communication more than an echo chamber? *Psychological Science*, 26(10), 1531–1542.

Beam, M. A. (2014). Automating the news: How personalized news recommender system design choices impact news reception. *Communication Research*, 41(8), 1019–1041.

Beam, M. A., & Kosicki, G. M. (2014). Personalized news portals: Filtering systems and increased news exposure. *Journalism & Mass Communication Quarterly*, 91(1), 59–77.

Benkler, Y., Faris, R., Roberts, H., & Zuckerman, E. (2017). Study: Breitbart-led right-wing media ecosystem altered broader media agenda. *Columbia Journalism Review*, 1(4.1), 7.

Blekesaune, A., Elvestad, E., & Aalberg, T. (2012). Tuning out the world of news and current affairs: An empirical study of Europe's disconnected citizens. *European Sociological Review*, 28(1), 110–126. doi:10.1093/esr/jcq051

Blumler, J. G. (1970). The political effects of television. In J. D. Halloran (Ed.), *The Political effects of television* (pp. 68–104). London, England: Panther.

Buckels, E. E., Trapnell, P. D., & Paulhus, D. L. (2014). Trolls just want to have fun. *Personality and Individual Differences*, 67, 97–102.

Chaffee, S. H., & McLeod, J. M. (1973). Individual vs. social predictors of information seeking. *Journalism Quarterly*, 50, 237–245.

Christakis, N. A., & Fowler, J. H. (2009). *Connected: The surprising power of our social networks and how they shape our lives – How your friends' friends' friends affect everything you feel, think, and do*. New York, NY: Little, Brown and Company.

Curran, J., Coen, S., Soroka, S., Aalberg, T., Hayashi, K., Hichy, Z., … Rhee, J. W. (2014). Reconsidering 'virtuous circle' and 'media malaise' theories of the media: An 11-nation study. *Journalism*, 15(7), 815–833.

DellaVigna, S., & Kaplan, E. (2007). The Fox News effect: Media bias and voting. *The Quarterly Journal of Economics*, 122(3), 1187–1234.

Duca, J., & Saving, J. (2012). *Has income inequality or media fragmentation increased political polarization?* Working Paper 1206. Retrieved February 18, 2017 from www.dallasfed.org/assets/documents/research/papers/2012/wp1206.pdf

Dvir-Gvirsman, S., Garrett, R. K., & Tsfati, Y. (2015). Why do partisan audience participate? Perceived public opinion as the mediating mechanism. *Communication Research*. First published August 17, 2015. doi:10.1177/0093650215593145

EBU. (2016). *Trust in media 2016*. The European Broadcasting Union Media Intelligence Service. Retrieved December 18, 2016 from www.ebu.ch/news/2016/08/ebu-research-shows-strong-public-service-media-contributes-to-a-healthy-democracy

Festinger, L. (1957/1964). *A theory of cognitive dissonance*. Stanford, CA: Stanford University Press.

Flaxman, S., Goel, S., & Rao, J. M. (2016). Filter bubbles, echo chambers, and online news consumption. *Public Opinion Quarterly*, 80(S1), 298–320. doi:10.1093/poq/nfw006

Fletcher, R. (2017). Polarisation in the News Media. *Reuters Institutes Digital News Report*. Retrieved July 17, 2017 from http://www.digitalnewsreport.org/survey/2017/polarisation-in-the-news-media-2017

Fuchs, C. (2015). *Culture and economy in the age of social media*. New York, NY: Routledge.

Gillespie, T. (2014). Facebook's algorithm – Why our assumptions are wrong, and our concerns are right. *Culture Digitally*, 4. Retrieved April 4, 2017 from http://culturedigitally.org/2014/07/facebooks-algorithm-why-our-assumptions-are-wrong-and-our-concerns-are-right/

Grabe, M. E., & Kamhawi, R. (2006). Hard wired for negative news? Gender differences in processing broadcast news. *Communication Research*, 33(5), 346–369.

Hall, S. ([1973] 1980). Encoding/decoding. In S. Hall, D. Hobson, A. Lowe, & P. Willis (Eds.), *Culture, media, language: Working papers in cultural studies, 1972–1979* (pp. 117–127). London, England; New York, NY: Routledge.

Hallin, D. C., & Mancini, P. (2004). *Comparing media systems: Three models of media and politics.* Cambridge, England: Cambridge University Press.

Herman, E. S., & Chomsky, N. (1988). *Manufacturing consent: The political economy of the mass media.* London, England: Random House Group.

Herman, E. S. & McChesney, R. W. (1997). *The Global Media: The New Missionaries of Corporate Capitalism.* London: Cassell.

Herman, E. S., & McChesney, R. W. (2004). *Global media: The new missionaries of global capitalism.* New York, NY: Continuum.

Himelboim, I., McCreery, S., & Smith, M. (2013). Birds of a feather tweet together: Integrating network and content analyses to examine cross-ideology exposure on Twitter. *Journal of Computer-Mediated Communication*, 18(2), 154–174. doi:10.1111/jcc4.12001

Hindman, M. (2009). *The myth of internet democracy*, Princeton, NJ: Princeton University Press.

Hmielowski, J. D., Beam, M. A., & Hutchens, M. J. (2015). Structural changes in media and attitude polarization: Examining the contributions of TV news before and after the Telecommunications Act of 1996. *International Journal of Public Opinion Research*, 28(2), 153–172.

Jamieson, K. H., & Cappella, J. N. (2010). *Echo chamber: Rush Limbaugh and the Conservative media establishment.* New York, NY: Oxford University Press.

Jang, S. M., Lee, H., & Park, Y. J. (2014). The more friends, the less political talk? Predictors of Facebook discussions among college students. *Cyberpsychology, Behavior, and Social Networking*, 17(5), 271–275.

Janis, I. (1982). *Groupthink* (2nd ed.). Boston, MA: Houghton-Mifflin.

Jun, Y., Meng, R., & Johar, G. V. (2017). Perceived social presence reduces fact-checking. *Proceedings of the National Academy of Sciences*, 114(23), 5976–5981. doi:10.1073/pnas.1700175114

Kaminska, M., Gallacher, J. D., Kollany, B., Yasseri, T., & Howard, P. N. (2017). *Social media and news sources during the 2017 UK General Election.* COMPRO Data Memo 2017.6, Oxford. Retrieved June 7, 2017 from http://comprop.oii.ox.ac.uk/wp-content/uploads/sites/89/2017/06/Social-Media-and-News-Sources-during-the-2017-UK-General-Election.pdf

Karlsen, R. (2015). Followers are opinion leaders: The role of people in the flow of political communication on and beyond social networking sites. *European Journal of Communication*, 30(3), 301–318.

Karppinen, K. (2013). *Rethinking media pluralism.* New York, NY: Fordham University Press.

Katz, E., & Lazarsfeld, P. (1955/2006). *Personal influence: The part played by people in the flow of mass communications.* New Brunswick, NJ: Transaction Publisher.

Knobloch-Westerwick, S., & Alter, S. (2007). The gender news use divide: Americans' sex-typed selective exposure to online news topics. *Journal of Communication*, 57(4), 739–758.

Lazarsfeld, P. F., Berelson, B., & Gaudet, H. (1944/1952). *The people's choice.* New York, NY: Duell, Sloan and Pearce.

Lelkes, Y., Sood, G., & Iyengar, S. (2015). The hostile audience: The effect of access to broadband internet on partisan affect. *American Journal of Political Science*, 61(1), 5–20. doi:10.1111/ajps.12237

McPherson, M., Smith-Lovin, L., & Cook, J. M. (2001). Birds of a feather: Homophily in social networks. *Annual Review of Sociology*, 27(1), 415–444.

Media Insight Project. (2017). *"Who shared it": How Americans decide what news to tryst on social media.* American Press Institute and the Associated Press, NORC Centre for Public Affairs Research. Retrieved May 28, 2017 from www.americanpressinstitute.org/publications/reports/survey-research/trust-social-media/

Media Reform Coalition. (2016). The bias of objectivity: The Evening Standard not so neutral after all. Retrieved August 17, 2017 from www.mediareform.org.uk/blog/bias-objectivity-evening-standard-not-neutral-mayoral-race-editor-claimed

Merton, R. K. (1949). Patterns of influence: A study of interpersonal influence and of communications behavior in a local community. In P. Lazarsfeld & F. Stanton (Eds.), *Communication research 1948–1949* (pp. 180–219). New York, NY: Harper and Brothers.

Messing, S., & Westwood, S. J. (2014). Selective exposure in the age of social media: Endorsements trump partisan source affiliation when selecting news online. *Communication Research*, 41(8), 1042–1063.

Mitchell, A., Gottfried, J., Barthel, M., & Shearer, E. (2016a). *Pathways to news: The modern news consumer.* Pew Research Center. Retrieved July 20, 2016 from www.journalism.org/2016/07/07/pathways-to-news/

Morley, D. (1980). *The nationwide audience: Structure and decoding* (British Film Institute Television Monograph No. 11). London, England: British Film Institute.

Mutz, D. C. (2002). Cross-cutting social networks: Testing democratic theory in practice. *American Political Science Review*, 96(1), 111–126. doi:10.1017/S0003055402004264

Nahon, K., & Hemsley, J. (2014). Homophily in the guise of cross-linking: Political blogs and content. *American Behavioral Scientist*, 58(10), 1294–1313.

Negroponte, N. (1995). *Being digital.* London, England: Hodder & Stoughton.

Newman, N., Fletcher, R., Levy, D. A. L., & Nielsen, R. K. (2016). *Reuters Institute digital news report 2016.* Retrieved December 3, 2016 from http://reutersinstitute.politics.ox.ac.uk/sites/default/files/research/files/Digital%2520News%2520Report%25202016.pdf

Newman, N., Fletcher, R., Kalogeropoulos, D., & Nielsen, R. K. (2017). *Reuters Institute digital news report 2017.* Retrieved July 3, 2017 from https://reutersinstitute.politics.ox.ac.uk/sites/default/files/Digital%20News%20Report%202017%20web_0.pdf?utm_source=digitalnewsreport.org&utm_medium=referral

Noelle-Neumann, E. (1974). The spiral of silence: A theory of public opinion. *Journal of Communication*, 24(2), 43–51.

Nyhan, B., & Reifler, J. (2010). When corrections fail: The persistence of political misperceptions. *Political Behavior*, 32(2), 303–330. doi:10.1007/s11109-010-9112-2

Pariser, E. (2011). *The filter bubble: What the Internet is hiding from you.* London, England: Penguin Books.

Patterson, T. E. (2016). News coverage of the 2016 National Conventions: Negative news, lacking context. Harvard Kennedy School. Retrieved May 20, 2017 from https://shoren steincenter.org/news-coverage-2016-national-conventions/

Pew Research Center. (2008). The news and daily life. Pew Research Center for the People and the Press. Retrieved November 17, 2016 from www.people-press.org/2008/08/17/the-news-and-daily-life/

Poindexter, P., Meraz, S., & Weiss, A. S. (2008). *Women, men and news: Divided and disconnected in the news media landscape.* Abingdon, England; New York, NY: Routledge.

Postman, N. (1986). *Amusing ourselves to death: Public discourse in the age of show business.* New York, NY: Penguin Books.

PR Newswire and Cambridge Analytica (2016). CA Congratulates Donald Trump and Mike Pence. *CA-political.com.* Retrieved January 20, 2017 from https://ca-political.com/news/ca-congratulates-donald-trump-and-mike-pence

Prior, M. (2007). *Post-broadcast democracy: How media choice increases inequality in political involvement and polarizes elections.* New York, NY: Cambridge University Press.

Purcell, K. (2013). *Online video 2013.* Pew Internet Project, Pew Research Center. Retrieved October 3, 2016 from www.pewinternet.org/files/old-media//Files/Reports/2013/PIP_Online%20Video%202013.pdf

Rainie, L., & Smith, A. (2012). Social networking sites and politics. Pew Research Center: Internet, Science & Tech. Retrieved 15 January, 2017 from www.pewinternet.org/2012/03/12/social-networking-sites-and-politics/

Schoenbach, K., & Lauf, E. (2002). The "trap" effect of television and its competitors. *Communication Research,* 29(5), 564–583. doi:10.1177/009365002236195

Schrøder, K. C., & Blach-Ørsten, M. (2016). *The nature of news avoidance in a digital world.* Reuters digital news report 2016. Reuters Institute for the Study of Journalism. Retrieved January 23, 2017 from www.digitalnewsreport.org/essays/2016/nature-news-avoidance-digital-world/

Slater, M. D. (2007). Reinforcing spirals: The mutual influence of media selectivity and media effects and their impact on individual behavior and social identity. *Communication Theory,* 17(3), 281–303.

Strömbäck, J., Djerf-Pierre, M., & Shehata, A. (2013). The dynamics of political interest and news media consumption: A longitudinal perspective. *International Journal of Public Opinion Research,* 25(4), 414–435. doi:10.1093/ijpor/eds018

Strömbäck, J., & Shehata, A. (2010). Media malaise or a virtuous circle? Exploring the causal relationships between news media exposure, political news attention and political interest. *European Journal of Political Research,* 49(5), 575–597. doi:10.1111/j.1475–6765.2009.01913.x

Stroud, N. J. (2007). Media effects, selective exposure, and fahrenheit 9/11. *Political Communication,* 24(4), 415–432. doi:10.1080/10584600701641565.

Stroud, N. J. (2010). Polarization and partisan selective exposure. *Journal of Communication,* 60(3), 556–576.

Sunstein, C. R. (2007). *Sunstein on the internet and political polarization.* Chicago, IL: University of Chicago. Retrieved November 7, 2016 from www.law.uchicago.edu/news/sunstein-internet-and-political-polarization

Sunstein, C. R. (2009). *Republic.com 2.0.* Princeton, NJ: Princeton University Press.

Tufekci, Z. (2015). How Facebook's algorithm suppresses content diversity (modestly) and how the newsfeed rules your clicks. *Medium.* Retrieved May 16, 2017 from https://medium.com/message/how-facebook-s-algorithm-suppresses-content-diversity-modestly-how-the-newsfeed-rules-the-clicks-b5f8a4bb7bab#.ojpcdiu0k

Valeriani, A., & Vaccari, C. (2016). Accidental exposure to politics on social media as online participation equalizer in Germany, Italy, and the United Kingdom. *New Media & Society,* 18(9), 1857–1874.

Van Aelst, P., Strömbäck, J., Aalberg, T., Esser, F., de Vreese, C., Matthes, J., … Stanyer, J. (2017). Political communication in a high-choice media environment: A challenge for democracy? *Annals of the International Communication Association, 2017,* 41(1), 3–27.

Wonneberger, A., Schoenbach, K., & van Meurs, L. (2012). Staying tuned: TV news audiences in the Netherlands 1988–2010. *Journal of Broadcasting & Electronic Media,* 56(1), 55–74.

Yardi, S., & Boyd, D. (2010). Dynamic debates: An analysis of group polarization over time on Twitter. *Bulletin of Science, Technology & Society,* 30(5), 316–327.

Yoo, S. W., & Gil de Zúñiga, H. (2014). Connecting blog, Twitter and Facebook use with gaps in knowledge and participation. *Communication & Society,* 27(4), 33–48.

Zuiderveen Borgesius, F. J., Trilling, D., Moeller, J., Bodó, B., de Vreese, C. H., & Helberger, N. (2016). Should we worry about filter bubbles? *Internet Policy Review,* 5(1). doi:10.14763/2016.1.401

3

WE ARE ALL JOURNALISTS NOW

Myth: the role of the journalist is merging with the role of the audience[1]

Critiques of the news media emphasise its one-way nature in which elites have had charge of the microphone and the people simply listen to the messages (Adorno, 1975; Thompson, 1995). Some argue that this problem was structured into the technology of mass media and that new technologies, in the hands of the audience, would automatically change that relationship (Enzensberger, 1970), the boundary between producers and consumers would start to blur and audiences would become "prosumers" (Toffler, 1970). Mark Deuze (2003) saw this change coming when he wrote of a: "fundamental shift in established modes of journalism, undermining the 'we write, you read' dogma of modern journalism". He was not the only person to foresee a complete change in the way in which news would be constructed in the future with "citizen journalists" taking their place alongside professionals, or simply replacing them (see also Beckett, 2008; Gilmore, 2004; Negroponte, 1995; Tapscott & Williams, 2006).

Journalists have often seen a rather different picture in which "prosumers", enjoying the chance of creative activity, or the opportunity to "have a say", gradually erode the opportunities for those who derive income from working as journalists or other media workers (Ritzer & Jurgenson, 2010). From this perspective, the possibilities for "co-creation" are not so much a force for liberation as a means by which the value of their work is degraded and corporations can replace a paid workforce with free labour, thereby reducing the costs of production (O'Sullivan & Heinonen, 2008). Interaction with the audience, on the other hand, is usually regarded as useful (Örnebring, 2013) even though most journalists see their own role as distinct, invoking "expertise, duty and autonomy" as claims to distinction (Örnebring, 2013).

There is a third position, which inverts the claim itself and asks whether it is reasonable to define everyone with a smartphone as a journalist? There certainly are changes in the way that journalism is now produced and delivered but the suggestion that we are all journalists misunderstands both the role of the journalist and the means by which the news industry has been disrupted. It also devalues the importance of what Jenkins (2016) refers to as "trans-media mobilisation" (or activism). Not every act of communication is an act of journalism. For Jenkins, the Internet has produced: "dramatic increases in grassroots access to resources for cultural production and circulation" (Jenkins, 2016, p. 17). However, he doesn't see this as a replacement for mainstream journalism. It is rather a means by which activist groups can "surf media flows" (ibid.). This chapter will examine these ideas and ask, to what extent have audiences actually started to blur the borderline with journalism?

Does technology turn citizens into journalists?

Adrienne Russell (2011), in her book *Networked*, suggests that journalism has fundamentally changed because:

> Journalism can be a conversation that takes place in the blogosphere; an interactive media rich interface on a mainstream or alternative news site that provides context to a breaking story; the work of any number of fact check sites; a tweeted camera-phone photo of a breaking news event; a comment or comment thread on a news site; a video game created to convey a particular news narrative, and so on.
>
> *(Russell, 2011, p. 22)*

The difficulty with definitions of journalism that are located, as this is, in technology, is that they are incapable of being separated from other activities that can be produced by the same technology and they fail to fully take into account the impact of changing business practices. Most of the tasks that Russell (2011), Glaser (2006) and Rosen (2008) describe as the defining attributes of citizen journalism are in fact activities that are regularly performed by journalists and can be performed by almost anyone else. Indeed, there has never been anything immanent in the technology that would make it impossible for others to perform the tasks required of journalism: pen and paper, typewriter, cameras, film and video cameras have always been used by people who are not journalists. Nor has there ever been a time in which the roles of journalist, commentator, political activist and diarist have not overlapped (Atton, 2010). The difference afforded by the Internet lies, not so much with the act of journalism, but in the ability to disseminate journalism and it is this new possibility for two-way communication and distribution that has led people, on the one hand to see a new and more democratic way of gathering and disseminating news, and on the other to see a threat to journalism as a fundamental plank of modern democracy.

The need to separate out a special category of "citizen journalism" is, for many of its exponents, part of the task of separating off those people who are attached to mainstream news organisations and those who have a more fluid relationship with the traditional media. For some scholars (Jenkins, 2006) the difference lies between those who are employed by mainstream media and are therefore answerable to editors and proprietors who are themselves part of the elite and those who are answerable to some definition of "the people". For others, the spectrum of the alternative covers anything from performance art to posters on lamp-posts (Downing, 2010). The US Senate, which has the task of drafting federal laws to protect journalists, has a similar definition but arrives at it from another perspective: the difference between a journalist and everyone else with access to the same tools boils down to their work status: "a salaried employee of, or independent contractor for" a business that produces journalism (Russell, 2011, p. 23). We would agree with Russell that this is an uncomfortable definition because journalism is not reducible to a particular business model. Indeed, it is perfectly possible to define oneself as a journalist and not be paid, or to be a journalist who is paid in one location and yet works for free in another (Atton, 2012).

Some have tried to define journalism through the lens of professionalisation. This has been particularly evident in the USA where successive waves of professionalisation introduced first, formal journalism education and, more recently, an attempt to codify professional behaviour through the Project for Excellence in Journalism (Kovach & Rosenstiel, 2007). The difficulty with using professionalism as an analytical term is that it fails to capture the variety and flexibility of journalism as an occupation. Professions require shared boundaries that are usually established by examinations and/or licensing. But in democracies, journalism cannot be fixed in this way, because that would immediately run into questions of legitimacy over who has the right to license freedom of speech (Phillips, 2014, p. 79; Carlson, 2007; Gerlis, 2008). Throughout the history of news production, there have been journalists dedicated to producing an account of events that is at odds with the established power hierarchy (Atton, 2012).

We would argue that, what best defines a journalist, as opposed to a bystander, witness, source, or political activist, lies in the process of journalism rather than in the tools or technology journalism employs (Larson, 1977; Örnebring, 2010). The term journalist is derived from the French word "jour" (day). It implies the daily observation and recording of events. The issue is not so much whether observers are paid (although that certainly helps if a job is to be done on a daily basis) but whether they dedicate a sufficient portion of their energy to this specialised activity. It is the regularity and therefore the intensity of what journalists do, their positioning as observers of, rather than participants in, events and their ability to broadcast to widespread audiences, that marks them out. Some journalists may operate at the periphery, many fail, but occasionally those on the outside find an audience that will sustain them (for example, the British magazine *Private Eye* or the *American Village Voice*), or are adopted by mainstream media, quick to spot a trend (as in the case of blogger Andrew Sullivan who became a newspaper columnist for *The Times*).

To claim these radical interventions as a new phenomenon, brought into being by the affordances of the Internet, as Glaser (2006) and Rosen (2008) suggest, is to misunderstand the rich variety of journalism historically. Independent journalists have always existed; cultural surfers riding on any new wave that they can catch. They may self-define as alternative, or independent, journalists but they are part of a rich tradition of individuals who use communication tools to circulate information on a regular basis to an audience. They are not a threat to journalism. They are part of journalism.

Counting the active audience

Having defined journalism as an activity, we now consider the degree to which the audience is interested in prosumer news activity, or able to interact with news producers. A United Nations report released in 2015 found that over 95 per cent of the global population were already covered by a mobile cellular system and 43.4 per cent were already online.[2] An estimated 2.95 billion are expected to be using some form of social media by 2020 (Statista, 2017). So the potential is there for very widespread engagement. A number of surveys have looked at the experience of audiences and asked what people are actually doing online and just how much they are interacting with journalists or producing news.

Jakob Nielsen (2006) developed an ad hoc rule for user participation: 90–9–1. He found that: "In most online communities, 90% of users are lurkers who never contribute, 9% of users contribute a little, and 1% of users account for almost all the action". Among those who set up blogs and therefore set up their own means of participation, the inequality was even greater: 95–5–0.1. When, in 2012, *The Guardian* published information about user participation in its comment section, it reported 70.6 million unique users that month, and 600,000 comments. Forty per cent of the comments were posted by 2,600 prolific commentators. In other words, fewer than 1 per cent of visitors ever interact with journalists, and only 1 per cent of *them* interact regularly (Elliott, 2012 in Phillips, 2014, p. 95). A BBC study found that only 0.05 per cent of the BBC audience contribute to "have your says" (Thurman, 2008). Nor is the audience interested in reading the work of other audience members. A seven-country study of audience preferences found "a strong disregard for participatory options such as user-generated content" (Boczkowski & Mitchelstein, 2013, p. 140).

With the advent of social media, with its ready-made user interface and simplified networking, more people are involved in interactivity – but they are not interacting directly with journalists and they are rarely intending to produce journalism. Mostly they are passing on (often with comments) material that has been written by journalists or by people who they believe to be journalists. Their key role lies in circulating and distributing the products of journalism. US research (Purcell, Rainie, Mitchell, Rosenstiel, & Olmstead, 2010) found that 37 per cent of people surveyed interacted in some way with news online but still only some 3 per cent actually created content, while 9 per cent commented. The rest posted links or tweets. An international review of the literature on "Media-User Typologies" (MUT) found a similar pattern. Only 5 per cent were identified as "Advanced Users". Most were categorised as Sporadics or Lurkers – rarely posting material themselves (Brandtzæg, 2010).

This fits well with work undertaken for the BBC by Wardle and Williams (2008). The researchers asked respondents how they would react if they were faced with a large fire and knew the emergency services had been called. Only 5 per cent said they would contact the media to let them know what was going on. A further 14 per cent would take a photo but only 6 per cent would send the photo to a news organisation, and the remaining 8 per cent would take a photo but not send it to a news organisation. An NBC news App called *breakingnews.com* attempted to organise citizens who stumbled upon breaking news events. The App alerted other users and breaking news editors to events happening nearby. After six years the service closed down because it didn't garner a big enough audience. As its editor Cory Bergman tweeted: "such a model doesn't fit with advertising, and despite a surge of interest in our premium data, the money has run out".[3]

By 2016, in a follow-up US study, there was still only 3 per cent who regularly posted their own photos or videos online, while another 16 per cent occasionally did so. Only 8 per cent regularly commented, though another 29 per cent occasionally did so. Most online activity now centres around distribution or consumption of material via linking (Mitchell, Gottfried, Barthel, & Shearer, 2016). A smaller Swedish study came up with similar results, finding that around 12 per cent of the population could be described as news sharers (Wadbring & Ödmark, 2016). While this has huge significance for what people see and how news is distributed it doesn't constitute a change in the production of news material. The material shared varies by country and media system. In the UK, Germany and France, over 50 per cent of material shared in a pre-election period came from professional sources (in the UK, the BBC was the most popular). In the USA only one-third came from professional sources and a similar proportion came from what the researchers classified as "junk news" sources (Kaminska, Gallacher, Kollany, Yasseri, & Howard, 2017).

Work by the Reuters Institute for the Study of Journalism (Newman, Fletcher, Levy, & Nielsen, 2016, p. 99) uses a different form of categorisation in which "Proactive Participators" include people who post, comment and blog on news websites and social media. As this is a much larger category it is harder to compare with other studies but the majority in this category were commenting on news rather than producing original content. What this study did find is a big difference in participation rates in different countries. The Japanese are the least participative nation. The most enthusiastic participators are in Turkey, Brazil and Greece: all countries that have experienced a degree of recent political turbulence and in all of which there are low levels of trust in the national media.

The study found a correlation between lack of trust and increased participation in all the countries surveyed and it is noteworthy that the USA is classified at the least trustful end of the spectrum alongside Spain and Italy, countries which are described as having politically aligned and partisan media systems (Hallin & Mancini, 2004). In these "politically polarized" news media systems, where opinion is not separated from fact, there has always been a more blurred distinction between journalism and comment, and the opportunities for greater participation afforded by social media have clearly been widely taken up. In those countries that have adopted the Northern European model, with state supported (and yet independent) public broadcasting, audience trust is higher and participation rates online and via social media are a great deal lower. The higher levels of both distrust and participation rates in the USA suggests that a Liberal (North Atlantic) news media system may have difficulty maintaining trust in the absence of a well-funded, public broadcasting system. These differences in the way in which news is delivered need to be kept in mind when considering the role of the audience.

What do active audiences produce?

While it is clear that the Internet has enabled large numbers of people to broadcast their views and to interact with one another, in most of their interactions online, they are acting in the capacity of audiences, not producers. For most people, the Internet is a tool which facilitates information seeking, rather than creative participation. When people are productive online, to what extent does journalism, or news-gathering, figure in their activities?

The prosumer

Alvin Toffler coined the term "prosumer" in 1980 to describe a consumer who is also a producer, capable of actively re-purposing or adding to media products produced for mass consumption. For Toffler this was a means of breaking down the divide between producers and consumers and heralded a return to a time before capitalist exploitation of labour, when individuals had more freedom to make, sell and consume on their own terms. Humphreys and Grayson (2008) describe the relationship between the companies that provide social media services and prosumers as the potentially exploitative "ideological recruitment of consumers into productive co-creation relationships [hinging] on accommodating consumers' needs for recognition, freedom, and agency" (p. 185).

The majority of activity online is social in nature (Örnebring, 2008, p. 783). Parents and friends produce most material, which is mainly viewed by close friends and family. The huge popularity of social media platforms is a testament to the desire of human beings to communicate and to create but the most common subject matter is friends and family doing everyday things: 58 per cent post videos with this kind of content; followed closely by videos of themselves or others doing funny things (56%) and videos of events attended (54%) (Duggan, 2013). Occasionally, a cute video escapes into the viral wild. Spotting the potential for cute videos to bring in vast audiences for advertisers, YouTube has been quick to exploit this potential and to offer a percentage of advertising cash to those people who manage to attract very large numbers of viewers. This has incentivised people who see an opportunity to make an income and changed the relationship so that a minority of the former audience are recruited, rather like Uber drivers, into a business relationship with YouTube.

In order to clock up the necessary number of viewings to start bringing in cash, it is nearly always necessary to be thoroughly professional. What we see here is the creation of a new field of highly commercial media content. At one end it covers those who make videos of their cats and of toddlers unwrapping toys; at the other it encompasses the growing specialist field of Vloggers. For many Vloggers, a self-produced video channel is a calling card to attract a management company who will then organise sponsorship deals and provide production expertise. But given that in October 2016 there were 276,000,000 style blogs, it takes more than just an interest in clothes and self-presentation to find an audience. Typing "style blogs" into Google brings up a page of intermediaries, usually mainstream media organisations that provide their own lists of top ten or "best" style blogs.

While anyone can create a blog, only an elite few will rise to the top. In a 2008 interview with Brian Stelter of *The New York Times*, a YouTube spokesman, Aaron Zamost, said: "hundreds of YouTube partners are making thousands of dollars a month". Stelter found one: Michael Buckley, who was earning over $100,000 from YouTube advertisements. However, he said: "I was spending 40 hours a week on YouTube for over a year before I made a dime" (Stelter, 2008).

Those who succeed are highly polished performers who have in many cases displaced the consumer, style and technology magazines that used to supply this market. This can be seen as a genuine disruption (Christensen, 1997) of the consumer magazine field on the one hand, and a genuine opportunity, on the other hand, for a small number of highly successful entrepreneurs to make a living that is relatively autonomous from mainstream media. It is not, however, autonomous from the market. Vloggers depend for their income on maintaining high enough audience figures to be able to offer brand endorsements. Those at the bottom of the food chain will earn nothing and even relatively successful style bloggers are either independently wealthy enough to buy new clothes on a very regular basis, or are dependent on their sponsors for access to the clothes they present (Stelter, 2008).

This is what BuzzFeed CEO, Jonah Peretti, had to say about prosumer material threatening mainstream publishers:

> User-generated content often is the most important in the early stages of a new distribution technology. But then people at companies like BuzzFeed and others can have full-time people who think a lot about the medium and can see the stuff that's working that's user-generated and make it better and improve upon it and learn more about it. I think over time, you will see professionals start to figure out how to do some of this in a way that you can't do if you just have a job and you're doing it part-time. So I think user-generated will be important. But you will start to see the biggest things won't necessarily be done by an average person. It will be done by celebrities, media companies and people who really understand how to connect with audiences.
>
> *(Yoshida, 2016)*

In 2015 *Technorati*,[4] which had been the gateway to the Bloggersphere, published their final list of the most influential bloggers. Of the top ten listed, all are now either major companies in their own right or are owned by major media companies. Five are tech related, two are sports related. A 2008 report also found that, although women and men both produced blogs, men were considerably more likely to appear in the lists of the most popular sites (Poindexter, Meraz, & Weiss, 2008). Research in *The Guardian* found that when women do write blogs they are also more likely than men to be subject to online abuse (Gardiner et al., 2016).

Conscious of how difficult it has become for ordinary people to be heard in the noise generated online, NGOs are entering the frame to help citizens who want to have their voices heard. One such is *Radar*, which describes itself as a citizen journalism support organisation. This is what it does:

> Radar has a number of ways of ensuring that what we publish is legitimate. Firstly, we work with trusted civil society networks to ensure that those put forward for training are already engaged with an issue or their communities to some degree. Secondly, we run intensive face-to-face training workshops, ensuring we find out who our reporters are and vice versa, which builds trust. We train people in the fundamentals of good journalism, including why we must report accurately and avoid plagiarism, hate speech and hearsay. Thirdly, our software guarantees we only ever receive and publish stories from the people we've trained, whose names and numbers we have programmed into our system. Finally, there is always the option of not publishing sensitive, provocative or unverified information. A story that needs extra research or is strong enough to be pitched to external media, is developed with Radar staff. This mentoring system improves reporters' skills and means their work can reach beyond social media channels.
>
> *(Klein, 2014, p. 32).*

While *Radar* is expanding the number of voices available to mainstream journalism, which is certainly a good thing, the effort involved belies the suggestion that it is possible for everyone to be a journalist just by being connected. What we are seeing here is a commendable effort to ensure that a wider variety of opinions and perspectives are made available but, in the absence of an expanding number of "external media channels", these views will still have to fulfil the requirements of traditional journalism and will still have to find a way through the "news funnel" in order to compete for the attention of news audiences.

> Professional media retain a powerful role in shaping agendas and legitimising and authorising political action. Digital technologies create many genuinely important and different opportunities for non-elite interventions in shaping agendas, but... these interventions are predicated on the very existence of professional media in the first place.
>
> *(Chadwick & Dennis, 2017, p. 54)*

Citizen news

In the arena of news, Peretti's prediction has even more resonance. The best-known attempt to establish an audience-powered news website is *OhmyNews*, which was started in South Korea in 2000. It recruited 70,000 registered citizen journalists and around 100 professional members of staff, who check and edit the work of the citizens as well as writing news stories (Nah & Chung, 2016). Nevertheless, most of the citizen content on *OhmyNews* is comment. Any news reports have to be double-checked and then edited by trained journalists because people who are not trained find it hard to understand how to gather evidence and present it. This actually raises costs rather than reducing them because work has to be done twice. Attempts to set up a similar international site foundered due to lack of interest.[5]

Mainstream news organisations, seeing what *OhmyNews* had achieved, considered harnessing the power of the audience as an opportunity to cut costs. Given that they already had newsrooms and journalists to pay for, most found that the value of user-generated content was "disproportionate to the excessive amount of management time which is taken up with trying to ensure it is accurate, balanced, honest, fair and – most importantly – legally safe to publish" (Singer, 2010, p. 134). The *Huffington Post* was one of the first to make it work. As a new "native" site without the encumbrance of a newsroom, it started using the free labour of engaged public intellectuals, enthusiastic amateurs and celebrities, alongside a judicious mix of curation (linking to other news sites and making use of their work without paying for it), and a small amount of paid editing (Deuze & Fortunati, 2011, p. 170).

HuffPo has a small team of journalists and editors and uses work from an estimated 100,000 "bloggers". Most of the material is commentary or reviews although the site sometimes makes use of amateur reporters, as they did with the OffTheBus blogging campaign during the 2012 US Presidential elections. The addition of extra, unpaid, reporters allowed HuffPo to cover a large number of election events that were off the main campaign trail and was at the time seen as a major breakthrough for citizen journalism. However, enthusiasm for helping out in this way is mixed. When AOL Time Warner bought the *Huffington Post* in 2011, a group of contributors sued for compensation for the value of their work. They lost, but their anger exposed the growing sense of unease among those who contribute for free to a company that makes revenue. Noah Baron, a HuffPo blogger, had this to say to the *International Business Times*:

> "I don't think that any company should be 'proud' that it doesn't compensate people for their labor. As pleased as I am with what I've written for Huffington Post, HuffPo ultimately generates substantial revenue off of my work and the work of many like me," said Baron. "I do wish I could be or had been paid for the material I write there. That said, I will likely continue to contribute because it allows me to spread a progressive message to a mass audience."
>
> *(James, 2016)*

Independent, local blogs, run on an unpaid (or low-paid) basis, often by non-professionals, perhaps come closest to what has been described as citizen journalism. *CGnet* in Swara, a rural area of India, appears to be a successful attempt to harness audience involvement directly in news-gathering. Established by an ex-BBC journalist, it uses phoned-in stories from local people that are checked and then released on the mobile phone network,[6] making a useful contribution to the local news ecology. In Rio de Janeiro, Brazil, the traditional mainstream media rarely send reporters into the favelas and neither the problems of infrastructure nor the behaviour of the police were being reported. Papo Reto stepped into the gap. The impetus behind the project was the extremely high number of police killings and the lack of any independent evidence to highlight such activity. Using smartphones and a computer this local independent outlet produces news "by the community, for the community", which is then checked and published on social media (Salomon, 2016).

Non-profit local newspapers or blogs have been established to try to plug the democratic gaps left by the closure of local papers, or as a means of providing an alternative form of democratic debate. *The Bristol Cable* or the *Brixton Blog* in the UK manage to keep going with a combination of grant and crowd-funding, self-exploitation and a modicum of local advertising. Partisan political sites provide new voices on the left and the right of politics but they depend heavily on mainstream journalism for content, which they then re-purpose for their particular audiences. Overall, the level of success does not seem to be any greater than that enjoyed by the alternative print press of the 1970s, some of which (like for example *Private Eye* in the UK) went on to establish themselves as a genuine alternative to the existing mainstream, but most of which enjoyed a brief flowering and then died away as enthusiasm waned (Phillips, 2007).

Apart from these much-publicised examples, audiences have not shown either the capacity, or the desire, to: "displace journalists as providers and analysts of civic information" (Singer, 2015, p. 85). The vast majority of so called "citizen journalism" sites are not engaged in reporting but instead link to and comment on material that is produced by paid journalists working for a dwindling number of mainstream news organisations. As Scott, Millard, and Leonard (2015) concluded: "online news systems are complex and interdependent, and most do not involve citizens to the extent that the terms used to describe them imply" (p. 737). Perhaps the most important issue however is that news organisations need to be sustained regularly, over the long term. While it is not impossible to do this on a voluntary basis, it does require a very high level of commitment, which can be very hard to sustain in the long term. A Knight Foundation study of non-profit news sites in the USA observed: "for the majority of organizations in the study, sustainability is just a premise on the distant horizon" (Knight Foundation, 2015, p. 23).

It is for this reason that the most successful new entrants into the field of "news" reporting have been the exponents of fake news. These people are entrepreneurs who have enough knowledge of social media to work the payments systems by writing stories that are likely to get shared. They are typically either "joke news", which people share for fun, or they are written to appeal directly to the fierce loyalty of political partisans. These stories are written to attract attention and to make it into the trending sections of Facebook or the top of the Google search engine.

Successful fake news entrepreneurs, such as Paul Horner, are said to be able to make a comfortable income from this entirely invented material (Dewey, 2016), which is often assumed to be true and passed on accordingly. The phenomenon of fake news came to public attention after the 2016 Presidential election in the USA and some efforts have been made by the Internet platforms to disrupt the business models of these entrepreneurs.

Partnership – Open journalism

Some scholars, recognising that unpaid journalists are not going to replace professionals, have looked instead to the emergence of an "ethic of participation", which "envisions audience integration as a normative goal of a truly digital journalism" (Lewis, 2012, pp. 851–852). Certainly audiences have a plethora of different possibilities for interaction with journalists: email, Twitter, Facebook or the comments below articles. However, they are often reluctant to use them.

There have been attempts to facilitate a more equal exchange, for example when *The Guardian* newspaper in the UK introduced Reality Check, a daily news story initiated by a journalist, in which readers were invited to send in information. The journalist and researchers would then comb through incoming comments and produce a rolling feature, incorporating the views of those audience members with knowledge of the subject. This project had some success for a short time but it was rare for a really well-informed member of the public to be able to provide useful material in the timescale required. It was often necessary to solicit information from known informants just to keep things going – which is exactly what a journalist would do routinely. Soon Reality Check stopped being a regular feature.

Some of the ideas of "open journalism" have kept going in liveblogs, which incorporate the audience voice, via material from social media, as events unfold. Journalist Matthew Weaver had this to say to *The New York Times* about the coverage of the Iranian uprisings in *The Guardian*: "first the tweets come, then the pictures, then the video and then the wires... What people are saying at one point in the day is then confirmed by more conventional sources four or five hours later" (Stelter, 2009). However, it is Weaver who is making the decisions, working as an editor (or curator) and incorporating voices that fit into the narrative he has established. Comment is Free, *The Guardian*'s comment platform, has also broadened the possibilities for individuals to make use of an international platform with a significant audience, but it is the editors who decide whose voice will be heard.

For a number of scholars, the limitations of open journalism lie in a form of protective inflexibility: "journalists resist relinquishing control over decisions about what passes through the news gate" (Singer, 2015, p. 86). But there are a number of reasons why journalists have not simply opened the gates to their audiences. For a start, journalists are themselves absolutely overwhelmed with information from electronic sources and find it very hard to comb through the amount of incoming material. As one political correspondent explained: "Being a journalist is rather like standing in the middle of a hurricane trying to pick out twigs. You are constantly looking around to see what's significant" (Phillips, 2010, p. 94).

While the two-way nature of the Internet has provided the means for interaction, the speed required to keep up with the ever-increasing flow of information online has reduced the time available to make contact with people. One result is that journalists tend to fall back on the sources that they know and which they have verified, through past experience, as reliable. A senior journalist on a British newspaper said:

> ...I can't think of a decent story that I've got from somebody that I'd never met or heard of before... maybe unsolicited in the respect in that I'd not actually heard of them before but it was a part of a relationship I built up with people in the area generally.
>
> *(Phillips, 2010, p. 92)*

The sheer scale of the material circulating online has also led to the increasing use of programmatic techniques for sorting out what is valuable. This immediately changes the power relationship. It is not the audience that is in charge of the interaction but the journalist, who trawls the Internet, using search engines that are specially built to surface stories and experiences that might be relevant. As information starts to emerge from social media it is usually the journalists, searching for relevant voices, who make the first contact using social media to solicit interviews. To facilitate this process, developers, working for news organisations, have produced specialist tools to identify worthwhile tweets. Other services allow journalists to search for key word clusters that help them home in on people who are tweeting at the scene of a news event (Doggett & Cantarero, 2016). For editors, the audience provides a useful source for digital news-gathering, rather than a means by which audience members can co-create (Hermida & Thurman, 2008).

Another side effect of the digital revolution has been the emergence of fact checking and verification as a specialised job. For some researchers this is all about the need to maintain editorial control and keep out interlopers.

> This desire for control is partly due to legitimate fears that, without such processes in place, some of the obscene, defamatory and libellous content that news websites receive will be published. It also stems from journalists and editors' long-held belief that they know what their readers want − and the associated traditions of selection and editing. These journalistic norms have played an important part in the implementation and regulation of participatory journalism in the mainstream. They betray the innate conservatism of newsroom culture − a culture forged during a long period of technological and financial stability − and a period that has now come to a sudden end.
>
> *(Thurman & Hermida, 2010, p. 27)*

As mainstream news organisations have become victims of deliberately planted "fake news", and manipulated material posted online for political ends, it has become necessary for them to protect the integrity of their product and avoid unintentionally circulating material that has been invented, or tampered with, in order to create propaganda or misinformation. This could be seen as a method of "boundary control" (Örnebring, 2013) and an attempt by mainstream news orga- nisations to maintain legitimacy in the field. However, it is arguably a worthwhile effort if genuine news organisations are to survive at all. Given competitive pressures online, processes of verification provide the "distinction" that is necessary to mark out a high-quality product from a fake news site.

Organisations such as Storyful (now owned by News International) employ staff to trawl the Internet (particularly in periods of civil unrest when many thousands of citizens are likely to take to social media) and use a variety of techniques to check whether the videos and photographs circulating actually relate to the events under scrutiny. Storyful then sells the verified material to news organisations, saving them hours spent checking material themselves.

Witnessing

The most potent and powerful material generated by "audiences" is what could be best described as witness content. These are images and video which are captured by passers-by who happen to be on the spot when events take place. Whether at a neighbourhood house fire, a revolution or a war, it has been the job of journalists to talk to witnesses in order to make sense of events because journalists are rarely on the spot when the event occurs. In the pre-mobile days, events that were important were missed because the people who did witness them did not have the knowledge, or the contacts, to ensure that their story was heard by those people who have the power to spread the word, nor the evidence to ensure that their version of events is believed.

The power of mobile technology in the hands of ordinary citizens has trans- formed witnessing, and ensured that events that in the past would have simply been overlooked, or filtered through the perceptions of elite sources such as the police or the army, can now be transferred, with a minimum of mediation, to an audience (Allan, 2006; Allan & Thorsen, 2009). The events that are most often uploaded to social media are rapid onset disasters.

> Twitter, Facebook, Instagram and Flickr lend themselves to the dramatic over the chronic; the earthquake or the long-term famine. It is not an accident that the disasters we have seen framed through the lens of user-generated content are ones like the tsunami, the Sichuan earthquake and the Haiti earthquake.
>
> *(Cooper, 2011, p. 36)*

Mostly they are the kind of disasters that would have been picked up by mainstream media anyway and the content, uploaded by citizens on the spot, adds to the depth and breadth of coverage in a way that no number of foreign correspondents ever could. However, when such an event occurs, it is the media that are in the driving seat, checking information and images and deciding what can be used. In exactly the same way they would check the veracity of verbal witness accounts.

There have been a few truly transformative moments in which mobile media drew attention to events that would never otherwise have been brought into public view: the death of newspaper salesman Ian Tomlinson during demonstrations in London in 2009 (Newman, 2009); the response to the shooting of Michael Brown in Ferguson in 2014, which was picked up on Twitter; and the subsequent shooting of Philando Castile in Indianapolis in 2016, which was livestreamed to Facebook by his girlfriend sitting in the car with him. In Brazil the shooting by police of a ten-year-old boy, Eduardo, in 2015 would have been covered up or presented as self-defence had the events not been filmed on mobile phones and then passed on via Papo Reto: "It took a mobile phone for people to be able to show what they had been saying for a long time. People used to just talk, now they show you what they see" (Salomon, 2016).

The importance of mobile witnessing cannot be underestimated but it can and often is misunderstood. Such events do not substitute for journalism, nor do they threaten journalism; they are a direct benefit to journalism and to audiences because they provide evidence that can be verified and, as such, they change the balance of power between ordinary people and the elite who so often seek to cover up their abuses of power. From the perspective of a journalist, verifiable evidence of an act of abuse of power is the best possible riposte to the authority of elite sources. The death of Ian Tomlinson was filmed by a passer-by, but it took a journalist, Paul Lewis, to track down the footage and it came to public notice through *The Guardian* (Newman, 2009, p. 33)

In the case of the Ferguson uprisings, the social media and mainstream media flows have been analysed (Hatlin & Vogt, 2014). Reports of the shooting and its aftermath were picked up on Twitter by journalists at the local newspaper who were down at the scene very quickly.[7] Events started being amplified by journalists on the scene, whose Twitter feeds have large followings and many of the tweets and re-tweets used the hashtag #blacklivesmatter. It was this amplification effect that ensured more and more people heard about the protests and came down to join them. It took several days for mainstream television news to pick up the events and the Twitter numbers then grew alongside the news, as people watched the news and tweeted about the events. Without that additional pick-up it is likely that a few people would have got angry, the police would have moved in and the entire protest would have been shut down in hours. Social media doesn't replace mainstream. It interacts with it.

Even in places such as China and Vietnam, where the media are controlled by the state, the act of witnessing is subtly changing the balance of power: not by bypassing the media but by providing a counter-balance to the power of the state. When journalists are able to access material from witnesses and link to that witness material online, their work is harder to censor. An article in *The New Yorker* compared media responses to the Sichuan earthquake of 2013 to coverage of a similar event in 2008 and noted that accurate information was reported in the media much faster – and official responses were also faster (Osnos, 2013). The gathering of witness material, that is clearly verifiable, is capable of tipping the balance against the elite sources that have always dominated news reporting. Nevertheless such material cannot simply be included unchecked. Research has found that "unreliable tweets" can compound problems and spread fear for those caught up in a disaster (Acar & Muraki, 2011, p. 392; Bruns & Burgess, 2014).

Singer (2015) sees the editorial insistence on verification of witness material as something journalists do just to protect professional boundaries: "in times of media instability, they also – even primarily – use ethics to distinguish between insiders and outsiders: who is or is not a journalist at all" (Singer, 2015, p. 4). It is verification that makes user-generated material powerful. It is the combination of the public ability to witness and the journalistic ability to verify and then disseminate, that challenges the power of elites and the power of the purveyors of fake news and misinformation.

The authoritative source

Journalists have always used sources: people who are either experts in the field, political actors or other members of the elite, whose testimony is used to build up an account of what happened or what is happening. This relationship is absolutely central to the production of liberal journalism. Ironically, as a result of the speed up in the news cycle, the decrease in the number of journalists and the exponential increase in the amount of circulating information, it has become more difficult for people without media contacts to be heard (Fenton, 2010). Even witnesses of, or participants in, a major event may find that it is hard to make much impact without a sophisticated understanding of how to manipulate social media.

Increasingly, people or organisations, feeling that their expertise is not heard, or is overlooked by journalists, are using the Internet and social media to appeal directly to audiences without the mediation of news organisations. NGOs and charities are particularly adept at this activity. Their websites are produced by public relations personnel, many of whom are ex-journalists, and they are dedicated entirely to getting information that will be of use to their organisations out to their supporters and to the public (Fenton, 2010). In some cases this activity is organised by third parties acting on behalf of organisations that are too small to manage their own public relations effort.

The affordances of the Internet provide campaigns, large or small, with the ability to provide a permanent showcase of their material, including detailed information about the particular cause they have espoused: from a neighbourhood campaign against environmental pollution to a major international campaign against the arms trade. While these websites are useful for providing information to activists, they also provide a very important resource for time-poor journalists. NGOs often have a frontseat view of the world's trouble spots and access to local voices, but their material is mainly produced for the purposes of advocacy or fundraising, with an inevitable focus on problems that require external intervention.

Reliance on uncorroborated NGO material may therefore produce a skewed picture of events on the ground (Wright, 2017). Similarly, when politicians speak directly to their voters without mediation, they are also producing a one-sided, positive picture of their intentions.

The availability of copious information that is easy to access has also, ironically, gone hand in hand with a decrease in face-to-face contact between NGOs and journalists (Davis, 2010; Fenton, 2010). The frantic speed of the news cycle means that journalists are more likely to trawl websites or listen to political debates online, rather than to take the time to attend press conferences and meet people in person (Davis, 2010; Phillips, 2010, p. 97). This reliance on online information sources, rather than face-to-face contact, means that the news media are producing more homogenous content based on the same online sources and are less likely to have the time to question the material they access (Davis, 2010; Phillips, 2010).

This failure to interrogate sources, or to conduct face-to-face interviews with people affected by political policy, is a trend that tends to favour elites. It also tends to lock journalists into the same kind of feedback loop as their audiences (described in Chapter 2). In the 2016 US Presidential elections for example, Donald Trump's Twitter feed became a major source of stories for journalists following the election. The organisation Social Flow calculated that Trump had managed to garner $380 million dollars of free publicity in the first weeks of the campaign by making provocative statements on social media that then got picked up and circulated by the traditional media (Lang, 2016). This focus on easily accessed, on-screen material, rather than interviews and investigation, meant that mainstream journalists focused even more intensely on established elite sources and their easily accessed social media accounts, rather than going out to interview voters about their concerns. This focus was, arguably, responsible for the media's failure to understand how the political landscape was shifting. A similar concentration on elite sources in the UK European Union referendum of the same year has also been blamed for the lack of any real sense of the public mood.

For journalists today it is hard to imagine doing the job without the rich resources of information provided by the Internet. It is a clear benefit to have online access to the proceedings of Parliament and its committees and to be able to check facts and dates on the websites of any reasonable-sized organisation. However, the existence of this rich mine of information doesn't in any way challenge the need for journalism. Arguably it makes it even more important. Direct access to an audience may be useful to elite players but it has also provided them with the means to side-step interrogation by journalists. While this lack of mediation may seem appealing to those who feel that they have been marginalised or misrepresented by mainstream bridging media, it also opens the door to uncorroborated and uncontested material. The journalists' relationship with sources is certainly open to criticism, but journalism without sources is not journalism at all and elites who are not prepared to hold themselves up to scrutiny by their fiercest critics are perhaps not people who should be trusted to take leadership roles in a democracy.

Activist media

It would be impossible to do justice here to the plethora of research on the role of alternative and activist media (Atton, 2001; Downing, 2001; Fenton, 2012; Harcup, 2012). Websites, blogs, Facebook and Twitter accounts provide the information and communication that keeps local civic action alive, as well as opportunities for intensifying bonds around campaigns and extending networks, so that activists can learn from one another. It can also provide an alternative news source, often focusing on the details of a particular local concern that will only be mentioned briefly in mainstream media.

Activist media has both gained and lost from the Internet and social media. It has gained the opportunity to publish at very low cost, but it is operating in the same competitive space as the major global companies and coping with the "winners-take-all" algorithms (Hindman, 2009) that ensure only the very biggest brands are easily discovered. It has also lost a source of income (through sales) that helped it to survive in the pre-Internet era. Publishing online costs not only the access to the Internet required to upload it, but also the time taken to write about, photograph or video events. The effort of keeping an online presence alive, on a continuous basis, requires dedication and an alternative source of income.

For local news journalists and subject specialists, activist media provide a mine of useful information, research and opinion. And the interaction with journalists on mainstream titles can provide the necessary bridge between pockets of activity and bubbles of interest and the broader, news-seeking public. Activism is a key ingredient of any healthy democracy; however, if it is not connected to the wider community through the news media that bridges activist bubbles, its value is much diminished. The tragic fire at Grenfell Tower in London in June 2017, which led to the biggest single loss of life in the capital since the Second World War, had been foreshadowed by the local activist blog *Grenfell Action Group*, which had been flagging up fire safety issues for some years. Unfortunately, the only surviving mainstream "news" organisation in the borough was a commercial free sheet, concerned mainly with cultural events and with no local reporters (Bell, 2017). It failed to cover this story and the local council felt free to ignore the complaints until a tragedy occurred. This is not an argument against mainstream journalism. It is an argument in favour of a renewed, responsible journalism, which is properly resourced and attuned to local needs.

Supporting journalism

By defining journalism as a set of practices, producing information for public circulation on a regular basis, some activities are excluded. A conversation with a group of friends on Facebook, including links, is publishing – not journalism. Those people who happen to pass the scene of a terrorist event and tweet pictures are certainly participating in the circulation of knowledge, but they pass by, or they pass through. They may have a point of view, they may have information to contribute, but the focus of their working lives is in some other realm. They may be sources, bystanders, participants or passers-by but they are not journalists and most would not define themselves as such. In most circumstances they are entirely reliant on journalists to circulate the knowledge that they have produced.

The desire to "speak back" to the elite is not new. The key difference lies not in the impulse but the ease and speed with which it is now possible to do it. The ability to debate, rebut or debunk journalism is a positive change but imagining it as a replacement for journalism is to misunderstand the role of both journalist and activist. Those who comment on and remix news and information may add to understanding, but they may also deliberately distort it and they are rarely held to account when they get things wrong.

Critiques of mainstream media are necessary and need to be rigorous but the assumption implicit in some critical commentary of mainstream media, by political activists of the right and left, and by some public figures, is that journalism itself needs to be replaced by partisan activism. There are many opportunities available for citizens to research, publish and debate issues that concern them. They are a welcome addition to civic life, but they do not replace journalism. Regular journalism is by no means perfect but we need to ensure that there continues to be a version (or versions) of events that have been checked and verified, by people who ask penetrating questions, backed up by ever more sophisticated means of data checking. These people need to be supported, so that they can focus on the key job of finding out what the elite is hiding. As trust in mainstream news is eroded, by those who would prefer that we don't know what is happening, the need to protect the job of journalism becomes ever more important, as does the need to hold journalism to account – wherever it takes place.

Notes

1 Domingo, D., Quandt, T., Heinonen, A., Paulussen, S., Singer, J. B., & Vujnovic, M. (2008). Participatory journalism practices in the media and beyond: An international comparative study of initiatives in online newspapers. *Journalism Practice, 2*(3), pp. 326–342.
2 Figures from the International Telecomunications Union (2015).
3 Cory Bergman, @corybe 5.49PM – 8 December 2016, accessed May 23, 2017.
4 Technorati listed and indexed all the blogs on the Internet based on a thousand-point ranking scale and divided into categories. Their final list of the top blogs is archived here: www.seocial.com/technorati-blog-directory-deleted-may-29/
5 As we are writing, in 2017, the founder of Wikipedia, Jimmy Wales, has announced the development of an international news site called *Wikitribune*, on a similar basis.
6 Jessica Elgot (2014), Indian Journalist Shu Choudary beat Edward Snowden to be digital activist of the year, for creating news for those who can't read, *Huffington Post*. www. huffingtonpost.co.uk/2014/03/21/india-shu-choudary_n_5007765.html
7 This was checked against the date-lined coverage of the *St Louis Post Dispatch* in the weeks after the event.

References

Acar, A., & Muraki, Y. (2011). Twitter for crisis communication: Lessons learned from Japan's tsunami disaster. *International Journal of Web Based Communities*, 7(3), 392–402. http://dx.doi.org/10.1504/ijwbc.2011.041206

Adorno, T. W. (1975). Culture industry reconsidered. *New German Critique*, 6, 12–19.

Allan, S. (2006). *Online news: Journalism and the internet*. Maidenhead, England: Open University Press.

Allan, S., & Thorsen, E. (2009). *Citizen journalism: Global perspectives*. New York, NY: Peter Lang.

Atton, C. (2001). *Alternative media*. London, England: Sage.

Atton, C. (2010). Alternative journalism: Ideology and practice. In S. Allan (Ed.), *The Routledge companion to news and journalism* (pp. 169–178). London, England: Routledge.

Atton, C. (2012). Foreword: Local journalism, radical reporting and the everyday. In T. Harcup (Ed.), *Alternative journalism, alternative voices* (pp. xi–xvi). London, England: Routledge.

Beckett, C. (2008). *Supermedia: Saving journalism so it can save the world*. Malden, MA: Wiley.

Bell, E. (2017). Grenfell reflects the accountability vacuum left by crumbling local press. *Guardian Media Blog*. Retrieved July 7, 2017 from www.theguardian.com/media/media-blog/2017/jun/25/grenfell-reflects-the-accountability-vacuum-left-by-crumbling-local-press

Boczkowski, P. J., & Mitchelstein, E. (2013). *The news gap: When the information preferences of the media and the public diverge*. Cambridge, MA: MIT Press.

Brandtzæg, P. B. (2010). Towards a unified media-user typology (MUT): A meta-analysis and review of the research literature on media-user typologies. *Computers in Human Behavior*, 26(5), 940–956.

Bruns, A., & Burgess, J. (2014). Crisis communication in natural disasters: The Queensland floods and Christchurch earthquakes. In K. Weller, A. Bruns, J. Burgess, M. Mahrt, & C. Puschmann (Eds.), *Twitter and society* (pp. 373–384). New York, NY: Peter Lang.

Carlson, M. (2007). Blogs and journalistic authority: The role of blogs in US election day 2004 coverage. *Journalism Studies*, 8(2), 264–279.

Chadwick, A., & Dennis, J. (2017). Social media, professional media and mobilisation in contemporary Britain: Explaining the strengths and weaknesses of the citizens' movement 38 Degrees. *Political Studies*, 65(1), 42–60.

Christensen, C. (1997). *The innovator's dilemma: When new technologies cause great firms to fail*. Boston, MA: Harvard Business Review Press.

Cooper, G. (2011). *From their own correspondent? New media and the changes in disaster coverage: Lessons to be learned*. Oxford: Reuters Institute for the Study of Journalism.

Davis, A. (2010). Politics, journalism and new media: Virtual iron cages in the new culture of capitalism. In N. Fenton (Ed.), *New media, old news* (pp. 121–137). London, England: Sage Publications.

Deuze, M. (2003). The web and its journalisms: Considering the consequences of different types of news media online. *New Media & Society*, 5(2), 203–230.

Deuze, M., & Fortunati, L. (2011). Journalism without journalists: On the power shift from journalists to employers and audiences. In G. Meikle & G. Redden (Eds.), *News online: Transformations and continuities* (pp. 164–177). Basingstoke, England: Palgrave Macmillan.

Dewey, C. (2016). Facebook fake-news writer: 'I think Donald Trump is in the White House because of me'. *Washington Post*. Retrieved November 18, 2016 from www.washingtonpost.com/news/the-intersect/wp/2016/11/17/facebook-fake-news-writer-i-think-donald-trump-is-in-the-white-house-because-of-me/

Doggett, E. V., & Cantarero, A. (2016). Identifying eyewitness news-worthy events on Twitter. *Proceedings of The Fourth International Workshop on Natural Language Processing for Social Media* (pp. 7–13), Austin, TX, November 1, 2016.

Domingo, D., Quandt, T., Heinonen, A., Paulussen, S., Singer, J. B., & Vujnovic, M. (2008). Participatory journalism practices in the media and beyond: An international comparative study of initiatives in online newspapers. *Journalism Practice*, 2(3), 326–342.

Downing, J. (2001). *Radical media: Rebellious communication and social movements*. Thousand Oaks, CA: Sage.

Downing, J. D. H. (2010). Audiences and readers of alternative media: The absent lure of the virtually unknown. In D. K. Thussu (Ed.), *International communications: A reader* (pp. 295–310). London, England: Routledge.

Duggan, M. (2013). Photo and video sharing grow online. Pew Research Center: Internet Science & Tech. Retrieved April 23, 2017 from www.pewinternet.org/2013/10/28/p hoto-and-video-sharing-grow-online/

Enzensberger, H. M. (1970). Constituents of a theory of the media. *New Left Review*, 64, 13–36.

Fenton, N. (2010). NGOs, new media and the mainstream news. In N. Fenton (Ed.), *New media, old news* (pp. 153–168). London, England: Sage Publications.

Fenton, N. (2012). The internet and radical politics. In J. Curran, N. Fenton, & D. Freedman (Eds.), *Misunderstanding the internet* (pp. 149–176). Abingdon, England: Routledge.

Gardiner, B., Mansfield, M., Anderson, I., Holder, J., Louter, D., & Ulmanu, M. (2016). The dark side of Guardian comments. *The Guardian*. Retrieved June 10, 2017 from www.theguardian.com/technology/2016/apr/12/the-dark-side-of-guardian-comments

Gerlis, A. (2008). Who is a journalist? *Journalism Studies*, 9(1), 125–128.

Gilmorc, D. (2004). *We the media: Grassroots media by the people, for the people*. Sebastopol, CA: O'Reilly Media, Inc.

Glaser, T. (2006). Your guide to citizen journalism. *Media Shift*. Retrieved January 19, 2017 from http://mediashift.org/2006/09/your-guide-to-citizen-journalism270/

Hallin, D. C., & Mancini, P. (2004). *Comparing media systems: Three models of media and politics*. Cambridge, England: Cambridge University Press.

Harcup, T. (2012). *Alternative journalism, alternative voices*. London, England: Routledge.

Hatlin, P., & Vogt, N. (2014). Cable, Twitter picked up Ferguson story at a similar clip. Retrieved April 3, 2017 from www.pewresearch.org/fact-tank/2014/08/20/cable-twit ter-picked-up-ferguson-story-at-a-similar-clip/

Hermida, A., & Thurman, N. (2008). A clash of cultures: The integration of user-generated content within professional journalistic frameworks at British newspaper websites. *Journalism Practice*, 2(3), 343–356. doi:10.1080/17512780802054538

Hindman, M. (2009). *The myth of internet democracy*, Princeton, NJ: Princeton University Press.

Humphreys, A., & Grayson, K. (2008). The intersecting roles of consumer and producer: A critical perspective on co-production, co-creation and prosumption. *Sociology Compass*, 2(3), 963–980.

James, B. (2016). Unpaid Huffington Post bloggers actually do want to get paid. *International Business Times*. Retrieved January 17, 2017 from www.ibtimes.com/unpaid-huffington-post-bloggers-actually-do-want-get-paid-2313744

Jenkins, H. (2006). *Convergence culture: Where old and new media collide*. New York, NY: New York University Press.

Jenkins, H. (2016). Youth voice, and political engagement: Introducing the core concepts. In H. Jenkins, S. Shresthova, L. Gamber-Thompson, N. Kligler-Vilenchik, & A. M. Zimmerman (Eds.), *By any media necessary: The new youth activism* (pp. 1–60). New York, NY: New York University Press.

Kaminska, M., Gallacher, J. D., Kollany, B., Yasseri, T., & Howard, P. N. (2017). *Social media and news sources during the 2017 UK General Election*. COMPRO Data Memo 2017.6, Oxford. Retrieved 7 June, 2017 from http://comprop.oii.ox.ac.uk/wp-content/uploads/sites/89/2017/06/Social-Media-and-News-Sources-during-the-2017-UK-General-Elec tion.pdf

Klein, A. (2014). Radar: From the margins to the front page. In G. Cooper, S. Cottle, L. Doucet, S. Duncan, B. Gormley, S. Joye, … R. Wynne-Jones (Eds.), *The future of humanitarian reporting*. London, England: City University London. Retrieved November 4, 2017 from http://fieldcraftstudios.com/wp-content/uploads/2015/03/The-Future-of-Humanitarian-Reporting-City-University.pdf#page=30

Knight Foundation. (2015). *Gaining ground: How non-profit news ventures seek sustainability*. Retrieved July 3, 2017 from https://s3.amazonaws.com/kf-site-legacy-media/feature_assets/www/nonprofitnews-2015/pdfs/KF_NonprofitNews2015.pdf

Kovach, B., & Rosenstiel, T. (2007). *The elements of journalism: What news people should know and the public should expect*. New York, NY: Three Rivers Press.

Lang, M. (2016). Presidential election circus: Is social media the cause? *Government Technology, San Francisco Chronicle*. Retrieved April 5, 2016 from www.govtech.com/social/2016-Presidential-Election-Circus-Is-Social-Media-the-Cause.html

Larson, M. S. (1977). *The rise of professionalism: A sociological analysis*. Berkeley, CA: University of California Press.

Lewis, S. C. (2012). The tension between professional control and open participation. *Information, Communication & Society*, 15(6), 836–866. doi:10.1080/1369118X.2012.674150

Mitchell, A., Gottfried, J., Barthel, M., & Shearer, E. (2016). The modern news consumer. Pew Research Center's journalism project. Retrieved June 17, 2017 from www.journalism.org/2016/07/07/the-modern-news-consumer/

Nah, S., & Chung, D. S. (2016). Communicative action and citizen journalism: A case study of OhmyNews in South Korea. *International Journal of Communication*, 10, 2297–2317.

Negroponte, N. (1995). *Being digital*. London, England: Hodder & Stoughton.

Newman, N. (2009). *The rise of social media and its impact on mainstream journalism*. Oxford, England: Reuters Institute for the Study of Journalism.

Newman, N., Fletcher, R., Levy, D. A. L., & Nielsen, R. K. (2016). *Reuters Institute digital news report 2016*. Retrieved December 3, 2016 from http://reutersinstitute.politics.ox.ac.uk/sites/default/files/research/files/Digital%2520News%2520Report%25202016.pdf

Nielsen, J. (2006). Participation inequality: The 90–9–1 rule for social features. *Nngroup*. Retrieved April 21, 2017 from www.nngroup.com/articles/participation-inequality/

Örnebring, H. (2008). The consumer as producer – of what? User-generated tabloid content in The Sun (UK) and Aftonbladet (Sweden). *Journalism Studies*, 9(5), 771–785.

Örnebring, H. (2010). Reassessing journalism as a profession. In S. Allan (Ed.), *The Routledge companion to news and journalism* (pp. 568–575). New York, NY: Routledge.

Örnebring, H. (2013). Anything you can do, I can do better? Professional journalists on citizen journalism in six european countries. *International Communication Gazette, 75*(1), 35–53. doi:10.1177/1748048512461761.

Osnos, E. (2013, April 20). The Sichuan earthquake test. *The New Yorker*. Retrieved November 13, 2017 from www.newyorker.com/news/evan-osnos/the-sichuan-earthquake-test

O'Sullivan, J., & Heinonen, A. (2008). Old values, new media. *Journalism Practice*, 2(3), 357–371. https://doi.org/10.1080/17512780802281081

Phillips, A. (2007). The alternative press. In K. Coyer, T. Dowmunt, & A. Fountain (Eds.), *The alternative media handbook* (pp. 47–58). London, England: Routledge.

Phillips, A. (2010). Old sources: New bottles. In N. Fenton (Ed.), *New media, old news* (pp. 87–101). London: Sage Publications.

Phillips, A. (2014). *Journalism in context*. London, England: Routledge.

Poindexter, P., Meraz, S., & Weiss, A. S. (2008). *Women, men and news: Divided and disconnected in the news media landscape*. Abingdon, England; New York, NY: Routledge.

Purcell, K., Rainie, L., Mitchell, A., Rosenstiel, T., & Olmstead, K. (2010). Understanding the participatory news consumer. Pew Research Center: Internet, Science & Tech, 1 March 2010. Retrieved April 11, 2017 from www.pewinternet.org/2010/03/01/understanding-the-participatory-news-consumer/

Ritzer, G. & Jurgenson, N. (2010). Production, consumption, prosumption: The nature of capitalism in the age of the digital 'prosumer'. *Journal of Consumer Culture*, 10(1), 13–36.

Rosen, J. (2008). A most useful definition of citizen journalism. *Pressthink*. Retrieved April 3, 2017 from http://archive.pressthink.org/2008/07/14/a_most_useful_d.html

Russell, A. (2011). *Networked: A contemporary history of news in transition* (1st ed.) Cambridge, England: Polity Press.

Salomon, J. (2016). Fighting injustice with smartphones in Olympic Rio. Retrieved October 29, 2016 from www.amnesty.org/en/latest/news/2016/07/fighting-injustice-with-smartp hones-in-olympic-rio/

Scott, J., Millard, D., & Leonard, P. (2015). Citizen participation in news. *Digital Journalism*, 3(5), 737–758. doi:10.1080/21670811.2014.952983

Singer, J. B. (2010). Quality control. *Journalism Practice*, 4(2), 127–142. doi:10.1080/17512780903391979

Singer, J. B. (2015). Out of bounds: Professional norms as boundary markers. In M. Carlson & S. C. Lewis (Eds.), *Boundaries of journalism: Professionalism, practices and participation* (pp. 21–36). Oxford, England: Routledge.

Statista. (2017). Social media – Statistics & facts. Retrieved June 3, 2017 from www.statista. com/topics/1164/social-networks/

Stelter, B. (2008). YouTube videos pull in real money. *The New York Times*. Retrieved November 25, 2016 from www.nytimes.com/2008/12/11/business/media/11youtube. html

Stelter, B. (2009, June 28). Journalism rules are bent in news coverage from Iran. *The New York Times*. Retrieved July 4, 2017 from www.nytimes.com/2009/06/29/business/media/29coverage.html

Tapscott, D., & Williams, A. D. (2006). *Wikinomics: How mass collaboration changes everything*. First Printing. New York, NY: Portfolio Hardcover.

Thompson, J. B. (1995). *The media and modernity*. Cambridge, England: Polity Press.

Thurman, N. (2008). Forums for citizen journalists? Adoption of user generated content initiatives by online news media. *New Media & Society*, 10(1), 139–157.

Thurman, N., & Hermida, A. (2010). Gotcha: How newsroom norms are shaping participatory journalism online. In S. Tunney & G. Monaghan (Eds.), *Web journalism: A new form of citizenship?* (pp. 46–62). Eastbourne, England: Sussex Academic Press.

Toffler, A. (1970). *Future shock*. New York, NY: Random House.

Wadbring, I., & Ödmark, S. (2016). Going viral: News sharing and shared news in social media. *Observatorio*, 10(4), 132–149.

Wardle, C., & Williams, A. (2008). *ugc@thebbc. Understanding its impact upon contributors, non contributors and BBC News*. Cardiff School of Journalism, Media and Cultural Studies. Retrieved November 13, 2017 from www.bbc.co.uk/blogs/knowledgeexchange/cardif fone.pdf

Wright, K. (2017). It was a simple, positive story of African self help, (manufactured for a Kenyan NGO by advertising multi-nationals). In M. Bunce, S. Franks, & C. Paterson (Eds.), *Africa's Media Image in the 21st Century*. London, England: Routledge.

Yoshida, T. (2016). BuzzFeed CEO Jonah Peretti talks Facebook and Ivanka Trump. *Digiday UK*. Retrieved October 2016 from http://digiday.com/publishers/buzzfeed-founder-jonah-peretti-talks-facebook-live-ivanka-trump/

4

THE WISDOM OF CROWDS?
HOW ALGORITHMS RULE ONLINE

Myth: the many are smarter than the few

One common thread connecting enthusiasts for a new technological "commons" was the assumption that the audience, when freed from the distorting effects of big media and editors, would produce a more participative, liberal and enlightened media (Barlow, 1996; Jenkins, 2008; Leadbeater, 2008). The news media they imagined would be built around individuals, freed by the interactivity of the Internet, to remodel the top-down, elite model of news production. The aggregation of these individual voices would allow us all to benefit from the "wisdom of crowds" (Surowiecki, 2004). In his Declaration of the Independence of Cyberspace, John Perry Barlow (1996) declared: "We will create a civilisation of the Mind in Cyberspace. May it be more humane and fair than the world your governments have made before".

This benign vision rested on the assumption that the structures embedded in the Internet are neutral and that whatever activity arises within those structures is merely a reflection of public sentiment, which is, by definition, a reflection of the people's will. The titles of popular books in the first decade of this century pick up this sentiment: *We the People* (Gillmor, 2006), *The Wisdom of Crowds* (Surowiecki, 2004) and *We Think* (Leadbeater, 2008). Few clouds passed across this rosy sunlit view, although Dan Gillmor, author of *We the Media*, showed signs of prescient uneasiness as he watched the traditional news organisations in the USA struggle to maintain their place against a rising tide of what he referred to as "news anarchy".

> A world of news anarchy would be one in which the big, credible voices of today were undermined by a combination of forces... There would be no business model to support the institutional journalism that, for all its problems, does perform a public service. Instead of journalism organisations with the critical mass to fight the good fights, we may be left with the equivalent of

countless pamphleteers and people shouting from soapboxes. We need something better.

(Gillmor, 2006, p. xxviii)

But on the whole, those who adopted the utopian narrative saw the Internet as the natural outcome of an egalitarian "co-evolution" between designers and users: "a complex, adaptive system, characterized by interdependencies, non-linear developments, emergence, and decentralized structures… which allows innovations at every node of the network, in other words by any user" (Just & Latzer, 2016, p. 7).

This perspective assigns a form of unproblematic agency to algorithms: "Automated algorithmic selection applications shape realities in daily lives, increasingly affect the perception of the world, and influence behaviour" (Just & Latzer, 2016, p. 17). While it is important to recognise that automated applications can indeed shape realities, it is equally important to recognise that they don't do so outside social systems and that they are subject to power differentials. Users, for example, have very little power in comparison with platform owners. On the whole, users conform to the pre-set list of possibilities that are embedded in the platform design. It requires technical knowledge beyond the possibilities of the vast majority of users to do anything other than passively accept the opportunities proffered by applications and platforms (Van Dijck, 2013, p. 33). These structures shape the "people's will" and can be manipulated by those with greater knowledge. While the elites who own and control the mass media can be identified and challenged, the structures of the Internet are more opaque.

So to what extent is the Internet a platform that gives back power to its users? How much has this myth obscured the operation of power and distracted policy makers from addressing the very real problems inherent in the growing centrality of privately owned Internet platforms in the organisation of political life? Could it be a problem for democracy that a handful of private companies should be given so much potential control over private data as well as the means of production and circulation of news? Should we be alarmed that these, mainly American, organisations are able to claim rights that cross national boundaries and take little account of national norms or local democratic organisations?

How the Internet grew up

In order to understand the way in which the structures of the Internet impact on decision-making and participation, it is necessary to understand that they are a reflection of the culture and the institutions from which they are produced (Williams, 1974) and follow the "institutional logics" of their field (Benson & Neveu, 2005; Bourdieu & Wacquant, 1992; Powell & DiMaggio, 1991). Tim Berners-Lee invented the World Wide Web within the unique constraints of the scientific field in which personal autonomy and the free exchange of ideas is a central legitimising narrative. Berners-Lee refused to patent his invention because he wanted it to be available, free to all (Berners-Lee, 2000). The next generation of Internet entrepreneurs also emerged from the field of science; indeed, the early years of both Google and Facebook were nurtured by universities with large endowments, giving these young inventors time, opportunities and encouragement. They too adopted the ideas of openness and sharing learned in that environment but this was a different time. Universities in the 1990s were under pressure to demonstrate that they were incubating technical innovation for industry, and the autonomy afforded by the university environment was inevitably contested by the requirements of commercial development.

These young software companies seemed to have little in common with the vast empires of computer technology such as IBM. Indeed, it could be argued that, in the early stages of development, software had more in common with the field of media and culture, which was itself contending with major technical change. Journalists and media reformers were early adopters of the Internet and were particularly delighted with what they saw as the democratising potential of these open, collaborative systems. Journalism Professor Jay Rosen (2006) described a world in which audiences would: "edit the news, and our choices [will] send items to our own front pages". Journalist Dan Gillmor (2006) looked towards an "emergent, self-assembling journalism" (p. xxix), which would also be a major challenge to the power of the established media. Benkler (2006) spoke of a "practice of producing culture [that] makes us all more sophisticated readers, viewers and listeners as well as more engaged makers" (p. 275).

However, the people who produced the platforms that sit on top of the original architecture of the Internet did not come from the liberal, humanities-inflected tradition of journalism, with its concerns for democratic accountability. The industry, looking for people with aptitude for coding, used personality screening which selected for those who "dislike activities involving close personal interaction (and) prefer to work with things rather than people" (Ensmenger, 2010, p. 17). Thus, it is argued, the industry gathered a workforce that was "particularly ill-equipped for, or uninterested in, social interaction" (Ensmenger, 2010, p. 17). This may be partly responsible for the bias towards a particular sub-group of male employees described by Kendall (2011) as exhibiting "facets of hypermasculinity by valorizing intellect over social or emotional intelligence."

A narrative of personal freedom and anti-elitism was combined with a particularly robust view of freedom of expression (Barlow, 1996), backed up by individual anonymity, and built into the organisational DNA of social platforms such as Reddit and search engines such as Google (Christopherson, 2007). As Mitch Kapor, the founder of Lotus and a past chairman of the Electronic Frontier Foundation, is said to have observed: "architecture is politics".[1] Algorithms were built to express this "techno/cyberlibertarian ethos, valuing the notion of a rational, autonomous individual and meritocratic idealism" (Massanari, 2015, p. 332). A populist conception of democracy was inscribed in the structure, so that in every niche it is the most popular post that is promoted, encouraging domination in the competition for the top spot, rather than differentiation or dialogue (Hindman, 2009).

Where collaboration is encouraged it is on the basis of similarity rather than difference – people gather together online in order to be with people who are like them. This populist conception of democratic behaviour, as a contest between individuals with opposing ideologies, gives no place to the kinds of rational deliberation that are the foundation of a Habermassian public sphere (Habermas, 1989). Nor does it provide protection for minorities or space for nuanced debate and compromise – indeed, it appears to actively promote polarisation (see Chapter 2). These patterns were not inevitable. They are the outcome of decisions taken by programmers who are in turn subject to the pressures of the institutions in which they are embedded. As the need to bring in money for shareholders built up, the platform entrepreneurs were inevitably pushed from the autonomy of their original position in the university, and the cushion of start-up cash, to look for ways of commercialising their product.

The narrative of personal and market freedom was maintained but gradually adapted to a commercialising logic, with a focus on free access for users, which would in turn provide income to platforms, applications and publications via advertising. Freedom to consume creative goods without cost was promoted at the expense of the producers of those creative goods, whose rights were simply brushed aside. Those who advocated relaxing copyright believed that they were aiding digital creativity (Lessig, 2005) but their campaigns have largely aided the platform owners. Freedom to remix and ease of consumption became the key benefits and the rights of creative workers to fair remuneration have been largely ignored. Questions of accuracy, depth, balance or fairness don't enter into the conceptual frame. As one researcher, basing her work on in-depth interviews with senior people in technology companies, found:

> The schemas clearly in the ascendant – the dominant market schema and the science-technology schema – provide little scope to raise issues of public welfare, fairness, or bias. Instead, they emphasize profit, in the case of the market schema, or progress and efficiency, in the case of the science-technology schema, or defence, in the case of the war schema.
>
> *(Van Couvering, 2007, p. 884)*

Soon the core value of privacy itself became a highly contested issue. The market required complete transparency and total access to private data, so that these "learning machines" were able to understand their audience and allow material to flow seamlessly between people who may not know one another. In order to manage these contradictions, a new ethos of personal transparency was developed. Foucault (1972, pp. 224–227) speaks of the way in which the institutional position of specific people gives them particular power to be heard. Mark Zuckerberg's position, as CEO of Facebook, gave him a pre-eminent position from which to speak and the power to "normalise" the loss of privacy in order to profit from the fruits of the sharing economy:

> People have really gotten comfortable not only sharing more information and different kinds, but more openly and with more people. That social norm is

just something that has evolved over time. We view it as our role in the system to constantly be innovating and be updating what our system is to reflect what the current social norms are.

(Zuckerberg, 2010)[2]

His views were not uncontested so, on the one hand, the freedom to propagate hate speech anonymously is defended as integral to the freedom of the Internet (Massanari, 2015), while on the other, private data is routinely harvested through the use of cookies (more code), which are quietly dropped into computers where they monitor every keystroke and send information back to help the machines learn better what the customer wants. And it is via their data, not their much-vaunted creative endeavours, that the audience are feeding back, as platform owners slice and dice personal information and match it with the advertising that most closely fulfils our desires and most lucratively fills the coffers of these new media intermediaries.

Network effects – how they work

The mass harvesting of data works best allied to the creation of monopolies because data is most useful at scale. The best search engine is the one that is most perfectly tailored to use and has access to the largest bank of information. A small-scale search engine is a less efficient search engine. It was therefore almost inevitable that the search engine that provided the most efficient service would take over the market. As is often the case, that search engine was not the first to be invented, but the one that refined the original idea and won the inevitable competition to dominate the market.

Google was launched publically in 1998, after a couple of years as part of the Stanford University website, where its founders were students. It was developed using a more sophisticated algorithm than earlier ones, based on page ranking – a means of working out the relationship between websites. This, at least theoretically, means that searches are ranked according to their level of influence, not merely the number of times a specific word is used. The sophistication of the search engine immediately speeded up the job of finding useful information and meant that it very swiftly became a near-monopoly provider of search results. In Europe, Google provides 90 per cent of search and in the USA 72 per cent.[3]

Facebook also started life on a university campus as a "hot or not" game allowing students to compare photographs of each other and rate them. It was closed down by the university but provided the basic idea for Facebook, which was launched in 2004 as a service for students at Harvard University. It was not the first social media site or, arguably, even the best but it quickly became the most influential because it traded on its exclusivity. In the initial stages it was open only to Ivy League students; it then expanded to include all universities. Within two years it had opened up to anyone with an email address. Indeed, its meteoric rise to become the most important social media site in the world is in itself an exercise in "virality". By opening up exclusively to the most important group of young "influentials", who used it as a means by which they could create social links with other people just like them, Facebook contained within it a means of creating social capital (Ellison, Lampe, Steinfield, & Vitak, 2011, p. 146). It embodied the aspirational and social factors that would propel it to global supremacy.

By 2014 almost two-thirds of Internet users in North America, Latin America, the Middle East and Africa had Facebook accounts.[4] It had become an inextricable part of social life, visited multiple times a day by its users, who are therefore open to influence by anything that turns up on their page, mixed in with messages from friends and loved ones. A female student from our interviews in 2014 expressed it like this:

> I do say I am going to have a massive exodus from my Facebook and call everybody but then I don't because it's more beneficial for me to not post anything, keep them as my friends, but have people that are informing me.
>
> *(Female student, UK)*

Neither Google nor Facebook initially made any money. They were supported by vast quantities of investment cash on the simple assumption that something that was that big and that popular would eventually succeed. By 2016 both Facebook and Google were in the top five of the Fortune 500, among the most valuable US companies on the planet. In working out how to monetise their companies, Google and Facebook, gave birth to an Internet industry that swept away the old relationships between news companies, their advertisers, and their audiences.

What does Google do?

- It connects people to the information that they want. It does so by embedding code that registers everything you click on and uses this information to filter out most of the rubbish that doesn't really interest you.
- It then sells all that knowledge about you as a service to advertisers, allowing them to place their wares in front of exactly the people who are most likely to buy.

This is how news organisations also operated but they did it blind. They guessed what you liked and presented it to you. If they guessed well, they could "sell" people to advertisers, who paid out large sums of money for the privilege of waving their wares in front of customers, hoping they would buy. The problem for news organisations lies in the fact that Google can do this better and far more cheaply because Google depends on accurately pairing millions of people with the things that they are already searching for online, via systems known as AdSense and DoubleClick. AdSense allows publishers to embed code in blogs and websites, which then links keywords in published copy to specific advertisements, which then appear on their sites. A small sum is then paid to the publisher when people reading an article then click on an advert. DoubleClick harvests data from users to help companies target their advertisements.

The two things that Google does so well have in turn engendered unexpected repercussions. The first was that they undercut and fatally challenged the business model of every news organisation. Advertisers were unwilling to pay premium prices to advertise directly on news webpages when they could get a more accurate service at a fraction of the price via Google. This meant that the income from digital advertising crashed to about one hundredth of the price of an advertisement in a printed news product. Google saw this as a fairer system that would help advertisers. Head of Viacom, Mel Karmazin, saw it rather differently, as a major threat to the legacy business model and told Google's founders: "You are fucking with the magic" (Auletta, 2009, p. 9). Legacy news organisations found that they were funding their newsrooms from the income generated by their failing print products rather than the increasing audiences online. The second thing was to encourage a new form of Internet business, aimed entirely at using the correct words to attract advertising. This was the first building block of the "fake news" boom.

What does Facebook do?

- Facebook allows people to pass on material that they find interesting to their friends.
- It also collects data from every "Like" and "Share" in order to pinpoint the particular preferences of its users. Using this information, it then serves more information and advertising to its users in the hope that they will themselves pass it on. For advertisers, sharing is the Holy Grail because it presumes a personal endorsement from a trusted source.

Facebook is not the only social media platform but it has become the dominant one outside China (where WeiBo, RenRen and WeChat are home-grown alternatives). Facebook's particular contribution to the changing behaviour of news audiences arrived with the inclusion of a Share button in 2006. This allowed people to link to articles or videos that amused them and pass them on to friends with a single click. This was at first a means by which people could gather online with their friends but a social gathering does not create income. Facebook found a way of opening up this private space so that companies could have access to social sharing via the Fan or Brand page. This allowed organisations to take part in the social media space and encouraged the growth of Facebook pages that are entirely dedicated to boosting the profile of a linked product or service. Material that was shared on Facebook had the additional value of being recommended by a friend but, just in case it isn't shared "organically", publishers are also able to leapfrog into news feeds by the simple expedient of paying to boost posts.

That was followed, in 2012, by Facebook Apps and Facebook Instant Articles, which allow news organisations to share stories directly onto an individual Facebook newsfeed. Those stories would then also be automatically shared to Facebook friends if they were clicked on. None of this was possible without changes to the original rigorous privacy settings. People who only want to share with a small group of friends were providing roadblocks to the vision of a totally viral system in which information (and the advertising that accompanies it) could be spread. Thus, with a series of adaptations, the affordances of the social media site were locked into place so that they forced the majority of people to interact and share material in very specific ways that would maximise profit for the company.

The sheer size and spread of Facebook meant that tying themselves to the Facebook juggernaut was irresistible to news publishers. They would get 70 per cent of any revenue from advertising served alongside their stories and they would find a whole new, and predominantly young, audience. *The Guardian* found that its referrals from Facebook rocketed from 2 per cent to 30 per cent in just four months of using the App (Cordrey, 2012). The downside was that Facebook would collect all the audience data and decide who would see which stories, based on that data (Phillips, 2012). They could also decide at any time to vary the terms of the deal – either cutting the advertising split or cutting the number of news stories fed to users. In 2015 for example, the Facebook traffic to its top 30 publishers dropped by 32 per cent (Moses, 2015).

A report for *Digital Content Next*, in 2017 (Moses, 2017a), found that premium publishers were making only 14 per cent of their advertising revenue from content displayed on platforms other than their own and most of that was from television. As media watcher Frederic Filloux said on the *Monday Note*, "Facebook is an unpredictable spigot, whose flow varies according to constantly changing and opaque criteria. A given news stream will see its conversion into clicks vary widely for no apparent reason" (Filloux, 2015). In 2017, *The Guardian* and *The New York Times* stopped using Facebook's Instant Articles, focusing instead on drawing readers to their own sites and their own advertisers. Nevertheless, Google and Facebook have become intermediaries for both mainstream organisations and new entrants, who depend on them to provide access to a large part of their audience. But this also set the stage for the entry of a new group of technically savvy entrepreneurs capable of using the speed, distribution and opacity of the platforms and their algorithms to their advantage.

How programmatic advertising feeds the trolls

A system of communication that allows for horizontal connection between people, based on social affinity, provided a fragmented and impossibly difficult prospect for advertisers who were used to placing ads in a relatively small number of mass-market outlets or in the niche products that catered directly to their audiences. So when Google launched AdWords in 2000, holding out the prospect of serving advertisements automatically by matching the advert to the needs of customers, advertisers were interested.

Pretty soon other data companies were getting in on the act, designing programmatic systems that analyse personal information from Web users and save it in data banks. They then began to sell their services to companies promising to create and then match relevant advertisements with prospective buyers. While the matching is taking place, an online auction is set up, so that advertisers bid against each other for the most advantageous positions right across the Web. Anywhere that an individual browser may go, they are trailing their data in their wake, like bait to catch fish. Only in this case what they are catching is adverts that will then be placed on the browser, smartphone or tablet in front of them. When it works well, the ads are tailored to fit the requirements of the browser and the targeting ensures that a reasonably high proportion of people click on them.

Critically the advertisements only appear on the websites or social media pages when the user visits the site. This means that, if a liberal-minded customer decides to visit a right-wing hate site in order to see what it is publishing, he or she may be surprised to find advertisements from well-known brands, NGOs and government departments appearing alongside extremely unpleasant content. This is because the advertisements are tethered to the customer, not the website. As long as the site in question is using the necessary embedded code to attract advertising, then whoever visits the site will see the advertisements that are meant for their eyes only. Publishers are roughly organised into categories, based on number of browsers and subjects covered, so that advertisers have some very general idea of where their products are displayed.

For advertisers who are only concerned with attracting people interested in their products, this matching is a boon. They pay for the privilege of using publishers' sites via a number of different metrics including the number of people who see their ads; more will be paid for a click through to the advertiser's site and the highest payments are for sales completed. This system allows advertisers to contact huge numbers of people at very modest costs per click. For traditional news organisations, even those with a big online and social media presence, the money earned is not enough to cover the cost of the operation. The income is really only viable for organisations or individuals who manage to attract very high visitor numbers with very low staff costs.

Content farms, as they were soon dubbed, such as Demand Media, exist only to provide material that will attract clicks. The information is gathered together using Google trending lists, and bespoke algorithms, to identify key words and subjects and find exactly which key words advertisers are likely to bid most on. This information is then followed by hasty Internet searches so that material can be written to answer the most likely questions, with long headlines and repeated use of key terms that push the material high up in any Google search; then it is "served" via apparently specialist websites (Bakker, 2012). A journalist in *Wired Magazine* highlighted how this works:

> To find out what terms users are searching for, it parses bulk data purchased from search engines, ISPs, and Internet marketing firms (as well as Demand's own traffic logs). Then the algorithm crunches keyword rates to calculate how much advertisers will pay to appear on pages that include those terms… Third,

the formula checks to see how many Web pages already include those terms...
Armed with those key words, another algorithm, called the Knowledge
Engine, dives back into the data to figure out exactly what people want to
know about the term.

(Roth, 2009)

It is hard indeed to find the power of the audience in these transactions. As Adorno
(1975 [2010]) said of mass media: "The masses are not primary but secondary, they
are an object of its calculation; an appendage of the machinery" (p. 16).

Other market entrants, like *BuzzFeed*, also capitalised on these new methods,
attracting millions of views with stories about cats and celebrities. They did well
because they were using social media platforms to expand audiences, spending very
little money on trained journalists and none on printing presses. However, as both
companies have found to their cost, depending on a third-party intermediary can
be very unreliable. Demand Media went public in January 2011, closing up 33 per
cent on the first day of trading. Then, according to a report in *Variety*, in April
Google changed its algorithm and traffic to the Demand sites was reduced by
40 per cent overnight (Wallenstein & Spangler, 2013). BuzzFeed did so well that it
was able to establish a serious investigative news team, paid for by the money
collected through programmatic advertising and via social media, but in early 2017
the *Financial Times* reported a similar change in fortunes as customers moved their
attention from their computers to mobile phones and tablets, where it is harder to
insert adverts (Garrahan, 2017).

For individual operators who game the system, there is still enough money to be
earned and it was through gaming and fraud (such as clickbots that generate clicks
automatically and therefore appear to increase the audience size) that advertisers
found themselves inadvertently providing financial support to fake news sites. In
2016, a BuzzFeed investigation traced 140 fake news sites to a town in Macedonia
called Veles. Although it is impossible to verify the amounts that were being
earned, it is clear that the people pushing the most improbable and sensational pro-
Trump stories in the run-up to the 2016 US elections were doing so simply in
order to generate advertising cash.

Several teens and young men who run these sites told BuzzFeed News that
they learned the best way to generate traffic is to get their politics stories to
spread on Facebook – and the best way to generate shares on Facebook is to
publish sensationalist and often false content that caters to Trump supporters.

(Silverman & Alexander, BuzzFeed, *2016)*

These sites, entirely invented to catch a political wave, were making use of the
rising tide of populism and in so doing helped to spread it. The US election
brought the fake news phenomenon rather forcefully to the attention of journalists,
news audiences, policy makers and the advertisers themselves. In the wake of the
election, according to industry publisher, *Digiday*, a number of advertisers became

aware for the first time that their advertisements were appearing alongside fake stories on dubious news sites but they didn't at that time have the necessary tools to prevent it happening.

> Brands that control all their ads through one demand-side platform can easily whitelist or blacklist entire publishers – often, many agencies recommend a list of "whitelisted" sites that are the only destinations ads can appear. But some exchanges do allow publishers to include blind inventory. So instead of seeing "Breitbart," you may just see "news site." There are also companies like Integral Ad Science that have a sliding scale of "risk tolerance" for brands. But while it's easy to filter out, say, curse words, it's harder to make subjective decisions like in the case of otherwise legitimate news sites.
>
> *(Pathak, 2016)*

The opaque nature of these transactions, added to the highly technical nature of programmatic advertising, has ensured that, just like the algorithms that power the search engines, the aspect of programmatic advertising that is emphasised is its phenomenal power and exponential growth. Executives with a background in rather more conventional advertising have no expertise in computing (Caffyn, 2017) but there is an additional problem too. Most people who do have the knowledge are soaked in the developer's ethos and concerned only with minimising friction and maximising profit (Van Couvering, 2007, p. 884).

A series of stories appeared in the press, early in 2017, written by journalists who visited hate sites and found a range of branded products from companies such as L'Oreal, Transport for London, *The Guardian* newspaper and *Sainsbury's Magazine, The Grocer* (Mostrous, 2017). The organisations and the advertising agencies involved immediately pulled their advertising off YouTube, the Google-owned video platform. According to Media Radar, advertising on the right-wing site, *Breitbart*, dropped 90 per cent over three months as marketing departments insisted on tighter "brand-safety" (Moses, 2017b). The response by Google has been to start de-listing websites that are considered problematic for advertisers. As Google tightens its grip on sites that can attract advertising, the diversity of the Internet will be reduced. It won't just be hate sites that lose money. Sites that represent minorities and minority issues, and individual bloggers writing on controversial subjects, will feel the impact as their source of funding is cut off (Allcott & Gentzkow, 2017) so options available for minority audiences will also be diminished.

Going viral

Every post is not equal. Only the most popular stories will rise to the top of the search page, appear on the trending column on Facebook, find themselves at the top of the Twitter feed or get upvoted on Reddit. The fact that a story is considered popular means that it will be more prominent and the greater visibility will ensure that even more people click on it or share it. This "winner-takes-all" pattern described by Matthew Hindman (2009) is what drives this exponential distribution effect in which one post is capable of being seen by millions of people in a very short space of time. The owners of such content don't just get noticed; they also get a share of the advertising revenue generated alongside their post. The Internet giants would like us to see this as a natural and unmanipulated outcome of individual choice.

> Google likes to claim that it is simply an algorithms-powered neutral inter-mediary that stands between a given user and the collective mind of the Internet. On its corporate website, Google compares the presentation of its search results to democratic elections, with the most-linked sites emerging on top. If the top results lead to sites that are politically incorrect or racist or homophobic, the fault is not Google's but the Internet's.
>
> *(Morozov, 2011)*

Far from being neutral, virality is supercharged by both the desire to make money and the desire to obtain influence. So working out what will "go viral" is now a very lucrative business. Jonah Berger and Katherine L. Milkman studied three months of content on *The New York Times* website to see what stories went viral. They found that the key factor was emotion. Positive stories were more likely to be shared than negative ones, but they also found material that evoked "high-arousal" was most likely to go viral. That is, people were more likely to share stories that made them angry, anxious or amazed. Stories that made people feel helpless were far less likely to be passed on (Berger & Milkman, 2012). This information can now be algorithmically verified but it doesn't vary a great deal from the assumptions made by editors and journalists on the most popular commercial newspapers who understand which stories sell. In 2003, *Guardian* columnist Nick Cohen quoted a memo to staff from the editor of the struggling tabloid newspaper, the *Daily Express*. He said:

> We are aiming to have six sex stories a week. In an ideal world we should have a 'Cabinet Minister affair' story... sex and scandal at the highest level of society always sells well, but these stories are notoriously difficult to get. We need to be constantly stirring things up... We must make the readers cross... the appalling state of the railways, the neglect of the health service, the problem of teenage pregnancies, the inability of bureaucrats to get enough done properly, etc. etc.
>
> *(Cohen, 2003)*

A group of Australian publishers analysed the stories from their own site that were shared the most and came up with a more precise formulation, which they refer to as the NIT model. They discovered that the most shared stories were either: News-breaking, Inspiring or what they refer to as "Teaming" (Crawford, Hunter, & Filipovic, 2015, p. 122). This overlaps with Berger's model but provides a clearer steer to those who want to write news in order to have it shared.

The news-breaking category is exactly as it appears, and researchers in Sweden have also found that this was a highly shared category (Wadbring & Ödmark, 2016). People tend to share news as it breaks but the Australians found that they also shared stories that are explanatory of breaking news and they share stories that commemorate or demonstrate fellow feeling. This would cover transmission of news about a natural disaster, explanatory materials about how it occurred and also the likes, hearts and expressions of sympathy that now accompany big breaking stories of this kind.

The authors describe an inspiring story as one that evokes awe or leaves the reader "spooked" or "heart-warmed". These are stories about cute kids, amazing floods, car crashes, or feats of human endeavour and they overlap with the emotional stories found by Berger and Milkman (2012). These are the stories that powered BuzzFeed's growth.

The third category however is perhaps the most important. "Teaming" is what might be called an act of recognition and a call to action to the people who you regard as members of your team. Very often these are also stories that make people feel angry and indignant. The Australian authors found that this category provided almost two-thirds of the stories that shared well. This category overlaps both with the emotional stories noted by Berger and Milkman (2012), and the controversial stories that were identified by the Swedish research (Wadbring & Ödmark, 2016). But it more accurately identifies the reason why they are so often shared.

When people share stories, they are not behaving simply as editors would. They are not interested in ensuring that their friends have a good mix of stories to read that cover a wide range of subject matter. The role of personal communication is different. And it is that personal recommendation system that makes Facebook so very valuable to marketers but also to populist politicians. As John Herrman (2016) explained in *The New York Times*:

> This strange new class of media organization slots seamlessly into the news feed and is especially notable in what it asks, or doesn't ask, of its readers. The point is not to get them to click on more stories or to engage further with a brand. The point is to get them to share the post that's right in front of them. Everything else is secondary.

This use of "teaming" and sharing on social media varies according to the news ecology in which it takes place. In the USA, stories that were entirely fabricated, and produced by people who have no journalism background, dominated social media in the months before the 2016 elections (Silverman, 2016). The top five shared fake stories were all pro-Trump or anti-Clinton: one suggested that the Pope endorsed Trump and the second most shared suggested that Clinton had sold weapons to ISIS. The top five mainstream stories that were shared were opinion pieces that supported Clinton or opposed Trump. The top headline was: "Trump's History of Corruption is Mind-Boggling. So why is Clinton supposedly the corrupt one?"

In the UK, data research for BuzzFeed found that the most shared stories in the period before the 2016 European Union referendum came from the populist pro-Brexit mass media. In the UK these stories were not entirely made up; they tended to contain a shred of truth, which was then manipulated to create a sensational and misleading impression (Waterson, 2017). This is not a new development in the UK. The propensity of the British press to produce misleading stories was flagged up by the European Commission as far back as 1992 when a special website was established to correct "Euromyths".[5]

What characterises both the fake news sites and the UK mainstream popular media is the understanding of what kind of material will be shared. In the UK, the most shared headline in the run-up to the European Union referendum came from the *Daily Express* and read: "Major leak from Brussels reveals that the NHS will be 'KILLED OFF' if Britain remains in the EU". This story aimed at "teaming" people in defence of a socialised health service had 464,000 interactions on Facebook and was, according to BuzzFeed data research, shared by far-right websites (Waterson, 2017). Teaming is a form of behaviour that fits in with other insights about how social media works. Zizi Papacharissi (2012) wrote of the way in which people use tweets as "Performances of the Self". In other words, they are not just using social media as a form of communication; they are using it as a way of presenting themselves to the world.

Those who feel that their identity is in some way threatened are most likely to focus on attitude-reinforcing material and avoid anything that contradicts their strongly held beliefs. So these performances become part of what Slater (2015) describes as "reinforcing spirals". This behaviour can then be manipulated, by political campaigners and by those seeking merely to make money from advertising, but also by the platforms, which optimise algorithms to encourage sharing. Thus, posts containing cute images or those featuring very strong language are identified and passed on more readily than more neutral posts containing reasoned discussion. It is this understanding of teaming behaviour and reinforcing spirals that animated the fake news sites and has allowed people to cash in on the manipulation of political sympathies.

Influencing the influentials

Viral posts are far more likely to be noticed if they are produced or shared by someone who is themselves influential. The key value of the influentials was graphically illustrated when Bin Laden was shot by US forces in May 2011. Social Flow (2011) analysed 14.8 million Tweets and bitly links posted in the time between the first announcement of a Presidential address and the address itself, just under two hours later. At 10.24 Keith Urbahn, the chief of staff of Donald Rumsfeld (retired defence chief to George W Bush) tweeted: "So I'm told by a reputable person that they have killed Osama Bin Laden". Urbahn had a following of only 1,016 people but they tended to be people who knew that he was very close to power. Within one minute of Urbahn's tweet it had been re-posted by

Brian Stelter at *The New York Times*. Stelter had 50,000 followers so the message was re-tweeted hundreds of times and spread exponentially. By the time Obama stepped up to the microphone most people already knew what he was going to say.

This cycle mimics the pattern that Stuart Hall observed in which "primary definers" are able to set "the initial definition or primary interpretation of the topic in question" (Hall, 1978, p. 58). Stelter recognised immediately that Urbahn was an authoritative source. He had no need to check that the information was bona fide. His existing knowledge of the power structure made it clear to him that this particular source would have access to believable sources of information. Then his own power as an intermediary ensured that the information was circulated as widely as possible.

This story is a useful demonstration of how a trusted source, added to an influential node in the network, can produce very powerful network effects that spread like wildfire. This is an effect that can happen organically, as in the case of the Bin Laden tweet, but it is increasingly subject to manipulation by intermediaries who have studied the way in which social media information travels. A source will gain credibility if he or she is attached to a trusted organisation or is a person who audiences feel they have come to know through celebrity, through fandom or simply through social affinity.

Advertisers have long understood the power of celebrity endorsement (Bergkvist, Hjalmarson, & Mägi, 2016) but the Internet and social media have provided an interactive model of celebrity endorsement which allows brands to match specific audiences with influentials to whom they have already demonstrated an affinity by liking, following or sharing. The circulation of influence has thus become a form of social capital, which is used to the economic advantage of both the influencer and the source. Where the source is a product, like women's clothing, trainers or technical gadgets, the value of personal recommendation is so high that companies are prepared to pay for it, sometimes in direct fees for tweets and mentions, sometimes with free products. Celebrities have their own reputations to consider and brands have learned that they can maintain more control over bloggers by selecting those who already have a following in the right demographic, with tastes that match their product range. They then promote those they favour by re-tweeting to their own brand followers and feeding them with material, which they can then pass on to their followers.

It is not just commercial organisations that use the power of intermediaries. The charity Save the Children took three influential "mummy bloggers" to Bangladesh to raise awareness about child poverty. All three already had a big online following and they were experienced in the use of influential intermediaries:

> The mummybloggers targeted well-known celebrities who tweet, asking them to mention #blogladesh. They included actor Stephen Fry (1.7 million followers), DJ Richard Bacon (1.3 million followers), TV host Davina McCall (375,000) and pop star Boy George (13,000). This inspired journalists such as India Knight to start tweeting, and interest from publications such as PR Week.
>
> *(Cooper, 2011, p. 33)*

Ten million people had been reached on social media by the end of the trip and the bloggers had been interviewed on major mainstream news networks. The success of the campaign depended on the interactivity of social platforms but it required the power of the influentials to create the initial momentum and to push the posts so that they "trended" and were then taken up in mainstream media, thus leaping across the barriers of friendship to appear at the top of news feeds where they would be seen by those who had no connection at all to the initial blog posts.

It is this interconnection between the bubbles of social connection and the mainstream that truly allows information to move from the desk of a person reading Facebook in their pyjamas into public consciousness. In this case the audience is rarely the instigator of the news. Its job in the news cycle is to spread what is already trending. Once again, it is the ability to make a post appear popular that will allow it to travel. And in the increasingly organised world of social media, popularity is produced by careful organisation and manipulation.

BuzzFeed's investigative team provided an insight into the way this manipulation is being fine-tuned by those who wish to influence political decision-making. Reporter Ryan Broderick (2017) managed to infiltrate the operation of an US right-wing group which had set itself the task of influencing the French elections of 2017. Their method was based on creating fake Facebook accounts and using them to add comments to the Facebook pages of the popular French press in areas that they felt were likely to be sympathetic to a right-wing message. By infiltrating large numbers of concocted messages that appear to come from a variety of different people, they hoped to create antipathy towards the centre right candidate and boost support for the National Front candidate, Marine Le Pen.

In this case, the social media organisers were piggy-backing off the popularity of the mainstream press where they knew they would have access to large numbers of what they chillingly refer to as "norms". In other words, people who are not involved in right-wing circles and who they are targeting in order to influence them. The organisers set down clear rules of engagement in which they concealed their far-right identity. The fake Facebook pages were to appear to belong to people who are: "ideally young, cute girl, gay, Jew, basically anyone who isn't supposed to be pro-[FN]" (Broderick, 2017).

The rules of engagement explained in the post pretty much mimic the tried and tested methods of commercial public relations, in creating the appearance of popularity and in so doing changing the nature of the debate. When a company uses these methods to promote a make of shoe, they are able to profit economically from the organisation of the Internet. When a political organisation does so, they are attempting to create new "social norms"; in the case mentioned above, they were attempting to normalise anti-immigrant attitudes. This effect is of far greater concern because, as Foucault has observed, power in contemporary society is exercised "not by law but by normalisation" (Foucault, 1980, p. 89). By this he means that the way to change the status quo is by encouraging people to believe that things they once thought abnormal are the new normal. If you change people's attitudes, the law will change to follow them.

Feedback effects

For the Internet utopians, the assumption has been that news organisations pay insufficient attention to audience preferences, and, by giving audiences more control, there would be different choices made and the power would tilt away from the editors and the elite. This difference between what journalists think and what audiences actually choose was the subject of research by Boczkowski and Mitchelstein (2013) who looked at 20 news sites in seven different countries. In every country, irrespective of the organisation or political leanings of the news media, there were big differences between what the editors believed to be important and what the audiences preferred to read. Journalists in all these countries were considerably more interested than their audiences in public affairs journalism (Boczkowski & Mitchelstein, 2013, pp. 17–18). The gap decreased at times of political activity, such as elections or crises, and then grew to nearly 20 percentage points between elections or when political crises were defused.

Some scholars, such as Schudson (1998), would see this as the reasonable behaviour of the monitorial citizen, who is happy to leave the governance of the country to experts in between elections. Boczkowski and Mitchelstein were concerned however about the impact of these changes on journalism as a profession, and on "the role of the media as a liaison between elite decision makers and consumers" (2013, p. 5). They feared that news organisations would be tempted to follow the lead of their audiences and abandon the role that they play in the public sphere as providers of information and space for public deliberation.

Pierre Bourdieu, commenting on the impact of commercial television on the news landscape in France, observed that: "One of the paradoxes is that competition has the effect... in fields of cultural production under commercial control, of producing uniformity, censorship and even conservatism" (2005, p. 44). As the Internet has lowered the cost of entry to almost zero, competition for audiences and advertising has increased. Just as Bourdieu (and Boczkowski & Mitchelstein) would have predicted, the legacy news providers, desperate to maximise the number of visitors and clicks, in order to bring in the now much reduced advertising cash, started to follow the organisational logic of the content farmers (Cherubini & Nielsen, 2016). *Private Eye*, the British satirical magazine, described how this works:

> News hacks are now sent a memo three or four times a day from the website boffins listing the top subjects being searched in the last few hours on Google. They are then expected to write stories accordingly and/or get as many of those key words into the first paragraph of their story. Hence, if the top stories being Googled are 'Britney Spears' and 'breast cancer', hey presto, the hack is duly expected to file a piece about young women 'such as Britney Spears' being at risk from breast cancer.
> (*Private Eye, 2008, p. 4, in Phillips, 2010, p. 60*)

Journalists in Taiwan and in mainland China have a similar experience. Editors "'watch where the opinions of internet users go'... Our high-ranking managers rely on readers for survival, so readers' click rates will even influence the arrangement of news in the print version of the newspaper" (Tong & Lo, 2017, p. 40). Just as Bourdieu would have predicted, the impact of increased competition for audiences has produced a narrowing of choice as news organisations, trying to cater to the now clearly expressed preferences of audiences, compete to produce coverage of trending topics as quickly as possible. Studies into the impact of this heightened competition found rising levels of duplication as reporters, working under pressure, cannibalised copy from rivals and posted it, slightly altered, online (Phillips, 2010). But audience pressure is having other effects too.

In a Swedish study of viral news, researchers looked at the kind of stories that are shared, and compared the audience decisions to those made by editors. They found that sharers were significantly more likely than editors to be drawn to material that is humorous, highly emotional, opinionated or designed to move the reader. However, over a one-year period, the percentage of positive to negative stories changed significantly. This was the period between 2014 and 2015 when digital native news sites started in Sweden, majoring on stories that are uplifting and inspirational (Wadbring & Ödmark, 2016). The researchers found that the success of the new viral news sites had in turn changed the kind of stories that were produced by the traditional tabloid news organisations. There had been a significant increase in positive news stories of the kind favoured by sharers. In this very short period of time, the legacy news organisations had learned the lessons of virality and were producing similar "heartwarming" content (Wadbring & Ödmark, 2016, p. 141).

It is not just the viral news sites themselves that have had an impact. News organisations also feed off social media as a news source. Every news organisation follows trending subjects on social media sites. If a subject is trending online, journalists are set to work to provide stories that will be picked up in the passing stream. Editors know that, with their very large social media following, they will then become part of the rising tide and bring people back to their sites in order to verify information and update themselves. If the newspaper can use the material to create a controversy, the story may then spill over onto the broadcast news networks and back again into social media. Feedback loops of this kind can massively enlarge the reach of a story that, in the days of analogue media, would probably not have gone beyond the pages of a single newspaper. When applied to the social media use of a Presidential candidate, the impact can be very significant indeed.

In the early stage of the 2016 US primaries, Trump was not expected to win the Republican nomination. His campaign had far less money than his rivals. He depended on social media and in particular on the ability of social media to bring in mainstream media. His Twitter feed depended largely on making outrageous and often unverified statements about his rivals, which were gleefully repeated on the mainstream media. Leslie Moonves, CEO of American news network CBS, summed up the mainstream media's interest in the synergistic effect of social media when he declared in February 2016 that Trump's candidacy: "may not be good for America, but it's damn good for CBS". He said: "The money's rolling in and this is fun… I've never seen anything like this, and this [is] going to be a very good year for us. Sorry. It's a terrible thing to say. But, bring it on, Donald. Keep going" (Gertz, 2016).

In responding to the Trump Twitter statements, the news programmes helped to create a climate of disapproval around Clinton. In media analysis around the primaries, Trump was quoted more often about Hillary Clinton's policies than she was: "Trump's claim that Clinton 'created ISIS', for example, got more news attention than her announcement of how she would handle Islamic State" (Patterson, 2016). A similar pattern seems to be emerging in India. Here, only 12 per cent of the population are active users of social media[6] and yet Prime Minister Modi has 26 million Twitter followers, and, according to an article in the *Financial Times* (Kazmin, 2017), holds no press conferences. He communicates via Twitter and his communiqués are then disseminated via mainstream media. There is concern that his followers are also using social media to launch online attacks on journalists who oppose Modi's policies (Chaturvedi, 2016). Derek O'Brian, a member of India's upper house from West Bengal, has accused Modi and his party of "mainstreaming hate" and suggested that Party officials should stop following abusive Twitter accounts (Kazmin, 2017).

Researchers at Stanford University (Allcott & Gentzkow, 2017) analysed the impact of false news in the 2016 American election and found little evidence that it was sightings of the fake news sites that swung the election because, as noted in earlier chapters, mainstream television is still the dominant source of news for the majority of people, particularly in the older age groups. However, when stories generated on social media, or indeed on fake news sites, draw attention from the mainstream, this feedback effect is instrumental in increasing audiences, who will often share stories disconnected from their context, thus emphasising precisely the points that the mainstream media had been attempting to de-bunk. The interconnection between the bubbles of social media and the mainstream therefore succeeds in amplifying the sensational and the angry over the calm and the dispassionate, thus deepening polarisation across all platforms.

Crowds and the journalism field

In conditions of extreme competition, within the particular institutional conditions of the Web, the wisdom of the crowd has turned out to be mainly the promotion of the popular, the cute and the angry. As Hindman (2009) observed, the "democracy" of the Internet has tended to reduce the number of mainstream news organisations because the particular logic of search algorithms and the push to promote only the most popular posts has ensured that, in every subfield of the news media, only the most popular survive. Some new brands have emerged online but most struggle to be financially self-supporting. Where innovation has taken place, it has mainly been through the manipulation of Search Engine Optimisation, which further popularises the news agenda and forces genuine news organisations to compete by popularising their own news offering.

The social media platforms have always maintained that they are not publishers and have no responsibility for the activities of people who use their platforms.

However, they do have responsibility for their own systems, which have allowed hate sites and fake news to be inadvertently funded by third parties. The only way that the platforms can prevent this happening is to de-list sites. This means that, rather than remaining neutral about which sites get funded by advertising, they are being forced to make decisions about which organisations are acceptable but that means, arguably, that they are becoming publishers, not merely pipes, and should be subject to the same regulatory and legal systems that govern the behaviour of publishers. This could have very far-reaching consequences for Net freedom as the means of monetising content would then be controlled by a very small number of very large, global companies. The advertisers would be happy about such a change because it protects their brand image. For those who dream of Net democracy it will be a further step backwards.

If one considers the World Wide Web as an institution, created by social forces and manipulated by different interests and power blocks, then it makes little sense to speak in terms of the interests of the crowd, or the interests of the people. The Internet, with its promise to provide a multitude of different sources of news, has in fact created a commercial platform in which the fierce competition for sources of income is reducing resources for basic news-gathering. Audiences can certainly share news more easily and they can do so in ways that challenge the power of editors to set the agenda, but the information they share will still come from a decreasing number of large (often global) companies; from political entities with the financial muscle to maintain a presence on the Web or companies that simply want to attract attention for the sake of making advertising cash.

In the past, technological developments in communication have very quickly become subject to state intervention and regulation. The means of regulation has differed according to political systems. In authoritarian regimes (discussed in more detail in the next chapter) this has implied censorship and state control but in democracies technologies have been judged on their impact on democracy. Where they have encouraged the development of monopolies (as was the case for the telegraph and television), governments have brought in controls or public owner-ship, to ensure that they are held in public trust, separate from the apparatus of the state. There has been no such debate about the role of the Internet platforms in Western democracies. The assumptions about the supremacy of free-market global economics have driven out all but the most timid discussions about the role of national governments in regulating these businesses, even as they threaten the existence of the news organisations that are critical to upholding democratic governance.

Notes

1 Mitch Kapor's Blog, April 22, 2006, http://blog.kapor.com/index9cd7.html?p=29. (this is now a dead link)
2 Mark Zuckerberg was speaking at the Talking at the Crunchie awards in San Francisco January 9, 2010.

3 2015 search engine market share by country. http://returnonnow.com/internet-market
   ing-resources/2015-search-engine-market-share-by-country/
4 Statista. www.statista.com/statistics/241552/share-of-global-population-using-facebook-
   by-region/
5 Euromyths is a website of the European Union which refutes specific inaccuracies published in the press. http://blogs.ec.europa.eu/ECintheUK/euromyths-a-z-index/
6 https://www.techinasia.com/india-web-mobile-data-series-2016

References

Adorno, T. W. (1975/2010). Culture industry reconsidered. *New German Critique*, 6,
   12–19.
Allcott, H., & Gentzkow, M. (2017). Social media and fake news in the 2016 election.
   Journal of Economic Perspectives, 31(2), 211–236.
Auletta, K. (2009). *Googled: The end of the world as we know it*. New York, NY: Penguin.
Bakker, P. (2012). Aggregation, content farms and Huffinization. *Journalism Practice*, 6(5–6),
   627–637. doi:10.1080/17512786.2012.667266
Barlow, J. P. (1996). Declaration of the Independence of Cyberspace. *The Electronic Frontier
   Foundation*. Retrieved June 2, 2017 from www.eff.org/cyberspace-independence
Benkler, Y. (2006). *The wealth of networks: How social production transforms markets and freedom*.
   New Haven, CT; London, England: Yale University Press.
Benson, R., & Neveu, E. (2005). *Bourdieu and the journalistic field*. Cambridge, England;
   Malden, MA: Polity Press.
Berger, J., & Milkman, K. L. (2012). What makes online content viral? *Journal of Marketing
   Research*, 49(2), 192–205.
Bergkvist, L., Hjalmarson, H., & Mägi, A. W. (2016). A new model of how celebrity
   endorsements work: Attitude toward the endorsement as a mediator of celebrity source
   and endorsement effects. *International Journal of Advertising*, 35(2), 171–184.
Berners-Lee, T. (2000). *Weaving the web: The original design and ultimate destiny of the World
   Wide Web*. New York, NY: HarperCollins.
Boczkowski, P. J., & Mitchelstein, E. (2013). *The news gap: When the information preferences of
   the media and the public diverge*. Cambridge, MA; London, England: MIT Press.
Bourdieu, P. (2005). The political field, the social science field, and the journalistic field. In
   R. Benson & E. Neveu (Eds.), *Bourdieu and the journalistic field* (pp. 29–47). Cambridge,
   England; Malden, IL: Polity Press.
Bourdieu, P., & Wacquant, L. (1992). *An invitation to reflexive sociology*. Chicago, IL: Polity
   Press.
Broderick, R. (2017). Trump supporters online are pretending to be French to manipulate
   France's election. *BuzzFeed News*. Retrieved March 10, 2017 from www.buzzfeed.com/
   ryanhatesthis/inside-the-private-chat-rooms-trump-supporters-are-using-to?utm_term=.
   dsvNRdZqL#.icm41gBqY
Caffyn, G. (2017). Confessions of a brand media chief: 'We're sheep'. *Digiday*. Retrieved
   January 26, 2017 from http://digiday.com/brands/confessions-brand-media-chief-sheep/
Chaturvedi, S. (2016). I am a troll: Inside the secret world of BJP's digital army, Juggernaut
   Books. Retrieved January 20, 2017 from www.business-standard.com/article/beyond-bu
   siness/i-am-a-troll-inside-the-secret-world-of-bjp-s-digital-army-116122801182_1.html
Cherubini, F., & Nielsen, R. K. (2016). Editorial analytics: How news media are devel-
   oping and using audience data and metrics. *Reuters Institute for the Study of Journalism*.
   Retrieved January 15, 2017 from http://digitalnewsreport.org/publications/2016/edi
   torial-analytics-2016/

Christopherson, K. M. (2007). The positive and negative implications of anonymity in Internet social interactions: "On the internet, nobody knows you're a dog". *Computers in Human Behavior*, 23(6), 3038–3056.

Cohen, N. (2003). Going nowhere fast. *The Guardian*. Retrieved March 2, 2017 from www.theguardian.com/politics/2003/oct/12/labour.tonyblair

Cooper, G. (2011). *From their own correspondent? New media and the changes in disaster coverage: Lessons to be learned*. Oxford, England: Reuters Institute for the Study of Journalism.

Cordrey, T. (2012). Tanya Cordrey's speech at the Guardian Changing Media Summit. *The Guardian*. Retrieved January 20, 2017 from www.theguardian.com/gnm-press-office/cha nging-media-summit-tanya-cordrey

Crawford, H., Hunter, A., & Filipovic, D. (2015). *All your friends like this: How social networks took over the news*. Sydney, Australia: HarperCollins.

Ellison, N. B., Lampe, C., Steinfield, C., & Vitak, J. (2011). With a little help from my friends: How social network sites affect social capital processes. In Z. Papsharissi (Ed.), *A networked self: Identity, community and culture on social network sites* (pp. 124–145). New York, NY: Routledge.

Ensmenger, N. (2010). Making programming masculine. In T. J. Misa (Ed.), *Gender codes: Why women are leaving computing* (pp. 115–142). New York, NY: John Wiley & Sons.

Filloux, F. (2015, April 6). Jumping in bed with Facebook: Smart or desperate? *The Monday Note*. Retrieved August 8, 2017 from https://mondaynote.com/jumping-in-bed-with-fa cebook-smart-or-desperate-936f95e3322

Foucault, M. (1972). *The archaeology of knowledge*. London, England: Tavistock.

Foucault, M. (1980). *The history of sexuality. Volume 1: An introduction*. New York, NY: Vintage.

Garrahan, M. (2017). BuzzFeed and online media rivals seek new models. *Financial Times*. Retrieved May 1, 2017 from www.ft.com/content/e1b7e23c-dde5-11e6-9d7c-be108f1c1dce

Gertz, M. (2016). Post-mortem: How 2016 broke political journalism. *Media Matters for America*. Retrieved February 2, 2017 from https://mediamatters.org/blog/2016/12/16/ post-mortem-how-2016-broke-political-journalism/214843

Gillmor, D. (2006). *We the media: Grassroots media by the people, for the people*. Sebastopol, CA: O'Reilly Media, Inc.

Habermas, J. (1989). *The structural transformation of the public sphere: an inquiry into a category of bourgeois society*. Cambridge, MA: Polity Press.

Hall, S. (1978). The social production of news. In S. Hall (Ed.), *Policing the crisis: Mugging, the state, and law and the order* (pp. 53–60). London, England: Macmillan.

Herrman, J. (2016). Inside Facebook's (totally insane, unintentionally gigantic, hyperpartisan) political-media machine. *New York Times Magazine*. Retrieved June 3, 2017 from www. nytimes.com/2016/08/28/magazine/inside-facebooks-totally-insane-unintentionally-giga ntic-hyperpartisan-political-media-machine.html?_r=0

Hindman, M. (2009). *The myth of internet democracy*. Princeton, NJ: Princeton University Press.

Jenkins, H. (2008). *Convergence culture: Where old and new media collide*. New York, NY: New York University Press.

Just, N., & Latzer, M. (2016). Governance by algorithms: Reality construction by algo- rithmic selection on the Internet. *Media, Culture & Society*. https://doi.org/10.1177/ 0163443716643157

Kazmin, A. (2017). 'I Am a Troll' by Swati Chaturvedi. India, cyber bullies and how social media is used to attack political opponents. *Financial Times*. Retrieved March 22, 2017 from www.ft.com/content/6dd90462-e3bd-11e6-8405-9e5580d6e5fb

Kendall, L. (2011). "White and nerdy": Computers, race, and the nerd stereotype. *The Journal of Popular Culture*, 44(3), 505–524. doi:10.1111/j.1540–5931.2011.00846.x

Leadbeater, C. (2008). *We-think: Mass innovation, not mass production.* London, England: Profile Books.

Lessig, L. (2005). *Free culture: The nature and future of creativity.* New York, NY: Penguin Books.

Massanari, A. (2015). #Gamergate and The Fappening: How Reddit's algorithm, governance, and culture support toxic technocultures. *New Media & Society*, October 9, 2015. doi:10.1177/1461444815608807

Morozov, E. (2011, July 13). Don't be evil. *New Republic.* Retrieved March 3, 2017 from https://newrepublic.com/article/91916/google-schmidt-obama-gates-technocrats

Moses, L. (2015, November 9). Facebook's traffic to top publishers fell 32 percent since January. *Digiday UK.* Retrieved February 6, 2017 from http://digiday.com/publishers/fa cebooks-traffic-top-publishers-fell-32-percent-since-january/

Moses, L. (2017a, January 24). Publishers made only 14 percent of revenue from distributed content. *Digiday UK.* Retrieved February 6, 2017 from https://digiday.com/media/pub lishers-made-14-percent-revenue-distributed-content/

Moses, L. (2017b, June 6). Breitbart ads plummet nearly 90 percent in three months as Trump's troubles mount. *Digiday UK.* Retrieved June 2017 from https://digiday.com/media/breitba rt-ads-plummet-nearly-90-percent-three-months-trumps-troubles-mount/?utm_medium= email&utm_campaign=digidaydis&utm_source=uk&utm_content=170606

Mostrous, A. (2017, March 17). Taxpayers are funding extremism. *The Times.* Retrieved March 21, 2017 from www.thetimes.co.uk/article/taxpayers-fund-extremism-csdn0npsf

Papacharissi, Z. (2012). Without you, I'm nothing: Performances of the self on Twitter. *International Journal of Communication*, 6, 1989–2006.

Pathak, S. (2016, November 22). In response to complaints, some brands are pulling ads placed on Breitbart. *Digiday.* Retrieved January 5, 2017 from http://digiday.com/market ing/brands-pulling-ads-placed-breitbart/

Patterson, T. (2016). If Clinton loses, blame the email controversy and the media. *LA Times.* Retrieved January 28, 2017 from www.latimes.com/opinion/op-ed/la-oe-patterson-clinton-press-negative-coverage-20160921-snap-story.html

Phillips, A. (2010). Old sources: New bottles. In N. Fenton (Ed.), *New media, old news* (pp. 87–101). London, England: Sage Publications.

Phillips, A. (2012). Sociability, speed and quality in the changing news environment. *Journalism Practice*, 6(5–6), 669–679. doi:10.1080/17512786.2012.689476

Powell, W. W., & DiMaggio, P. J. (1991). *The new institutionalism in organizational analysis.* Chicago: University of Chicago Press. Retrieved May 1, 2017 from www.press.uchicago. edu/ucp/books/book/chicago/N/bo3684488.html

Rosen, J. (2006, June). The people formerly known as the audience [Blog post]. Retrieved May 1, 2017 from http://archive.pressthink.org/2006/06/27/ppl_frmr.html

Roth, D. (2009, October 19). The answer factory: Demand media and the fast, disposable, and profitable as hell media model. *Wired Magazine.* Retrieved November 9, 2017 from www.wired.com/2009/10/ff_demandmedia/

Schudson, M. (1998). *The good citizen: A history of American civic life.* New York, NY: The Free Press.

Silverman, C. (2016). This analysis shows how viral fake election news stories outperformed real news on Facebook. *BuzzFeed News.* Retrieved January 25, 2017 from www.buzz feed.com/craigsilverman/viral-fake-election-news-outperformed-real-news-on-facebook? utm_term=.vlwVYJXDn#.xfv20pZGR

Silverman, C., & Alexander, L. (2016). How teens in the Balkans are duping Trump supporters with fake news. *BuzzFeed News.* Retrieved January 24, 2017 from www.buzzfeed. com/craigsilverman/how-macedonia-became-a-global-hub-for-pro-trump-misinfo?utm_ term=.ai3Vv569X#.fcQOZ2G0M

Slater, M. D. (2015). Reinforcing spirals model: Conceptualizing the relationship between media content exposure and the development and maintenance of attitudes. *Media Psychology*, 18(3), 370–395.

Social Flow. (2011). Breaking Bin Laden: Visualizing the power of a single tweet. Retrieved January 27, 2017 from www.socialflow.com/breaking-bin-laden-visualizing-the-power-of-a-single/

Surowiecki, J. (2004). *The wisdom of crowds: Why the many are smarter than the few*. London, England: Abacus.

Tong, J., & Lo, S. (2017). Uncertainty, tabloidisation, and the loss of prestige: New media innovations and journalism cultures in two newspapers in mainland China and Taiwan. In Tong, J. & Lo, S. (Eds.), *Digital technology and journalism: An international comparative perspective*. London, England: Palgrave.

Van Couvering, E. (2007). Is relevance relevant? Market, science, and war: Discourses of search engine quality. *Journal of Computer-Mediated Communication*, 12(3), 866–887.

Van Dijck, J. (2013). *The culture of connectivity: A critical history of social media*. New York, NY: Oxford University Press.

Wadbring, I., & Ödmark, S. (2016). Going viral: News sharing and shared news in social media. *Observatorio*, 10(4), 132–149.

Wallenstein, A., & Spangler, T. (2013). Epic fail: The rise and fall of demand media. *Variety*. Retrieved May 13, 2017 from http://variety.com/2013/biz/news/epic-fail-the-rise-and-fall-of-demand-media-1200914646/

Waterson, J. (2017). Fake news sites can't compete with Britain's partisan press. *BuzzFeed News*. Retrieved January 24, 2017 from www.buzzfeed.com/jimwaterson/fake-news-sites-cant-compete-with-britains-partisan-newspape?utm_term=.jbByMEAWB#.enA8MQ2Av

Williams, R. (1974/1999). The technology and society. In H. Mackay & T. O'Sullivan (Eds.), *The media reader: Continuity and transformation* (pp. 43–57). London, England: Sage Publications.

5

GLOBALISATION

Myth: the Internet has produced the "global village" envisioned by McLuhan

When McLuhan (1964) predicted the attainment of a "global village" in which information and experience would be freely available for all to share, he argued that "as electrically contracted, the globe is no more than a village. Electric speed in bringing all social and political functions together in a sudden implosion has heightened human awareness of responsibility to an intense degree" (McLuhan, 1964, p. 5). He saw this change as a challenge to power structures by ordinary people who, with their new sense of connection to people in other places, would exercise their power to produce a more equal and compassionate world.

As news media have increasingly moved online, some scholars have identified an emerging "networked" structure of news that resembles computer networks in breadth of distribution and rhizomatic spread. They argue that such "networked journalism" blurs formerly rigid lines between national news spaces (Heinrich, 2012). Others claim that this network structure is changing the power structures in the world. Whereas nation states used to be the dominant social organisation that concentrated power and managed resources, Carnoy and Castells find this power located in media because "Only at this point in history was a technological infrastructure available to make it possible" (Carnoy & Castells 2001, p. 3).

Hannerz (1996) argues that such a change would require something more than networks: "genuine cosmopolitanism is first of all an orientation, a willingness to engage with the Other. It entails an intellectual and aesthetic openness toward divergent cultural experiences, a search for contrasts rather than uniformity" (p. 103). Embrace of cosmopolitanism therefore implies access to what Putnam (2000) would refer to as bridging social capital, which seeks connection between different groups.[1] Norris and Inglehart (2009), referring to Hannerz's work, suggest that cosmopolitanism can be understood to reflect both *values* and *identities*, and claim that:

cosmopolitans express tolerance and trust of people from other countries, rejecting the politics of fear and xenophobia. Cosmopolitan orientations should lead to a willingness to understand other peoples and places, expressed, for example, by an interest in foreign travel or working abroad and tolerance of immigrants, strangers, and visitors from other nations.

(Norris & Inglehart, 2009, p. 182)

However, far from enabling cosmopolitanism and an increase in bridging capital, Hafez (2016) suggests that "the new uncertainties of the information flow are generating an often 'virtual' knowledge of the world, which is almost impossible to harmonize with verifiable reality" (p. 50). He is concerned that we are in fact becoming "virtual cosmopolitans", who watch reality programmes about owning a home in the sun, rather than citizens organising collectively in civil society and having our voices heard in multilateral organisations beyond the boundaries of the nation-state.

The structure of the Internet does indeed allow news to flow across national boundaries and people to follow real-time news of events in New York, Istanbul and Moscow from anywhere in the world. We have access to news at any time and in any place via mobile phones and Internet cafes. Diasporas also have access to news media in their homeland online and via satellite television, and news from other countries is available in a range of languages. The impact of media globalisation on audiences is the subject of an increasing abundance of research, from a multitude of different perspectives, which we will examine here but does it mean that we now live in a global village in which borders are no longer important for the way we consume and use news? Has the Internet and globalisation allowed us to participate in a cosmopolitan democracy operating not only within states, but also among states and at the global level? Or has it simply made us voyeurs of other people's suffering while we turn inwards and focus only on our own national concerns? Have we become more cosmopolitan? Do we see a convergence of media systems, a Westernisation or both of these things? Have we left local communities and moved into a global village or have we merely created new walls around us while using our global connections for shopping?

Homogenisation towards Westernisation?

In his book *No Sense of Place*, Meyrowitz (1985) argued that electronic media move people informationally to the same "place" and he pointed to an on-going homogenising process. "Where one is now", he suggested, "has less to do with who one is, because where one is now has so little to do with what one knows and experiences" (p. 158). This homogenising of the news audiences has been discussed as a process in which individuals become more global, but the argument leaves unexamined what it would mean for us all to be "in the same place" when that sense of place is in fact dominated by global flows of power. If it were ever possible for everyone in the world to view each other from the same place, it has been argued, that place would almost certainly be America. The export of media products, mainly from the USA, has been claimed to destroy authentic, traditional and local culture in many parts of the world (Tunstall, 1977). The globalising tendency of large media corporations has been well documented (Herman & McChesney, 2004). Global news flows are still dominated by predominantly Western giants, some old and some new: the BBC, CNN, News Corp. Pearson Publishing and the three news agencies: Reuters, Agence France Presse and Associated Press, are still mainly responsible for the coverage of foreign stories for news media across the world. They are all Western and they pass on stories about the world framed from a Western perspective.

The relative newcomers: Apple, Facebook and Google, also all global companies based in the USA, increasingly structure the way we are exposed (or not) to news. These multinational (media) companies also take most of the world's online advertising, diverting it from the support of local media products. These global companies choose to locate in national contexts where they don't have to pay tax (or pay very little), and they do not have to spend money on producing news and information. The flows from individuals, via social media such as Twitter, are provided without cost and are gathered up and re-purposed by mainstream news organisations, both national and international. In this way the Internet platforms are benefitting from mainstream media producing the news and people who share it online.

The move from offline to online has also increased the possibilities for national *soft power*, the ability of one country to get "other countries to want what it wants" (Nye, 1990, p. 167). According to Nye (2010), cultural diplomacy, such as international news production, can serve as an instrument of public diplomacy and an "important soft power tool". Western states, especially the UK and the USA through the BBC World Service and CNN (a commercially funded service) were the first to distribute television worldwide when capabilities became available. Globally, the BBC World Service reaches 246 million users around the world each week (2015 figures). In that year 320 million people worldwide, or one in every 16 adults, used the BBC's international news services (World Service, World News Channel, bbc.com and social media), which is now available in 30 languages including English. BBC News is also the biggest news provider on Facebook with more than 40 million "likes" in April 2017. CNN International started broadcasting in 1985, primarily for US business travellers in hotels across the world. Today CNN International offers news in English, Arabic and Spanish to 425 million households or hotel rooms (2016 figures). CNN is also the second biggest news provider on Facebook, with more than 27 million followers (in April 2017).[2]

For critical theorists (Schiller, 1969), this media globalisation goes hand in hand with cultural imperialism, in which the ideas of the West are transmitted across the world. However, Tomlinson (1996) claims that globalisation may not be firmly in the cultural grip of the West and that the prospects for the developing world may be less determined than the critical pessimism of the "Westernisation" thesis predicts. Tomlinson does not deny the economic dominance of the West, but he concludes that globalisation is not a process firmly in the cultural grip of the West and that the global future is much more radically open than the discourse of homogenisation and Westernisation suggest.

Norris and Inglehart (2009) agree with this less pessimistic view. By analysing data from the World Values Survey and the European Values Survey, they found that "the people of the world have come to share certain cultural icons and contemporary fashions, and increasing amounts of information and ideas about people and places, but this does not mean that they will lose their cultural heritage" (p. 310). The news media are an important agency for cultural values, but this does not imply convergence. Distinct national identities and cultural practices do not appear to be dissolving. Indeed, they suggest that convergence of national cultures around Western values is only one possible outcome of cosmopolitan communication and that "distinctive identities, values and ways of life in each society are more deeply rooted and resilient in the face of the impact of global media than is often claimed" (Norris & Inglehart, 2009, p. 298).

Norris and Inglehart (2009) suggest four possible reactions to the flow of media messages: convergence or fusion on the one hand but polarisation around political differences or outright rejection on the other. There is evidence of all four tendencies. A study of coverage of the Greek, US and Chinese elections of 2012 in China, Japan, the UK, Germany and the USA found very striking convergence in coverage. The only substantial difference was in the reporting of the Chinese election. The four democracies reported in very similar terms, giving guarded approval to the new regime (Curran, Esser, Hallin, Hayashi, & Chin-Chuan, 2017). Curran et al. (2017, p. 124) were particularly struck by the adherence to what they describe as "the international neo-liberal hegemony" in the reporting of the Greek elections won by the anti-austerity party, Syriza.

This level of unanimity in coverage may demonstrate a uniformity in response to global financial instability, but discourses can also diverge and polarise around political and cultural differences, as news travels across international borders. An international research project looked at the way in which drawings of the Prophet Muhammad, published in a Danish newspaper in 2005, were discussed around the world (Eide, Kunelius, & Phillips, 2008). The differences in this case were not binary; they operated around a set of scripts in which various positions on press freedom, tolerance of religious difference and anti-imperialism were adopted, both between countries and within them. Some of the elite, the English-language press of Pakistan, for example, took a similar line to the Western press (evidence perhaps of convergence), while others showed evidence of polarisation, focusing on what they took to be the double standards of the Western news media that protects some minorities and persecutes others (Eide et al., 2008).

Attempts by Western governments and civil society organisations to spread news information that is seen to be at odds with the interests of authoritarian regimes have been met by rejection using fiercely defensive protective measures (Fenton, 2012). Eighteen authoritarian regimes with Internet penetration above 40 per cent were found to have blocked content related to political or religious themes (Pan,

2017). China blocks a large number of websites and news organisations and in June 2017 halted video streaming on three major Internet platforms. Almost all social media traffic takes place on locally owned platforms which are subject to censorship and to removal if material is considered inimical to the interests of the regime. Researchers found that Chinese censors tend to leave some critical material in place but remove posts with "collective action potential" (King, Pan, & Roberts, 2014). However, outside China and Iran, which have built their own successful and popular social media platforms, states have far less ability to control material, because social media sites are owned by US firms (Pan, 2017).

A more potent use of state power to reject unwanted messages is the threat to arrest those who post opposition messages online. In Iran, Egypt, Turkey and Singapore (to name just a few places) there have been examples of activists being arrested because they have published their opinions on social media, or they have been identified via pictures published on their profiles on social media. The network structure of social media also makes it relatively easy to trace the networks of political activists, which in turn makes it easy for authoritarian regimes to disrupt these networks. In 2009, the Iranian government formed a cybercrime team to find what they defined as false information (not supportive of the regime), and Iranian police hunted the Internet for photos and videos that showed faces of protesters, which they published on news media websites asking for public help to identify the individuals (Morozov, 2011). After the revolution of the Arab Spring in Egypt in 2011, and the coup attempt in Turkey in the summer of 2016, hundreds of bloggers and journalists were imprisoned. Miller et al. (2016) found that such actions have the effect of creating self-censorship: "Social media leads to an interweaving of the social and political fabric, to the extent that state surveillance overlaps and is reinforced by the social surveillance of friends, acquaintances or family members" (p. 149). The Reuters Institute for the Study of Journalism noted a 10 per cent drop in the use of Facebook for news in Turkey in the year of the coup and an 8 per cent rise in the use of WhatsApp, which is a more secure and less public system of communication. (Newman, Fletcher, Kalogeropoulos, & Nielsen 2017, p. 98).

Russia uses less direct action to get rid of content internally. An independent social media company, Vk.com, became the object of intimidation when its founder refused to censor material. The company is now wholly owned by allies of the government (Pan, 2017). Russia has also used network effects (described in Chapter 4) to organise Troll attacks (Global Voices, 2015) on domestic liberal media, forcing them to disable their comment sections, or abusing those with "unpatriotic" views. These tactics result in the majority of liberal, or simply moderate, websites opting to disable their comments sections altogether, thus depriving the online community of the opportunity to exchange with genuine unfiltered views. On websites where comments remain open, one anti-Putin statement is counteracted by a flurry of offerings in the spirit of Kiselyov's "militant pseudo-patriotism", leading to a feeling of isolation for those who fully or partially disagree with policies pursued by Putin (Irisova, 2015).

Global counter-narratives

While authoritarian regimes use various methods to reject the flow of material coming into their countries, we are also now seeing the spread of counter-narratives from regimes that, in the past, have been excluded from the global news hegemony. Daya Thussu (2010) refers to these as "subaltern flows". These regimes have recognised the value of increasing their own soft power by spreading news and information across the world, first through satellite television networks, and then the Internet. In 1996, Al Jazeera,[3] a worldwide Arabic satellite television network with headquarters in Qatar (owned by the government of Qatar), was launched. Al Jazeera rapidly established an audience, principally from the Arabic-speaking world but increasingly, and significantly, among the international community, as "the international status has improved over time and it has become clear that Al Jazeera speaks with an independent voice and has its own viewpoints, at least when Qatari foreign policy goals are not involved" (Si, 2014, p. 16). Al Jazeera had more than 9 million followers on Facebook in April 2017, which is considerably fewer than the Western global broadcasters but still a significant addition to the mix.

In Russia the focus of soft power intervention intensified after the invasion of Ukraine in 2014. The Russian media were used to shape domestic support and the administration increased the reach of English-language programming, through the government-controlled broadcaster Russia Today/RT, which circulates global news from a Russian point of view. It has been claimed that the unifying character of RT "is a deep scepticism of Western and American narratives of the world and a fundamental defensiveness about Russia and Mr. Putin" (Erlanger, 2017). RT's head of communications in Moscow, Anna Belkina, said: "We want to complete the picture rather than add to the echo chamber of mainstream news; that's how we find an audience" (in Erlanger, 2017).

In China, which also has a rejectionist policy towards foreign news media, "soft power" and "going out" began to appear in policy documents in the early 1990s (Jiang, 2014; Xue, 2012). According to Jirik (2016, p. 3539), "the strategy of going out and soft power are inextricably linked, as they represented the material and ideological dimension of the Chinese polity's decision to increase China's engagement with the outside world". In 2001, CCTV9, a global 24-hour, English-language news service was developed (Xu, 2002 in Liu, 2006). In 2009, the *South China Morning Post* of Hong Kong reported that the Chinese government was intending to spend 45 billion Yuan (USD $6.6 billion) to promote the international development of its major media institutions and thus improve the Chinese national image all over the world. In December 2016, the national broadcaster in China, China Central Television (CCTV), launched China Global Television Network (CGTN) offering Chinese news in English, Spanish, French, Arabic and Russian.[4]

However, there is a question about audiences for all of these international media, including the BBC, CNN, Al Jazeera, CGTN and RT. In his early work, Nye (1990) wrote that soft power depends on the state's culture and ideological attractiveness, because this will make others more willing to follow it. Conversely,

"If the content of a country's culture, values and policies are not attractive, public diplomacy that 'broadcasts' them cannot produce soft power" (Nye, 2010, para 5).

National media flows and global elites

The number of people potentially connected to global news flows is vast and increasing. Social network use worldwide is expected to increase to 2.72 billion in 2020 (Statista, 2017), which is approximately half of the adult (15 years and older) population of the world. A recent study from Reuters (Newman, Fletcher, Levy, & Nielsen, 2016) including data from 26 countries shows that 44 per cent of the survey respondents said that they use Facebook for news. YouTube is also a key network for news (19 per cent), while Twitter is favoured by journalists, politicians, and heavy news users in particular (10 per cent) and is a key platform for people who are news influentials (see Chapter 4). However, although the use of social networks allows for global exposure to news, there is no evidence to suggest that they are actually used to any significant extent to access global news, or that, when they do so, the news received is coming from alternative sources. Nor is there any evidence that, as Xenos, Vromen, and Loader (2014) suggest, social media is "the great equalizer" transforming existing patterns of social inequality by lowering the threshold for civic engagement for all people.

Although increasing access to both local and global news makes it easier to cultivate either a local or a global news orientation, the main change in news exposure is that individuals across the Western world are spending less time on news (politics and current affairs) today than 10–20 years ago (Blekesaune, Elvestad, & Aalberg, 2012; Prior, 2007), and the media consumption is more specialised. Now that it is easier to create your own news diet, recent research shows that fewer individuals in the US and Norway are omnivores when it comes to orientation towards local, national and international news (Elvestad & Shaker, 2017). This may be at least partly due to the amount of heterogeneous information available which makes it more difficult to find relevant material. A recent study from Germany shows that younger people in particular are susceptible to "information overload" (Schmitt, Debbelt, & Schneider, 2017). There may be more international news available, but audience interest has not kept pace with that expansion.

A study of media interest in Kenya, Egypt, Senegal, India and Pakistan found that citizens prefer news about local and national affairs to international news (Geniets, 2011). In times of national and international crises, people across the populations of these countries also tend to watch news from international providers such as the BBC and CNN, because it is perceived to be more reliable than local news (Geniets, 2011). But on the whole, they prefer indigenous programming. There are also national differences according to access and use of international news. In Denmark, Germany and France, interest in international news is considerably higher than in the UK and the USA (Levy, 2012). In the UK and USA, the amount of overseas coverage in the mainstream media has declined as access has increased (Hamilton, 2004; Moore, 2010; Pew, 2012). UK audiences are relatively uninterested in international news and are even less likely to come across overseas news stories online than in news bulletins, where stories are chosen for them (Fenyoe, 2010; Sambrook, 2010).

The ability of news searchers to access foreign news is also often related to being able to speak a language other than their own. The potential for being a cosmopolitan, or getting access to global news, differs both within countries (according to individual levels of proficiency in English or another "world language") and across countries (in relation to the standard and spread of second language teaching). Geniets (2011) found, for example, that the language used in most international stations that are relayed in Kenya (mainly English) was perceived as a hindrance, as many Kenyans are not comfortable with the English language.

Direct access to foreign-language news, via any platform, remains the privilege of small knowledgeable elites or immigrants who manage several languages. Micklethwait and Wooldridge (2000) talk about a global info-elite of high-income "cosmocrats", claimed to number around 50 million people across the world. These are the real winners of globalisation, who they claim are worryingly disconnected from local communities. According to Sparks (2000), the so-called global media's audience is, "too small, too rich and too English-speaking to be considered inclusive" (p. 86). On an individual level, Norris and Inglehart (2009) found that citizens with English-language skills are more likely than non-English-speaking citizens to use radio, TV, newspapers and the Internet. Geniets (2011) also found that, while the transnational news providers, such as CNN, were highly trusted in Kenya, Egypt, Senegal, India and Pakistan, they were only regularly used by the socioeconomic and educational elite.

National media systems also vary in the depth and quality of their international news coverage. A cross national study in eleven countries across five continents shows that the more market-oriented media systems and broadcasters give less time to international news, and that the international news offered by these commercial broadcasters more often focuses on soft rather than hard news (Aalberg et al., 2013). This study also shows a positive relationship between the amount of hard international news coverage and citizens' level of foreign affairs knowledge, which implies that national media environments can explain individual differences in knowledge about the world outside their country. The impact of exposure to mass media on cultural values is strongest in societies that are most integrated into global markets and networks, with internal media freedom and widespread access to media technology (Norris & Inglehart, 2009). In countries with a strong public service broadcaster and media-rich environments on the national level, high Internet access and high general trust, citizens are also more likely to show a cosmopolitan awareness.

Television and the Internet are the main news sources in most Western countries, and surveys suggest that less than a quarter of news items on TV and the Internet are devoted to foreign news (Curran et al., 2013, p. 88; Stepinska, Porath, Mujica, Xu, & Cohen, 2013, p. 9). Two decades of cable news and the Internet has not increased international knowledge in the USA (Curran, Coen, Aalberg, & Iyengar, 2012). In their study of Americans and citizens from five European countries, Curran et al. found that Americans underachieved in response to international hard news questions. They did relatively well if the news had a particular resonance in the USA but US graduates gave a lower percentage of correct answers to international news questions than Dutch and British citizens who had not been to university (p. 83). One of the explanations given by the researchers (Curran et al., 2012) is that hard news knowledge gaps are closely aligned to axes of inequality, and the USA is significantly more unequal than the EU countries in this study, and in particular compared to the welfare democracies of northern Europe.[5] Overall, recent studies suggest that interest in foreign news and knowledge about international hard news questions are heavily dependent on the conditions in the country of origin, the trust in mainstream media and the depth of coverage available via mainstream sources (Elvestad, Phillips, & Feuerstein, 2017; Esser et al., 2012).

Glocalising the news

People prefer national news sources, both offline and online (Alexa, 2017; Newman et al., 2016). According to Jirik (2016, p. 3544), "A global news channel has two options to make itself culturally proximate. One is to create a programming model that is as culturally neutral as possible, thereby appealing to the greatest number of people possible regardless of cultural differences". This is what the big global broadcasters aim for. The alternative is to put culturally proximate fare and faces on air in different cultural settings within a global framework, a form of news "glocalization" (Robertson, 1992) that refers to global form and local content.

The large global players (all products of national media systems and operating within the professional assumptions and the frames of their "home" countries) are still responsible for most of the news that circulates globally but increasingly they employ local journalists with an understanding of the local culture and political systems for national editions of their websites or television channels (Thussu, 2010, p. 229). For example, *The Guardian* newspaper employs Australian journalists for their Australian edition. The BBC broadcasts in 40 languages, including Russian. This allows international media organisations to tailor their news to a local audience. Local journalists act as intermediaries, reading global accounts and filtering them for local use.

A national focus in the framing of foreign news is typical for coverage of international news online as well as in traditional media (Nossek, 2004). The argument is that news audiences are not very interested in international news without local adaptation. Thus, natural disasters tend to get greater coverage in the news media if witnesses from the home country can be interviewed because there will be a greater sense of audience identification. In a comparative study of leading news websites in nine nations,[6]Curran et al. (2013) show that online news (in common with television and newspaper news) is strongly nation-centred in its foreign news coverage, and that it focuses on great powers and neighbouring countries, and is much more inclined to cite the voices of authority than those of civil society and the individual citizen. The researchers also found that the USA "accounts for 26 percent of all international hard news in the nine websites, and for higher proportions in some countries, most notably Japan where the USA accounts for half of foreign web hard news and Australia where it constitutes 45 percent" (Curran et al., 2013, p. 889).[7] This convergence is due to the way in which leading media conglomerates have extended their hegemony across technologies. It also reflects the constraints exerted by the wider societal context across all media (Curran et al., 2013).

According to Hafez (2007), who suggests that media globalisation is a myth, there are few events in the news media which are global events and these are locally framed. Hafez (2007) claims that "even today national media agendas [are] in synch with the world only in a very superficial way" (p. 169). Based on empirical research he shows how the numbers of such global events are few, and that the framing of these events differs across national borders. The globalisation of economy, governance and culture has not been accompanied by a similar globalisation of the public sphere. Opinion formation is still very much tied to the level of national political institutions (Hjarvard, 2001, p. 19). Those events which are reported all over the world are usually "domesticated" by national interest groups (Hafez, 2007, p. 169), viewed through domestic frames (Eide et al., 2008; Nossek, 2004) and usually based on the countries' cultural familiarity with the news event (Galtung & Ruge, 1965; Herman & Chomsky, 1988). In the process of localising news, stereotypes of the world and people from different countries are reproduced (Galtung & Ruge, 1965). When news and information are produced for a domestic audience, usually a national group of consumers typified by national interests, reservations, stereotypes and cultural expectations, media respond to these and end up reproducing them (Hafez, 2007).

Diasporic communities and global news

Diasporic communities are now more able to access news from their country of origin (Tufte, 2003; Zuckerman, 2013) and several scholars have pointed out how following the news from "home territories" is a way of negotiating a multi-identity for ex-patriot families and individuals. The Internet and other transnational media channels provide opportunities for linking back to the communities they have left behind (Christiansen, 2004, p. 201). However, this does not necessarily make these communities more global or cosmopolitan in their orientation: "Information may flow globally, but our attention tends to be highly local and highly tribal; we care more deeply about those with whom we share a group identity and much less about a distant 'other'" (Zuckerman, 2013, p. 58).

A study of young adults from the Vietnamese diaspora in Norway showed how when access to satellite television from Vietnam became available, there was a change in their parents' media exposure (Elvestad, 2007). When these young adults were growing up, soap operas and novels were used to keep up the Vietnamese identity in the families, while the Norwegian public broadcasters or local and national newspapers were their main medium for news. After 2004, many of the parents replaced the Norwegian public broadcaster with Vietnamese television channels (Elvestad, 2007). This study shows how the preference for homeland media is so strong that even after 20 years in a host country, if the possibility for tuning in to your homeland is there, some will be prepared to leave the local media frames of the new nation.

Several researchers have discussed how national broadcasting has played a pivotal role in creating a national "culture in common". Aksoy (2006) highlights the symbolic power (and indeed expectation) of the national broadcaster as a producer of a sense of shared reality. However, not all people feel included in symbolic membership of the nation represented in its mediated culture, and Morley (2000) argues that the tie to "home" may be a response to feelings of alienation in their newly adopted country rather than a reflexive conservatism. The framing of immigrants or ethnic minorities in the national mainstream media can be exclusionary. A study of Danish ethnic minorities showed that racism, a feeling of being excluded from the flow of national news and lack of sufficient Danish language skills were all mentioned as reasons why Danish television news broadcasts are not their most prominent sources of news (Christiansen & Sell, 2000). As Christiansen (2004, p. 201) points out:

> When immigrant or diaspora populations are excluded, as targets for nation-wide public service television, it can both reinforce their general feeling of exclusion from their present society, and reduce possibilities of pursuing their own interests as minorities. Instead, the transnational social space presents itself as an opportunity for developing enduring relations and acquiring relevant information and news.

The use of homeland media is thus a consequence of feeling excluded by media in their adopted land. In a more recent study of migrants in Sweden, Christensen (2012) claims that "some instances of feeling Othered both within the diasporic community and by the larger society leads to a search for alternative means of sociality, particularly using online platforms" (p. 896).

Milikowski (2000) interviewed 50 Turkish-Dutch people between 1997 and 1998 about their experiences of Turkish satellite television. She argues that exposure to homeland media was not separating them from the nation in which they live. On the contrary, she found that for many Turkish immigrants, and for their children in particular, Turkish satellite television helped them "to liberate themselves from certain outdated and culturally imprisoning notions of Turkishness, which had survived in the isolation of migration" (Milikowski, 2000, p. 444). She showed how watching Turkish television in a Dutch context helped the young immigrants to show their parents that "young people are out of control" in both Turkey and the Netherlands, and this helped to *de-ethnicise* rather than ethnicise the viewers' perception of cultural difference.

Ethnicization and de-ethnicization in modern multicultural societies are to be viewed, in sum, as opposite forces in a series of boundary games played under new conditions and by unsettled rules. While ethnicization works at reproducing and strengthening ethnic social boundaries, de-ethnicization works at undoing them.

(Milikowski, 2000, p. 448).

However, attitudes towards national or diasporic media may change in reaction to external world events. Aksoy (2006) found that Turkish migrants in London initially developed a "transnational sensibility" but she found that the events of September 11, 2001 changed the way that migrants related to host media and homeland media, and the discussion of homeland media exposure. Before September 11, Turkish migrants in London did not find the complexities of identity problematic, but September 11 and the world's awareness of Turkey as an Islamic country changed that. She shows how the immigrants had to do a lot of thinking on their own, because of their scepticism about both Turkish and British media. She also showed how the emergence of transnational broadcasting after September 11 has called into question a sense of belonging to the national family of the "host" country. Media coverage started to express a fear that immigrants would use the news media environment and the opportunities to access media from their homelands to consolidate their belonging to their transnational communities (Aksoy, 2006).

Aksoy suggests that these events "regenerated a moral-cum-political discourse around national 'us' versus a dangerously different 'them'" (Aksoy, 2006, p. 924). A situation where the "morality of exclusion" was articulated into a question about loyalty to the British nation and to "Western civilisation", where immigrants' engagement in media systems based in other parts of the world was translated into suspicions about their loyalty to Britain. Hafez (2007) suggests that greater avail ability of news from home may be strengthening internal community bonds, rather than creating global citizens or cosmopolitans, and may also ultimately encourage conservative, nation-based, and chauvinistic cultures.

Arguably, the impact of access to global media will have varying effects on diasporic communities, dependent on both world events and events in their country of settlement. It might be equally pertinent to suggest that mainstream, bridging media, that fails to include diversity in its projected image of a homeland, and continues to provide a platform for the strident voices of anti-immigrant parties, pushes minority communities into a defensive attachment to the culture that offers acceptance. If audiences prefer to view the world through a national frame then the way the nation is framed by media and the degree of inclusivity it projects are important.

Political and social movements

For Castells, the Internet should be the means by which people express their concerns about the legitimacy of national governments and take on issues of global justice:

"The global civil society now has the technical means to exist independently from political institutions and from the mass media" (Castells, 2010, p. 42). He points to a long list of NGOs and global movements that have organised via the Internet on issues such as global warming, global poverty and women's rights and have used their own networks to disseminate information.

The global environment movement has certainly used the Internet in order to organise protests but the necessary change must still take place through the laborious application of traditional democratic systems, and the production of social pressure on governments still requires the involvement of the media. Certainly there have been instances in which news of political events have been drawn to global public attention via the horizontal networks of social media, but it is rare for news generated within social movements to be disseminated beyond those groups without the involvement of mainstream, bridging media. The worldwide mobilisation against the war in Iraq in 2003 is often held up as an example of global mobilisation and indeed it is true that events were coordinated so that they happened on the same day, but it was the mass media that took those events to a global audience. Similarly the organisation around the events in Ferguson, Missouri, in 2015, and the development of Black Lives Matter have also been cited as evidence that parallel social networks are capable of disseminating news globally. To some extent this is the case; however, it was the involvement of mainstream, bridging media that initially brought the events to global attention (Hitlin & Vogt, 2014).

Global media technologies cannot by themselves rejuvenate democracy. This is partly because they are shaped by social systems and carry the imprint of existing power relationships, but also because, as we discuss in greater detail in Chapter 2, social media systems are designed around "homophilous bonding social capital" (among actors who are similar), rather than around "heterophilous bridging social capital" (among actors who are dissimilar) (Lin, 2001; McPherson et al., 2001). People link to groups of people who are like them, strengthening bonds and pulling together to create political movements that are inward facing, not outward facing. This effect has been useful for both progressive and nationalist organisations because it allows for rapid mobilisation among like-minded people, but as we discuss in the chapter on Personalisation (Chapter 2), it also tends to polarise rather than encouraging debate or compromise.

The movements that seem to have been best able to make use of the horizontal structures of the Internet and social media have been nationalist movements that thrive because the bonding nature of social media and the tendency to form tightly knit, inward-looking groups lends itself to organisation which is tightly focused on activating like-minded people and on creating anger and focusing it. Miller et al. (2016) in their eight-country project on the use of social media found that most interviewees across the samples avoid serious discussion on social media, for fear of causing offence (we discuss this further in Chapter 2). In the English sample, humour was the mode of choice in political discussion, but they also found that some of those in the lowest income group were involved in promotion of nationalist causes "such as supporting the army or banning immigrants" (Miller et al. 2016, p. 147). In the USA, a nationalist social sub-group has been galvanised to re-post news stories supporting their cause through a network of Internet sites and social media, all of which are linked to the Alt Right website Brietbart and to the cable television station Fox News (Benkler, Faris, Roberts, & Zuckerman., 2017).

The blogospheres in authoritarian regimes are also teeming with nationalism and xenophobia, sometimes so poisonous that official government policy looks cosmopolitan in comparison (Morozov, 2011, p. 86). In China, some hoped that the Internet would bring a more open and democratic society. However, Hyun and Kim's (2015) study of Chinese Internet users suggests that public use of the Internet for political expression contributes to sustaining the existing Chinese system rather than undermining it.

> Respondents' online political expression enhanced their nationalistic and system-supportive attitudes. The more frequently they expressed their political opinions online, the stronger is the likelihood that they would report nationalistic attitudes and support for the existing system.
>
> *(Hyun & Kim, 2015, p. 774).*

For example, Nyíri, Zhang, & Varrall (2010) describe the way in which Chinese students studying abroad used social media to coordinate activities in defence of China in the spring of 2008 when pro-Tibetan demonstrators disrupted the torch parades in the run-up to China's Olympics. Their heroics were passed around on social media and also disseminated, with approval, by the mainstream, government-controlled media. The Miller et al. (2016) study suggests that there is a very good reason for this. In the context of Turkey they found that "such activity as there is on social media is usually at a national level and is conducted mainly by supporters of the current government, since people are aware of state surveillance online" (p. 143).

When attempting to spread globally, these organisations come up against the problems inherent in the structures that suit them so well. A reporter for BuzzFeed joined a chatroom organised by Trump supporters to assist right-wing activists campaigning for the far-right party in France. The level of intimate cultural knowledge required in order to be effective in another country made it hard to operate without close collaboration with French nationalists (Broderick, 2017). Nationalism doesn't work very easily on a global basis. It thrives best on self-reinforcing spirals in an echo chamber of unchallenged beliefs.

The Internet and social media has not created a global village

The Internet and social media have not turned the world into a global village. Indeed, events across the world suggest that there is a growing polarisation between those who see themselves as cosmopolitan subjects of an open world and those for whom the Internet and social media have provided greater opportunities for joining with others to defend national identities and borders. There is no "global public sphere" liberated from specific national and cultural influences (Hafez, 2007;

Hjarvard, 2001). Transnational news producers such as CNN, BBC and Al Jazeera are not common public spheres for all people across the world. Cross-border media communication is easier online but people still tend to access news through the lens of nationalism. Global media networks have not reduced the responsiveness of societies, even democratic ones, to propaganda (Hafez, 2007; Morozov, 2013). We are not global villagers but rather we are localised and bonded around particular ideas of identity, nation or religion, which cause polarisation rather than unity and parochialism instead of a globalised news audience.

Notes

1 Putnam refers to bridging and bonding social capital. Bonding social capital on the other hand refers to the tighter ties between members of a group or a family (Putnam, 2000).
2 Popularity of international news sources online (in ranked order) in May 2017: BBC, CNN, *The New York Times, The Guardian,* CCTV, *Huffington Post,* Fox News, RT, Reuters, Al Jazeera (Alexa, 2017).
3 As we write, Al Jazeera is under threat from a coalition of Middle Eastern powers that are pressuring the Qatar government into closing the station. If they succeed this would seriously damage the flow of counter-narratives and increase the power of the global news hegemony.
4 On October 1, 2004, CCTV added a 24-hour shared French and Spanish service, which it split into separate services three years later, on October 1, 2007. CCTV Arabic went to air in July 2009, and CCTV Russian was launched on September 10, 2009 (Jirik, 2010, as cited in Jirik, 2016).
5 OECD (2008) in Curran et al. (2012).
6 Australia, Colombia, Greece, India, Italy, Japan, Norway, South Korea and the United Kingdom.
7 "The Norwegian website is the most outward looking of the nine websites, devoting 48 percent of its total news to foreign topics and events. The most insular are websites in South Korea, India and Italy, which allocate between 13 and 25 percent of their news to foreign stories. The websites most inclined to relate foreign news reports to domestic affairs are in Japan, United Kingdom and Greece" (Curran et al., 2013, p. 889).

References

Aalberg, T., Papathanassopoulos, S., Soroka, S., Curran, J., Hayashi, K., Iyengar, S., Jones, P. K., Mazzoleni, G., Rojas, H., Rowe, D. & Tiffen, R. (2013). International TV News, Foreign Affairs Interest and Public Knowledge. *Journalism Studies,* 14(3), 387–406. doi:10.1080/1461670X.2013.765636

Aksoy, A. (2006). Transnational virtues and cool loyalties: Responses of Turkish-speaking migrants in London to September 11. *Journal of Ethnic and Migration Studies,* 32(6), 923–946. doi:10.1080/13691830600761487

Alexa (2017). Retrieved April 27, 2017 from www.alexa.com/

Benkler, Y., Faris, R., Roberts, H., & Zuckerman, E. (2017). Study: Breitbart-led right-wing media ecosystem altered broader media agenda. *Columbia Journalism Review,* 1(4.1), 7.

Blekesaune, A., Elvestad, E., & Aalberg, T. (2012). Tuning out the world of news and current affairs: An empirical study of Europe's disconnected citizens. *European Sociological Review,* 28(1), 110–126. doi:10.1093/esr/jcq051

Broderick, R. (2017). Trump supporters online are pretending to be French to manipulate France's election. *BuzzFeed News.* Retrieved March 10, 2017 from www.buzzfeed.com/

ryanhatesthis/inside-the-private-chat-rooms-trump-supporters-are-using-to?utm_term=.
dsvNRdZqL#.icm41gBqY

Carnoy, M., & Castells, M. (2001). Globalization, the knowledge society, and the Network State: Poulantzas at the millennium. *Global Networks*, 1(1), 1–18. doi:10.1111/1471-0374.00002

Castells, M. (2010). Globalisation, networking, urbanisation: Reflections on the spatial dynamics of the information age. *Urban Studies*, 47(13), 2737–2745. doi:10.1177/0042098010377365

Christensen, M. (2012). Online mediations in transnational spaces: Cosmopolitan (re)formations of belonging and identity in the Turkish diaspora. *Ethnic and Racial Studies*, 35(5), 888–905.

Christiansen, C. C. (2004). News media consumption among immigrants in Europe: The relevance of diaspora. *Ethnicities*, 4(2), 185–207. doi:10.1177/1468796804042603

Christiansen, C. C., & Sell, L. (2000). *Godt stof eller medborger? Nyheder og etniske minoriteter i Danmark* [Good copy or citizen? News and ethnic minorities in Denmark]. Copenhagen, Denmark: Socialforskningsinstituttet/Danmarks Radio.

Curran, J., Coen, S., Aalberg, T., Hayashi, K., Jones, P. K., Splendore, S., … Tiffen, R. (2013). Internet revolution revisited: A comparative study of online news. *Media, Culture & Society*, 35(7), 880–897. doi:10.1177/0163443713499393

Curran, J., Coen, S., Aalberg, T., & Iyengar, S. (2012). News content, media consumption, and current affairs knowledge. In T. Aalberg & J. Curran (Eds.), *How media inform democracy: A comparative approach* (pp. 83–97). London, England: Routledge.

Curran, J., Esser, F., Hallin, D. C., Hayashi, K., & Chin-Chuan, L. (2017). International news and global integration. *Journalism Studies*, 18(2), 118–134. doi:10.1080/1461670X.2015.1050056

Eide, E., Kunelius, R., & Phillips, A. (2008). *Transnational media events: The Mohammed cartoons and the imagined clash of civilizations*. Göteborg, Sweden:Nordicom.

Elvestad, E. (2007). Ressurs eller flukt? Unge norsk-vietnameseres bruk av "hjemlandsmedier" [How do young Norwegians with parents from Vietnam use "homeland" media?]. *Norsk medietidsskrift*, 14(1), 4–26.

Elvestad, E., & Shaker, L. (2017). Media choice proliferation and shifting orientations towards news in the United States and Norway, 1995–2012. *Nordicom Review*, 38(1), 1–17. doi:10.1515/nor-2016-0390

Elvestad, E., Phillips, A., & Feuerstein, M. (2017). Can trust in traditional news media explain cross-national differences in news exposure of young people online? *Digital Journalism* (Published online June 16, 2017). doi:10.1080/21670811.2017.1332484

Erlanger, S. (2017). Russia's RT network: Is it more BBC or K.G.B.? *New York Times*. Retrieved April 15, 2017 from www.nytimes.com/2017/03/08/world/europe/russias-rt-network-is-it-more-bbc-or-kgb.html?_r=0

Esser, F., de Vreese, C., Strömbäck, J., van Aelst, P., Aalberg, T., Stanyer, J., … Reinemann, C. (2012). Political information opportunities in Europe: A longitudinal and comparative study of 13 television systems. *International Journal of Press/Politics*, 17(3), 247–274. doi:10.1177/1940161212442956

Fenton, N. (2012). The internet and radical politics. In J. Curran, N. Fenton, & D. Freedman (Eds.), *Misunderstanding the internet* (pp. 149–176). Abingdon, England: Routledge.

Fenyoe, A. (2010). *The world online: How UK citizens use the internet to find out about the wider world*. London, England: International Broadcasting Trust.

Galtung, J., & Ruge, M. H. (1965). The structure of foreign news: The presentation of the Congo, Cuba and Cyprus crises in four Norwegian newspapers. *Journal of Peace Research*, 2(1), 64–90. doi:10.1177/002234336500200104

Geniets, A. (2011). *Trust in international news media in partially free media environments: A case study of five markets in Africa and South Asia.* Working paper. Oxford, England: Reuters Institute for the Study of Journalism, University of Oxford.

Global Voices. (2015). Social network analysis reveals full scale of Kremlin's Twitter bot campaign. Retrieved April 3, 2017 from https://globalvoices.org/2015/04/02/ana lyzing-kremlin-twitter-bots/

Hafez, K. (2007). *The myth of media globalization.* Cambridge, England: Polity Press.

Hafez, K. (2016). The 'global public sphere' – A critical reappraisal. In K. Merten & L. Krämer (Eds.), *Postcolonial studies meets media studies: A critical encounter* (pp. 43–66). Bielefeld, Germany: Transcript.

Hamilton, J. (2004). *All the news that's fit to sell: How the market transforms information into news.* Princeton, NJ: Princeton University Press.

Hannerz, U. (1996). Cosmopolitans and locals in world culture. In U. Hannerz (Ed.), *Transnational connections: Culture, people, places* (pp. 102–111). Florence, KY: Routledge.

Heinrich, A. (2012). What is 'Network Journalism'? *Media International Australia,* 144(1), 60–67. doi:10.1177/1329878X1214400110

Herman, E. S., & Chomsky, N. (1988). *Manufacturing consent:The political economy of the mass media.* London, England: Random House Group.

Herman, E. S., & McChesney, R. W. (2004). *Global media: The new missionaries of global capitalism.* New York, NY: Continuum.

Hitlin, P., & Vogt, N. (2014). Cable, Twitter picked up Ferguson story at a similar clip. *Pew Research Center, Fact Tank News in the Numbers.* Retrieved January 3, 2017 from www. pewresearch.org/fact-tank/2014/08/20/cable-twitter-picked-up-ferguson-story-at-a-sim ilar-clip/

Hjarvard, S. (2001). News media and the globalization of the public sphere. In S. Hjarvard (Ed.), *News in a globalized society* (pp. 17–40). Göteborg, Sweden: Nordicom.

Hyun, K. D., & Kim, J. (2015). The role of new media in sustaining the status quo: Online political expression, nationalism, and system support in China. *Information, Communication & Society,* 18(7), 766–781. doi:10.1080/1369118X.2014.994543

Irisova, O. (2015). Drowning in a sea of propaganda and paranoia. *New Eastern Europe,* 6, 117–123.

Jiang, S. (2014). Chinese investment in the EU. *Working Paper Series on European Studies,* 8(1). Institute of European Studies, Chinese Academy of Social Sciences. Retrieved June 2, 2017 from http://ies.cass.cn/webpic/web/ies2/en/UploadFiles_8765/201401/201401 1009510935.pdf

Jirik, J. (2016). CCTV News and soft power. *International Journal of Communication,* 10, 3536–3553. doi:1932–8036/2016FEA0002

King, G., Pan, J., & Roberts, M. E. (2014). Reverse-engineering censorship in China: Randomized experimentation and participant observation. *Science,* 345(6199). doi:10.1126/ science.1251722

Levy, D. A. (2012). Evidence on interest in and consumption of foreign news. *Reuters Institute for the Study of Journalism.* Retrieved November 1, 2016 from www.digitalnewsrep ort.org/essays/2012/evidence-on-interest-in-and-consumption-of-foreign-news/

Lin, N. (2001). *Social capital: A theory of social structure and action.* New York, NY: Cambridge University Press.

Liu, G. (2006). *From China to the world: The development of CCTV International in the age of media globalization* (Unpublished master's dissertation). University of Westminster, London, England.

McLuhan, M. (1964). *Understanding media: The extensions of man.* London, England: Routledge & Kegan Paul.

McPherson, M., Smith-Lovin, L., & Cook, J. M. (2001). Birds of a feather: Homophily in social networks. *Annual Review of Sociology*, 27(1), 415–444.

Meyrowitz, J. (1985). *No sense of place: The impact of electronic media on social behavior*. New York, NY: Oxford University Press.

Micklethwait, J., & Wooldridge, A. (2000). *A future perfect: The challenge and hidden promise of globalization*. New York, NY: Oxford University Press.

Milikowski, M. (2000). Exploring a model of de-ethnicization: The case of Turkish television in the Netherlands. *European Journal of Communication*, 15(4), 443–468. doi:10.1177/0267323100015004001

Miller, D., Costa, E., Haynes, N., Tom, M., Nicolescu, R., Sinanan, J., … Wang, X. (2016). *How the world changed social media*. London, England: UCL Press.

Moore, D. (2010). *Shrinking world: The decline of international reporting in the British press*. Media Standards Trust report. Retrieved January 3, 2017 from http://mediastandardstrust.org/wp-content/uploads/downloads/2010/11/Shrinking-World-FINAL-VERSION.pdf

Morley, D. (2000). *Home territories: Media, mobility, and identity*. London, England: Routledge.

Morozov, E. (2011). *The net delusion: The dark side of internet freedom* (1st ed.). New York, NY: Public Affairs.

Morozov, E. (2013). *To save everything, click here: The folly of technological solutionism*. New York, NY: Public Affairs.

Newman, N., Fletcher, R., Levy, D. A. L., & Nielsen, R. K. (2016). *Reuters Institute digital news report 2016*. Retrieved December 3, 2016 from http://reutersinstitute.politics.ox.ac.uk/sites/default/files/research/files/Digital%2520News%2520Report%25202016.pdf

Newman, N., Fletcher, R., Kalogeropoulos, D., & Nielsen, R. K. (2017). *Reuters Institute digital news report 2017*. Retrieved July 3, 2017 from https://reutersinstitute.politics.ox.ac.uk/sites/default/files/Digital%20News%20Report%202017%20web_0.pdf?utm_source=digitalnewsreport.org&utm_medium=referral

Norris, P., & Inglehart, R. (2009). *Cosmopolitan communications: Culture diversity in a globalized world*. Cambridge, England: Cambridge University Press.

Nossek, H. (2004). Our news and their news: The role of national identity in the coverage of foreign news. *Journalism*, 5(3), 343–368. doi:10.1177/1464884904044941

Nye, J. S. (1990). Soft power. *Foreign Policy*, 80, 153–171. doi:10.2307/1148580

Nye, J. S. (2010). Soft power and cultural diplomacy. Retrieved April 2, 2017 from www.publicdiplomacymagazine.com/soft-power-and-cultural-diplomacy/

Nyíri, P., Zhang, J., & Varrall, M. (2010). China's cosmopolitan nationalist: "Heroes" and "Traitors" of the 2008 Olympics. *The China Journal*, 63, 25–55.

Pan, J. (2017). How market dynamics of domestic and foreign social media firms shape strategies of internet censorship. *Problems of Post-Communism*, 64(3–4), 167–188. doi:10.1080/10758216.2016.1181525

Pew (Pew Research Center) (2012). Interest in foreign news declines. Retrieved June 7, 2017 from www.people-press.org/2012/06/06/interest-in-foreign-news-declines/

Prior, M. (2007). *Post-broadcast democracy: How media choice increases inequality in political involvement and polarizes elections*. New York, NY: Cambridge University Press.

Putnam, R. D. (2000). *Bowling alone*. New York, NY: Simon & Schuster Paperbacks.

Robertson, R. (1992). *Globalization: Social theory and global culture*. London, England: Sage Publications.

Sambrook, R. (2010). *Are foreign correspondents redundant? The changing face of international news*. Oxford, England: Reuters Institute for the Study of Journalism. Retrieved November 14, 2017 from https://dsl-review.ga/articles/download-free-are-foreign-correspondents-redundant-the-changing-face-of-international-news-by-richard-sambrook-pdf.html

Schiller, H. I. (1969). *Mass communications and American empire*. New York, NY: Kelley.

Schmitt, J. B., Debbelt, C. A., & Schneider, F. M. (2017). Too much information? Predictors of information overload in the context of online news exposure. *Information, Communication & Society*, 1–17. doi:10.1080/1369118X.2017.1305427

Si, S. (2014). *Expansion of international broadcasting: The growing global reach of China Central Television*. Working Paper. Oxford, England: Reuters Institute for the Study of Journalism, University of Oxford.

Sparks, C. (2000). The global, the local and public sphere. In G. Wang, A. Goonasekera, & J. Servaes (Eds.), *The new communications landscape: Demystifying media globalization* (pp. 75–96). London, England: Routledge.

Statista. (2017). Social media – Statistic & facts. Retrieved June 3, 2017 from www.statista.com/topics/1164/social-networks/

Stepinska, A., Porath, W., Mujica, C., Xu, X., & Cohen, A. (2013). The prevalence of news: Domestic, foreign and hybrid. In A. Cohen (Ed.), *Foreign news on television* (pp. 23–38). New York, NY: Peter Lang.

Thussu, D. K. (2010). Mapping global media flow and contra-flow. In D. K. Thussu (Ed.), *International communication: A reader* (pp. 221–238). London, England: Routledge.

Tomlinson, J. (1996). *Cultural globalisation: Placing and displacing the West. European Journal of Development Research*, 8(2), 22–36.

Tufte, T. (2003). Minority youth, media uses and identity struggle: The role of the media in production of locality. In T. Tufte (Ed.), *Medierne, minoriteterne og det multikulturelle samfund: Skandinaviske perspektiver* [The media, minorities and multicultural society: Scandinavian perspective](pp. 181–196). Göteborg, Sweden: Nordicom.

Tunstall, J. (1977). *The media are American: Anglo-American media in the world*. London, England: Constable.

Xenos, M., Vromen, A., & Loader, B. D. (2014). The great equalizer? Patterns of social media use and youth political engagement in three advanced democracies. *Information, Communication & Society*, 17(2), 151–167. doi:10.1080/1369118x.2013.871318

Xue, L. (2012). *China's dilemma in its soft power: How to build its national image?* (Unpublished master's dissertation). Aalborg Universitet, Aalborg, Denmark. Retrieved May 4, 2017 from http://projekter.aau.dk/projekter/files/65554672/the_whole_thesis1.docx

Zuckerman, E. (2013). *Rewire: Digital cosmopolitans in the age of connection*. New York, NY: W.W. Norton.

6

COMMUNITIES ONLINE ARE
REPLACING COMMUNITIES OFFLINE

Myth: real social solidarity online has displaced the imagined solidarity of the mass news media

In the 1920s, Robert Park and Max Weber talked about the integrating function of news media – bringing together individuals in great industrialised societies. At the same time, John Dewey (1927) argued that communication media is fundamental for the building and sustaining of polities, and that politics is the work and duty of each individual in the course of his daily routine. It is not enough, therefore, for individuals to consume news. In order for news to fulfil its democratic potential, it should also be judged on its ability to stimulate the kind of behaviour that creates positive social solidarity or political activity. Newspaper readership was seen as an important part of being a community member (Janowitz, 1952) and essential to the idealised public sphere of communication which Habermas considered necessary for participation in democratic political processes (Habermas, 1989). While local media function as a tie between lifeworld and system in local communities, national media tie citizens to society at the national level.

The improved access to information on the Internet has been variously claimed to improve political participation, by reducing the political knowledge differences between people of different socioeconomic status, men and women, and youth versus older age groups (cf. Delli Carpini, 2000; Delli Carpini & Keeter, 1996), and to provide greater opportunities for what Putnam (2000) described as bonding social capital, which builds links between likeminded people (Jenkins, 2008). Jenkins argues that: "in the context of a many-to-many networked communication system, the potential for direct contact between participants is different from what could have been achieved among readers of the Times" (Jenkins, 2016, p. 37). He suggests that, for young people who don't accept an agenda constructed by the mass media, the Internet will provide interest-based communities which may be as much an indicator of civic participation as offline participation is for older people.

But it has also been argued that the flight from conversation to online environments, where we only talk with likeminded people in insulated bubbles, could be a threat for democracy (Turkle, 2015), that the use of online media reinforces the knowledge gap that exists between people with high and low levels of education and with and without interest in politics and news (van Aelst et al., 2017), and that the erosion of the mainstream press, particularly at the local level, can cause "news deserts" across entire regions with significant long-term political and social consequences for a community (Abernathy, 2016). It has been noted in the USA that people who lose their local newspaper become less engaged in their communities (Shaker, 2014). Similar concerns have been raised about the situation in Europe (Howells, 2015; Nielsen, 2015b). Although communities today may not all be defined by geography and proximity, local communities are still central to our governance and society (Macedo & Karpowitz, 2006).

This chapter will consider whether virtual and connected communities on the Internet mean that we do not need mainstream media for democracy any more and it will ask whether mainstream media is still important in people's identity construction and for their belonging to and engagement in a community. In most Western democracies, people are less likely to read local newspapers (print and online) than they used to 10 or 20 years ago. Should we be concerned or does the Internet replace or improve on organised public media as a means of integrating people into political life? We will look at the evidence for and against the integrative possibilities of the Internet and consider the proposition that community solidarity is promoted when social media and mass media reference one another, but is likely to be damaged when social media silos are left un-bridged.

News integration and belonging

Anderson (1983) described the importance of media in creating a sense of nationalism through the production of "imagined communities" of people who never meet, but feel connected to one another because they consume the same media. This idea was further developed with the concept of "media events" which produce collective awareness, social solidarity and cultural memory (Dayan & Katz, 1992). Dayan and Katz's account emphasises the role of media events in integrating society, affirming its common values, legitimating its institutions, and reconciling different sectional elements.

Couldry (2003, p. 9) reminds us to be wary of assuming the existence of a common, mediated centre that produces a common culture: "There is no underlying organising social 'presence' from which they [the media] derive their reality, only the continuous material process whereby myths and rituals are produced, circulated and legitimated". Many media users feel unrepresented in and through media and have doubts about how their voice is reflected in the media, if it is at all (Costera Meijer, 2010; Couldry, 2007). Nevertheless, shared, common accounts, even when they are interpreted differently, do produce a connecting narrative, albeit a narrative from which groups or individuals may dissent on the basis of their own differing experiences (Morley, 1980), and it is in relation to this account that, in Couldry's words, people seek, or avoid "public connection".

The newspaper as an integrating mechanism for people moving to the big cities was very much at the forefront of Park's 1929 study of the role of the immigrant press in assimilating migrants into the culture of the American city (Stamm, 1985, p. 4). Park's thinking was later formulated into what has been called the "community integrating" hypothesis of Morris Janowitz (1952). According to Janowitz, newspapers are one of the institutionalised social mechanisms through which the individual is integrated into his residential community. A few years earlier, Robert K. Merton (1949) offered a spatial hypothesis about community integration and newspaper reading: "locals", people who orientate towards local society, tend to read more local newspapers, while cosmopolitans (orientating out of the local community) read more national and international news.

While Park and Janowitz argued that the importance of newspaper reading precedes the development of community ties, Merton turned this around in his theory of how community ties can explain differences in newspaper reading. In the 1970s and 1980s there was a growing interest in the relationship between newspaper use and the individual's ties with local community, and Keith R. Stamm (1985) followed up the theories of Park, Janowitz and Merton. He offered an alternative theory showing how Park, Janowitz and Merton's theories should be combined into a dynamic theory where community ties and newspaper use are reciprocally related. The mobility of individuals shows how community ties are far from static.

Stamm's study of citizens in the US (1985) showed us how newspapers were of importance for local communities as they create bonds between readers and citizens. This study shows that "anticipated length of residence" was a stronger predictor of local news exposure than past length of residence. More recent studies have also shown how reading a local newspaper is positively correlated with community ties (Elvestad, 2006; Hoffman & Eveland, 2010). Based on a US national panel survey, researchers found a clear correlation between community attachment and local news media use, but the causal ordering of the relationship is not clear (Hoffman & Eveland, 2010). Moreover, in their study of residential areas in Los Angeles, Ball-Rokeach, Yong-Chan, & Matei (2001) found that the most important factor in creating belonging was found to be an active and integrated storytelling system that involves residents, community organisations, and local media. In a later study, Kim and Ball-Rokeach (2006) found that the relative importance of integrated storytelling systems for the likelihood of participation in civic activities is significantly higher in unstable or ethnically heterogeneous areas than in stable or ethnically homogeneous areas.

In a qualitative study with local television audiences in the Netherlands, Costera Meijer (2010) found that city residents of Amsterdam expect their local TV station to perform seven social functions: supplying background information (unbiased, reliable, good-humoured, fast and multi-perspectival); fostering social integration, or giving citizens insight into how the city "works"; providing inspiration; ensuring representation ("voice", recognition and "mirroring"); increasing local understanding; creating civic memory; and contributing to social cohesion, or a sense of belonging. Costera Meijer (2010) stresses that local media, since they are close to their audience, "give more voice to groups that are currently underexposed or systematically misrepresented, 'hard to reach' or less easy to satisfy – such as youngsters, those who are 'socially disappointed', and first and second-generation migrant groups" (p. 338). Citizens expect their local media to be "good neighbours" (Poindexter, Heider, & McCombs, 2006), and they expect local journalists to care about community (Nielsen, 2015b).

Studies of immigrants' media exposure have shown how local media can be useful for integration and civic engagement. For instance, a Norwegian study showed that Vietnamese immigrants used Norwegian national and local news media as part of an integration process into their new society (Elvestad, 2007). However, mass media can also play a role in connecting individuals to former places of residence, homeland or diasporas (see Chapter 5). Studies of news exposure among immigrants, exchange students and national students who move away to study show how news media can be important to sustain ties to their former residence, creating a kind of "ontological security" (Giddens, 1991).

In his study of exchange students in the USA, Sampedro (1998) shows how the newspaper section in the university library was a place many students visited frequently to be informed about news from their homeland. A study among Norwegian students, who had moved away from their original domicile to study, shows how people can have ties to various communities and consider several local newspapers as "their own". The students who read the local newspaper, either in print or online, from their former home showed stronger ties to this place. Students who read both the local newspapers at home and at their place of study ("multi-locals"), showed local ties to both communities (Elvestad, 2006).

In a 2014 study of students' use of local newspapers (Elvestad, 2015), the ties to local communities were still of importance for newspaper exposure. However, what was more interesting was the increasing share of students (who have moved away to study) who now read local newspapers from their former home. This can be explained by the availability of local news online and its relative popularity in Norway (Høst, 2017). For the students who move away to study, the local newspapers are one way of keeping a connection to their former local community, which again can make it easier to move back or to join conversations with family and friends when they are back on vacation. Stamm (1985) stresses the importance of local newspapers to serve the neighbourhoods in creating a "perceived homogeneity", that is "the extent to which persons in a local area identify with one another" (p. 184).

News, ritual and sociability

Drawing on the uses and gratifications approach, Lee (2013) found that people consume news for more reasons than to be informed. Her findings were also found in a much earlier study of news audience. In one of the classic papers of media sociology, Bernard Berelson (1949) studied what happened to the New Yorkers who could no longer get their daily news. During the 1945 newspaper strike in New York, the citizens had alternative news sources, most notably radio news;

they could also get newspapers from other cities, but most of those who normally read one or more newspapers daily suddenly had none. Berelson and his colleagues used this unique opportunity to interview 60 New Yorkers who had an involuntary period without their daily newspaper.

They discovered that people talked about how important it is to follow the serious news of national and international affairs, but they also found that for readers, newspapers are more than news about politics and current affairs. Many of the readers couldn't come up with a specific topic at a national or international level which they wished to have more information about, but they still missed their newspaper. Berelson claimed that the newspaper audience shared a "ritualistic and near-compulsive" attachment to the newspaper. People read newspapers at the same time every day, and if they are used to reading while they are eating their breakfast, they would feel that they were missing something if they didn't have a newspaper to read.

In new media environments, fewer people read a daily printed copy of a newspaper with their morning coffee. This does not imply that their ritualistic attachment to news has ended. Today online media and social media have replaced newspapers, in particular among young people. On smartphones, news is always available and it is easy to get news in the morning. In our own research, we found that the students from the UK and Norway visited social media before they got out of bed in the morning, and several of them expressed a ritualistic and near-compulsive attachment to social media. First, they checked what their friends were up to and shared, and then many of them (especially the Norwegian students) turned to online mainstream news. Without the serenity or security of that news-reading ritual, people were emotionally unprepared to face the day (Glasser, 2000).

Berelson (1949) also found that following the news can be a kind of social interaction in itself and the study highlighted how important news media information can be for entering into social conversation. News consumption and the information people receive from it can function as an important facilitator of informal interaction, or "sociability" (Simmel, 1949). The Internet does not change the fact that we live in neighbourhoods and societies where we meet people and talk, and much of this talk is about what is in the mainstream media. For these meetings, what people have seen, heard or read in the mainstream media is a relevant resource for conversation and in the construction of social relations and our sense of social identity (Fiske, 1987; Lee, 2013).

In a US study, Hoffman and Eveland (2010) found that in more densely populated communities, increased local news use is associated with increased feelings of community attachment. Moreover, they argue that local news can provide a common experience for people to share when they meet occasionally, particularly when they reside in densely populated areas. Couldry, Markham, and Livingstone (2007) also found that one of the common uses of news among his interviewees was the simple desire to share through talk and that: "the idea that public issues are in principle social in their relevance seemed therefore to be universal" (p. 114).

News exposure from alternative news sources online does not imply a rejection of mainstream news sources (Elvestad, Phillips, & Feuerstein, 2017). For those who do share links and discuss or "like" news in social media, news sharing is often part of socialising and identity construction. By sharing news online, they can signal to friends and potential friends their opinions and interests. Turkle argues that sharing in social media is a symptom of a new way of being: "I am sharing, therefore I am" (Turkle, 2012). By sharing different types of news, individuals express something about themselves and the relationship between the sender and the receiver. Andrew Hunter and his colleagues categorised the most shared news in the USA, the UK and Australia and distinguished between different kinds of news. "Inspiring" news describes a traditional "altruistic" notion of sharing ("here is something special for you" type of distribution) whereas "teaming news" is shared to pass judgement, to take a stand and be seen to be taking a stand. Two-thirds of the news that was shared was teaming news, which demands: "Are you for or against me?" According to Hunter et al., "this is sharing to define group identity and values" (2015, p. 123).

News exposure and cultural capital

We don't only consume news to be informed, or even to feel connected. Bourdieu (1986) wrote about the way in which cultural taste and consumption distinguishes different social groups in society and contributes to what he describes as social and cultural capital and the position of individuals in social fields. A US study from 1998 found that news consumption operated as a means of distinguishing between people with high versus low cultural capital resources (Holt, 1998). People with low cultural capital preferred local newspapers, while people with high cultural capital found the local newspaper to be poorly written and a parochial substitute for big-city papers (Holt, 1998). Lizardo (2006) found that people use cultural resources in different ways. While popular cultural consumption is useful for making more diverse connections with others (weak-tie network density), more "highbrow" cultural consumption intensifies connections within specific groups of people and excludes others (strong-tie density). Diverse news exposure can therefore function in different ways to create weak ties and also to intensify stronger ties within the cultural group.

Costera Meijer found, for example, that young people in the Netherlands used news as incentives for a chat with friends: "they are interested in particular in shocking, bizarre, funny and abnormal events" (Costera Meijer, 2007, p. 102). This "popular" news is, in this context, used to strengthen ties among young people, but these young people also knew the distinction between important and trivial news and quality information and entertainment. They were also aware of the different quality of news brands, signifying A-quality and B-quality news media and programmes (Costera Meijer, 2007). Others have argued that there has been a qualitative shift in the basis for marking elite status, from snobbish exclusion to omnivorous appropriation (Peterson & Kern, 1996). The omnivores have a diverse cultural competence or cultural capital that allows them to participate in diverse social networks. Individuals who follow both local, national and international news closely will have competence about society at all these levels. These news omnivores are closer to the real "cosmopolitans" that Hannerz (1996) talks about (for further details, see Chapter 5).

Interest in local news shows a positive correlation with interest in and participation in local politics (Barthel, Mitchell, & Holcomb, 2016; Elvestad, 2015), and interest in local news is therefore not necessarily something we should associate with low cultural capital (as Holt, 1998 did in his study). Some recent studies show that news omnivores, who are interested in both local, national and international news, are more likely to have higher levels of education (Elvestad, 2009; Elvestad & Shaker, 2017). In Norway, highly educated people read more than one newspaper more often on an average day than do people with lower levels of education (Vaage, 2017). The higher share of news subscription to morning papers among Swedes with high socioeconomic status (Wadbring, Weibull, & Facht, 2016) also confirms this. A Swedish study shows how political interest has become a more important determinant of news consumption in today's high-choice media environment (Strömbäck, Djerf-Pierre, & Shehata, 2013). Van Aelst et al. (2017) conclude that "the increasing supply has made for a better match with the demand for political information among the most politically interested and the demand for non-political information among those not interested in politics" (p. 18). News audiences have become more polarised over time between news-seekers and news-avoiders, but also more specialised (Elvestad & Shaker, 2017).

News exposure is in many social situations an important resource for access to conversations (Bourdieu would describe this as knowledge skills or cultural capital useful for entrance in different "fields"); however, it has become increasingly clear that the way people use news as a form of cultural capital differs online. The decision to share news is very different from the decision to talk face to face. Couldry (2006) noted that the number who reported sharing talk about public issues online rather than in person was "strikingly low". With the advent of widely used social media, the numbers sharing online have risen but talk about political matters is still constrained. People are found to be less likely to disagree with someone on a social media platform than they would be over their own kitchen table (Jang, Lee, & Park, 2014). They are often anxious about sharing their ideas online for fear of being identified as part of a particular political group, or saying something that would lead to ostracism, or derision. Miller et al. (2016), in a nine-country research project, found that: "Informants were concerned with maintaining or strengthening relations with their social media contacts, and did not want to risk damaging friendships or relationships with extended family or work colleagues" (p. 145). In our own 2014 research (Elvestad, 2015; Elvestad, Phillips, & Feuerstein, 2017) among university students, this sort of comment was typical of those students who were reluctant to post on Facebook:

> ... it's not necessarily based on insecurity, the desire to not be judged. It's just the fact that I don't want people to automatically assume certain things based

on, er, little information. I don't want to risk it, especially on a private Facebook
account which has … my family members on there as well.

(UK male, 18)

We found that British and Norwegian students moved to media platforms such as
Messenger if they wanted to share or discuss news, to avoid the public attention
they could receive on Facebook or Twitter. For instance, a female Norwegian
student teacher told us that she never shared news on Facebook. When she saw
news of interest for education students, she shared it on Messenger with her friends
in her study group. Several of the students also said that people that share a lot of
news online sometimes turn out to be classified as preachy, disrupting or
troublesome.

The sharing of news on social media is therefore both a kind of civic engagement and an expression of being an engaged individual in a greater community
online, but it can also be something you share discretely, in more closed forums
that can strengthen ties in these groups. From a democratic perspective, the sharing
of news and discussions of news in closed communities online can end up like echo
chambers, but they can also play important roles in developing "safer" forums for
dialogue and countercultures (cf. Sunstein, 2009). For the Norwegian student
teacher, the sharing and discussion of news on Messenger with real friends made
her feel more comfortable about discussing the news.

News exposure and public disconnection

Putnam's *Bowling Alone* thesis (2000) and Turkle's *Alone Together* thesis (2011)
suggest that what Couldry (2003, p. 9) describes as "public connection" is fatally
undermined, rather than being enhanced, by modern media. Putnam (2000)
claimed that increased television consumption was one of the reasons why Americans
have become increasingly disconnected from each other. Television watching is
something people more often do alone and they prefer entertainment instead of
news, which is associated with civic disengagement. He found that it was those
Americans "most marked by this dependence on televised entertainment who were
most likely to have dropped out of civic and social life". He also found that they
"spent less time with friends, were less involved in community organisations, and
were less likely to participate in public affairs" (Putnam, 2000, p. 246). Sherry
Turkle (2012, 2015) argues similarly that the use of new media technologies,
particularly among the young, is replacing conversation with a new solitude.
Turkle (2011) found that new media technology is breaking down community
connections, as we have thousands of "friends" but they don't inform us or make
us feel more integrated and included in society.

Dana Boyd (2014), who studied networked teens in the USA, says "It's complicated". The adolescents Boyd studied told her how bonds were intensified
online. They could meet friends there, and for them this was a substitute for
meeting them in person. It was a way of being social with their friends without

interruptions from their parents, and for some, who had parents who didn't allow them to go to the mall, or other gathering places, this was one way of meeting friends outside school. However, although the Internet and social media have opened up possibilities for interaction with like-minded people, and more choices, the extreme level of personalisation means that it may be less likely that individuals will find common ground with people from different age groups or socioeconomic backgrounds (discussed in Chapter 2).

Research into news consumption suggests that the breakdown in social solidarity seen by Turkle has its echo in news consumption. Sunstein warns against "information cocoons" and "echo chambers" wherein people avoid the news and opinions that they don't want to hear (Sunstein, 2009) and create and strengthen "idiocultures" that turn inward rather than making outward connections that typically enhance social solidarity (Fine, 1979; Lizardo, 2006). However, the reasons for disconnection, where it occurs, are also more complicated, and not always a result of being social loners. Couldry et al. (2007) talk about how "public connection", a shared orientation to a public world where matters of common concern are (or at least should be) addressed, is mediated through shared media consumption. In their research, the group they describe as "weakly connected" showed neither a strong orientation to a media world, nor to a public world independent of media, and its members were more likely to be orientated overall by family and social networks (Couldry et al., 2007, p. 113). While Couldry et al. (2007, p. 15) argue "that media consumption, important though it is, can only be one part of the solution to contemporary citizenship's problems", and Woodstock (2014) claims that some "news resisters" are both knowledgeable and politically active, we argue that increasing news avoidance is a democratic problem.

A study of disconnected individuals in Europe shows that news avoidance tends to be coupled with low social and political capital (Blekesaune, Elvestad, & Aalberg, 2012). The researchers argue that these disconnected citizens "are not only disconnected from the society at large but they are also disconnected from more personal networks such as family, friends and work colleagues", and they also found that they are "less likely to have political interest, [they] show less political efficacy and [they] fail to vote" (Blekesaune et al., 2012, p. 122). In a UK study among teenagers, Livingstone and Sefton-Green (2016) found that the experience of disconnections and blocked pathways caused by class and cultural differences is often more common than that of connections and new opportunities in the digital age.

Informed citizens and civic engagement

We have discussed the ways in which exposure to news is important for reasons of ritual, sociability and cultural capital and status. It also has a vital function for democratic engagement and the move towards online engagement, and in particular engagement via social media is altering the ways in which people access news and the way in which they make use of what they understand. Some of these changes are certainly positive but, as we demonstrate above, some are also negative and it's important to understand the pros and cons because, as Aalberg and Curran (2012, p. 3) point out, access to political information ensures that citizens make responsible, informed choices rather than acting out of ignorance or misinformation. Considerable social scientific research has demonstrated that use of traditional, bridging news outlets increases political knowledge, efficacy and engagement (e.g. Chaffee & Schleuder, 1986; Delli Carpini, 2004; Eveland & Scheufele, 2000; Strömbäck & Shehata, 2010) and that exposure to public television news and broadsheet newspapers (news outlets with high levels of political content) is found to contribute to political knowledge gains and increases the propensity to turn out to vote (de Vreese & Boomgaarden, 2006).

Boulianne (2009, p. 205) concluded that the effect of Internet use on political engagement is positive when those being measured are reading news online rather than engaging in a more general way. By using three-wave panel data from the American election study (2008–2009), Boulianne (2011) examined the roles of different media in both stimulating and reinforcing political interest. She found that those respondents who were already interested and talking about politics were more likely to watch television news. There is a positive feedback loop (reciprocal process) between television watching and talking politics; however, watching television news as an activity does not have a significant direct effect on stimulating political interest among those who are not particularly interested (Boulianne, 2011, p. 155). Boulianne also found that print and online news use stimulates political interest, which in turn has a significant, positive effect on the level of political talk. In a 2015 meta-analysis of 36 studies she found that the correlations of social media and political participation could be spurious. However, she was also concerned that the interaction between social media and mainstream news is complex and requires more detailed analysis (and mixed methods).

Boulianne hypothesised that the Internet's information-sharing functions may stimulate political interest, which could again explain why the relationship between online news exposure and the stimulation of political interest appears to be a reciprocal process, while this is not the case with television news. In a later study of the impact of social media, Boulianne (2016) found that there is a significant indirect effect (via civic awareness) on civic and political engagement. She hypothesises that mainstream news, passed on through social media, could have a positive effect on the knowledge required to engage in civic life. In a Swedish study, Holt, Shehata, Strömbäck, & Ljungberg (2013) also found that both political social media use and attention to political news in traditional media increase political engagement over time. However, a study of the US election in 2012 found that, although watching a televised debate is good for knowledge gain, the effect of debate viewing is dulled when simultaneously engaging in social media multitasking (Gottfried, Hardy, Holbert, Winneg, & Jamieson, 2017). This could indicate that those engaged in sharing are less likely to be interpreting what they hear and may instead be looking for information containing heuristic clues confirming their prior beliefs in order to share it.

The Internet also allows for users to participate in the news dissemination process through community "gatewatching", where users in online communities can share links with each other (Bruns, 2003). However, in their study of news exposure and sharing of online news, Beam, Hutchens, and Hmielowski (2016) found evidence that the reading of news and sharing of online news have different effects. Reading online news shows a positive correlation with factual political knowledge, whereas sharing online news is positively related to a kind of structural knowledge by which they mean that sharers are better able to connect disparate pieces of information and understand how they relate to one another. The researchers suggest that: "News sharers might be viewing a stronger diet of attitude consistent information that is building their understanding of disparate news items but through an incorrect or incomplete set of facts" (Beam et al., 2016, p. 218).

A multi-method research project by Conroy, Feezell, and Guerrero (2012) looked at Facebook's impact on political engagement and found that while online political engagement is correlated with offline political participation, there was no similar correlation with political knowledge. The researchers suggest that this might be due to the poor level of the information content online: posts were found to be very poor, generally lacking support for their claims, incoherent, or simply opinionated. In other words, political group members are exposed to little new or well-articulated information about the political causes around which these groups form. The information is more likely to be reinforcing and therefore mobilising, but not enlightening and therefore educational.

These studies demonstrate that the interaction between news sources and platforms is complex. While social media can contribute to political and civic engagement, it doesn't necessarily improve knowledge and that having a consistent and available source of news is important whether or not news is received directly or via social media. Mainstream local news, in particular, is important for citizen engagement in local communities and the erosion of news-gathering is likely to have a deleterious effect on political knowledge and engagement. A study in the UK, where local news media are under pressure and a quarter of local government areas have no dedicated local source of news (Media Reform Coalition, 2014, p. 3), found "a vocal desire in local communities for better communication and local news". It suggested that: "many of our communities feel disempowered, unheard or irrelevant" (Fenton, Metykova, Schlosberg, & Freedman, 2010, p. 3). In his study of local political information environments in Denmark, Rasmus Kleis Nielsen (2015a) argued that daily local newspapers have become more important even as their editorial resources and audience reach is diminished. He agrees with Ekström (2006 in Nielsen, 2015a), who claimed that local newspaper coverage is hardly hard-hitting investigative watchdog journalism, but argues that local newspapers are still the only kind of independent ongoing and diverse news about local politics available in the community (Nielsen, 2015a, p. 68). For citizens to know their local politicians and who to vote for, local newspapers are still the most important information source in Norway (Karlsen, 2017).

There are few studies of what happens if a local society loses its local newspaper. From a natural experiment in the USA, Lee Shaker (2014) offers an important contribution to the field. Using data from 2008 and 2009, Shaker (2014) examines the civic engagement of citizens in US cities that lost their newspaper (Denver and Seattle) and cities that did not lose a newspaper, over the same time period. Shaker's analysis shows a clear negative effect of newspaper death on civic engagement. In both Seattle and Denver, civic engagement dropped significantly from 2008 to 2009. This decline was not consistently replicated in the other cities examined in the study, even after controlling for several other alternative explanations (Shaker, 2014).

A recent Pew Research Center study confirms that the civically engaged are more likely than the less engaged to use and value local news (Barthel et al., 2016). Local community attachment and regular local voting connect strongly to local news habits. Americans with a strong connection to community are much more likely always to vote in local elections. The study also finds that Americans with one of these two attributes consistently display stronger local news habits across a range of measures such as news interest, the number and types of news sources they turn to and news attitudes. Another trait closely associated with broad community attachment is how well one knows one's neighbours. Barthel et al. (2016) found that 52 per cent of those who know all their neighbours follow local news very closely, compared with 32 per cent who don't know any of their neighbours. Moreover, 71 per cent of those who know their neighbours say that the local media are in touch with their communities versus 49 per cent of those who don't know their neighbours. The decline in local newspaper circulation and the online news sites that they typically support, in the USA and other countries, does therefore give rise to great concern.

Nielsen (2015a) argues that the local newspapers are not only of importance to local democracy. They are keystone media, and they have an important function in getting local stories, which might otherwise be overlooked, into the public domain (Nielsen, 2015a, p. 51). While there have been some attempts to make good this deficit via local community organisations and informal hyperlocal news sites (see more in Chapter 3), without stable funding these efforts to maintain news coverage of local democracy struggle (Schaffer, 2007; Williams & Harte, 2016). Without a reliable source of news information, online or offline, offered regularly, by local journalists, it seems likely that local civic engagement will decrease.

Social media, mainstream media and elections

The importance of media for the outcome of elections has long been a subject of study. The way John F. Kennedy mastered the television medium in 1960 is claimed to be one reason why he won against the less "television charismatic" Nixon. The introduction of Fox News in 20 per cent of states in 1996 is thought to be one of the reasons for the higher popularity of the Republican Party in these states (DellaVigna & Kaplan, 2007), and in 2008, Obama's successful use of social media especially mobilised young voters and is considered to be one of the reasons why he won this election.[1] In 2016 President Trump was also considerably more active on social media than his rival, Hillary Clinton (Allcott & Gentzkow, 2017), and he used social media to attract the attention of both journalists and supporters. Nevertheless, only 13.8 per cent of voters identified social media as their most important source of news during the election (Allcott & Gentzkow, 2017).

In Norway and the UK, their public broadcasters (BBC and NRK) are still the most important news sources for citizens about the election, and are more important than social media (Enders Analysis, 2017; Karlsen, 2017; Karlsen & Aalberg, 2015). Social media, such as Facebook, has become more important for receiving information about the elections (Karlsen, 2017). However, in the UK the most shared news articles overall came from the mainstream press (Enders Analysis, 2017).

In the UK elections and the European Union referendum, most of the material shared came from political parties or mainstream media and the level of junk news in circulation was relatively low (Kaminska, Gallacher, Kollany, Yasseri, & Howard, 2017). In the US elections, one-third of the material circulated on Twitter came from junk news sites that had been established for the purpose of exploiting the interest in election news (Allcott & Gentzkow, 2017; Kaminska et al., 2017). Clearly, those US citizens circulating, or receiving, junk news were not being informed in any sense of the word. The majority of voters in these elections were getting news from mainstream (albeit partisan) news sources in addition to what they saw in their Facebook and Twitter feeds and yet, as Boulianne (2011) demonstrated, the effect of receiving news in an online environment appears to be more effective in encouraging political participation.

During the 2010 US congressional election, researchers from Facebook and the University of California in San Diego used a randomised controlled trial with 61 million users of at least 18 years of age in the USA, who accessed the Facebook website on the day of the US congressional elections, to test the hypothesis that political behaviour can spread through an online social network. In this study, the users received a message encouraging them to vote, provided a link to find local polling places, showed a clickable button reading "I Voted", showed a counter indicating how many other Facebook users had previously reported voting, and displayed up to six small randomly selected "profile pictures" of the user's Facebook friends who had already clicked the "I Voted" button. The informational message group was shown the message, poll information, counter and button, but they were not shown any faces of friends. The control group did not receive any message at the top of their news feed.

The researchers found that political mobilisation messages "influenced political self-expression, information seeking and real world voting of millions of people" (Bond et al., 2012, p. 295). The researchers also found that the messages didn't only influence the Facebook users that received them, but also their friends and friends of friends. This study shows how mobilisation in online networks is significantly more effective than informational mobilisation alone. If you have strong ties to friends on social media and they are showing you that they are voting, you are more likely to vote.

Online mobilisation works because it primarily spreads through strong-tie networks that probably exist offline but have an online representation. In fact, it is plausible that unobserved face-to-face interactions account for at least some of the social influence that we observed in this experiment.

(Bond et al., 2012, p. 298)

Taken together, the evidence demonstrates that social media has strong effects in stimulating individual political action but much weaker effects in informing citizens about the political parties, policies (and what might be wrong with them) and candidates. The mainstream media are still important sources of information during election campaigns.

Future pathways to news and civic engagement

Prior (2007, p. 270) warns that the transition from low-choice media environments, dependent mainly on television, to high-choice media environments, with a greater reliance on the Internet and social media, has major ramifications for the political environment and, hence, processes of knowledge dissemination and acquisition in post-industrial democracies (for further details, see Chapter 1). Blekesaune et al. (2012, pp. 122–123) suggest that these effects might be compounded over time, leading to greater news inequality and polarisation because, in societies where almost the entire population reads the news (e.g. Norway), being a non-reader carries a greater stigma than in countries where non-reading is more common (e.g. Greece). In countries where only a small elite "tune in", media use of the news on television, radio and especially in newspapers, may contribute to a kind of "bonding social capital" among the elite only, creating even larger social inequality. Based on a review of recent research about the inequality in political knowledge, Van Aelst et al. (2017, p. 18) also conclude that:

> As media use increasingly moves online, and as studies suggest that motivation is more decisive for learning from online compared to offline media, there is a risk that growing differences in media use will lead to wider knowledge gaps.

The orientation towards local news seems to be dwindling – even where people do have access to local news, as well as other news sources, they seem to be shifting towards national and international news (Elvestad & Shaker, 2017). This shift has been rapid in the UK and the USA (Nielsen, 2015a), where many local news organisations have closed, or reduced local coverage due to loss of advertising funding, and there has been a sharp drop in the number of journalists employed locally (Ramsay & Moore, 2016). A study from 2012 showed that a majority of Americans thought that it would have no impact on their knowledge about their local community if the local newspaper closed down, even as the same research project showed the multiple ways in which local citizens actually depend on newspapers (Rosenthiel et al., 2012, as cited in Nielsen, 2015b).

While those countries with well-funded public service media have so far resisted the polarisation of news attention and political opinion that is growing in the higher-choice environments, there is reason to be concerned that changing news consumption patterns are beginning to have an impact even in countries that are well served. The regularity of news consumption, for many people, is dependent on others. For example, Couldry et al. (2007) show how Andrea, a 25-year-old British nurse, in 2004 depended on her male partner to bring home the daily newspaper from work and her parents to pass on information from the local newspaper. When consumption is private, the impetus to share is left to the sharer, and individuals with lower levels of news interest may simply not encounter news at all.

For children, the habit of news consumption is learned and there is some concern that there has been a break in the ways in which children have been socialised into consuming news. The great majority of the children who grew up in literate families in the 1960s and 1970s had at least one newspaper either delivered to their door in the morning, or brought home in the evening. Many of the newspapers offered comics and pages for children to encourage them to read newspapers and to teach them where to find information about their society. In the 1980s and early 1990s, television took over in many countries as a shared family medium for news. Today, printed newspapers on the breakfast table are not as common any more, fewer families watch television news together and the online consumption of news is increasing. Adults' news consumption is therefore often hidden from their children. This is changing the way in which children can be introduced to politics and current affairs and citizenship, but children brought up in a digital world still need to be guided (for more discussion see Chapter 8). Parents are still the most important source of information about what is going on in society and they play an important role in teaching children how to find useful information for becoming integrated citizens in societies (Marchi, 2012).

We found in our own research that some of the UK and Norwegian students spontaneously mentioned that their parents, or another key adult, routinely provided them with news information by email or via social media. Those who did not have the advantage of engaged parents were not less interested in news, but appeared to be less confident in their use of news information. For example, a male UK student, whose parents rarely accessed news, explained that he had tried to find information about who to vote for in a local election but "I found it very hard to find, um, first of all, I found it very hard to find solid information on who was running where".

As communal news consumption disappears from the home, parents and educators will have to look for different opportunities to engage children in debate about news events and matters of social concern, if they are to be able to engage effectively with news information online. Those who are less interested in news are likely, in the future, to have fewer opportunities to encounter broadly non-partisan news without actively searching for it.

News media and solidarity

In this chapter we have argued that there are several reasons for being critical of the idea that the Internet and social media technology on its own is the solution to integrating and engaging citizens in democracies. We argue that the traditional journalistic news media and public service broadcasters are still important for producing social cohesion and politically skilled citizens and that traditional journalism still plays an important role both online and offline. Local news reporters are still the key medium in local communities (Nielsen, 2015a), and freedom from interference by market forces and government seems to lead to a form of public broadcasting that is markedly "better" than its commercial rivals (Soroka et al., 2013).

> In short, given that public affairs knowledge appears to be significantly improved through the publicly-funded provision of news (here, on television, but potentially online as well), then governments' decisions about funding for public broadcasters seems in many cases to be very much like decisions about just how well informed their citizens will be.
>
> *(Soroka et al., 2013, p. 733)*

Local and national democracy depends on citizens who have a feeling of belonging to and are engaged in communities at these levels. Mobile technology not only moves people's habits from print to the Internet, but also, from public to private and it seems, from local to national (Wadbring & Bergström, 2015). However, our society is still geographically organised and governed, and "commitment to local news and information cannot be abandoned" (Shaker, 2014, p. 146). We may be virtual and connected, but we still need mainstream mass media at a local and national level, to tie citizens to each other and their communities. Without such media where does a newcomer go to join the imagined community of her new local society? How will political information reach those who believe important information will come to them without having to search for it? Zaller (2003) will probably argue that the media "burglar alarm" will solve this, but not all will agree with him (see for instance Bennett, 2003). Moreover, even if the most important news (the candidates in an election or natural disasters) reaches almost every citizen, it is not enough to ensure the ideal of informed citizens.

Couldry et al. (2007) also stressed that we must not ignore the long-term nature of the process by which media technologies get embedded in daily practice. New social habits of online news exposure will also occur. If those habits are developed inside opposing bubbles, with low levels of exposure to cross-cutting material, the prospects for social division are likely to intensify. While there is no reason to suggest that normative public media can, on their own, produce a more representative politics, there seems to be even less reason to believe that the Internet and social media will do better.

Note

1 Obama was in fact building on the knowledge and online organisation of the 2004 Howard Dean campaign, organised by Joe Trippi, in which Meetup.com was used to

organise campaigners on the ground (Jenkins et al., 2016, p. 210). For Obama it was the interaction between online organisation (for fundraising and communication) and on the ground campaigning that made the difference.

References

Aalberg, T., & Curran, J. (2012). *How media inform democracy: A comparative approach*. London, England: Routledge.

Abernathy, P. M. (2016). *The rise of a new media baron and the emerging threat of news deserts.* Chapel Hill, NC: University of North Carolina Press.

Allcott, H., & Gentzkow, M. (2017). Social media and fake news in the 2016 election. *Journal of Economic Perspectives*, 31(2), 211–236.

Anderson, B. (1983). *Imagined communities: Reflections on the origin and spread of nationalism*. London, England: Verso.

Ball-Rokeach, S. J., Yong-Chan, K., & Matei, S. (2001). Storytelling neighborhood: Paths to belonging in diverse urban environments. *Communication Research*, 28(4), 392–428.

Barthel, M., Holcomb, J., Mahone, J., & Mitchell, A. (2016). Civic engagement strongly tied to local news habits. *Pew Research Center: Journalism & Media*. Retrieved March 25, 2016 from www.journalism.org/2016/11/03/civic-engagement-strongly-tied-to-local-news-habits/

Beam, M. A., Hutchens, M. J., & Hmielowski, J. D. (2016). Clicking vs. sharing: The relationship between online news behaviors and political knowledge. *Computers in Human Behavior*, 59(June), 215–220.

Bennett, W. L. (2003). The burglar alarm that just keeps ringing: A response to Zaller. *Political Communication,* 20(2), 131–138. doi:10.1080/10584600390211145

Berelson, B. (1949). What missing the newspaper means. In P. Lazarsfeld & F. Stanton (Eds.), *Communication research 1948–1949*. New York, NY: Harper and Brothers.

Blekesaune, A., Elvestad, E., & Aalberg, T. (2012). Tuning out the world of news and current affairs. An empirical study of Europe's disconnected citizens. *European Sociological Review*, 28(1), 110–126. doi:10.1093/esr/jcq051

Bond, R. M., Fariss, C. J., Jones, J. J., Kramer, A. D. I., Marlow, C., & Settle, J. E. (2012). A 61-million-person experiment in social influence and political mobilization. *Nature*, 489 (7415), 295–298. doi:10.1038/nature11421

Boulianne, S. (2009). Does internet use affect engagement? A meta-analysis of research. *Political Communication*, 26(2), 193–211. doi:10.1080/10584600902854363

Boulianne, S. (2011). Stimulating or reinforcing political interest: Using panel data to examine reciprocal effects between news media and political interest. *Political Communication*, 28(2), 147–162. doi:10.1080/10584609.2010.540305

Boulianne, S. (2016). Online news, civic awareness, and engagement in civic and political life. *New Media & Society*, 18(9), 1840–1856. doi:10.1177/1461444815616222

Bourdieu, P. (1986/2001). The forms of capital. Reprinted in R. Sweberg & M. S. Granovetter (Eds.), *The sociology of economic life* (pp. 96–111). Boulder, CO: Westview.

Boyd, D. (2014). *It's complicated: The social lives of networked teens*. New Haven, CN: Yale University Press.

Bruns, A. (2003). Gatewatching, not gatekeeping: Collaborative online news. *Media International Australia*, 107(1), 31–44. doi:10.1177/1329878X0310700106

Chaffee, S. H., & Schleuder, J. (1986). Measurement and effects of attention to media news. *Human Communication Research*, 13(1), 76–107.

Conroy, M., Feezell, J. T., & Guerrero, M. (2012). Facebook and political engagement: A study of online political group membership and offline political engagement. *Computers in Human Behavior*, 28(5), 1535–1546.

Costera Meijer, I. (2007). The paradox of popularity: How young people experience the news. *Journalism Studies*, 8(1), 96–116. doi:10.1080/14616700601056874

Costera Meijer, I. (2010). Democratizing journalism? Realizing the citizen's agenda for local news media. *Journalism Studies*, 11(3), 327–342. doi:10.1080/146167009035 00256

Couldry, N. (2003, May). *Television and the myth of mediated center: Time for a paradigm shift in television studies*. Paper presented at the Media in Transition 3 Conference, Boston, USA.

Couldry, N. (2006). *Listening beyond the echoes: Media, ethics and agency in an uncertain world*. London, England: Paradigm.

Couldry, N. (2007). Media and democracy: Some missing links. In T. Dowmunt, M. Dunford, & N. Van Hemert (Eds.), *Inclusion through media* (pp. 254–264). London, England: Goldsmiths University of London.

Couldry, N., Markham, T., & Livingstone, S. (2007). *Media consumption and public engagement: Beyond the presumption of attention*. London, England: Palgrave Macmillan.

Dayan, D., & Katz, E. (1992). *Media events: The live broadcasting of history*. Cambridge, MA: Harvard University Press.

DellaVigna, S., & Kaplan, E. (2007). The Fox News effect: Media bias and voting. *The Quarterly Journal of Economics*, 122(3), 1187–1234.

Delli Carpini, M. X. (2000). Gen.com: Youth, civic engagement, and the new information environment. *Political Communication*, 17(4), 341–349.

Delli Carpini, M. X. (2004). Mediating democratic engagement: The impact of communications on citizens' involvement in political and civic life. In L. L. Kaid (Ed.), *Handbook of political communication research* (pp. 357–394). Mahwah, NJ: Lawrence Erlbaum Associates.

Delli Carpini, M. X., & Keeter, S. (1996). *What Americans know about politics and why it matters*. New Haven, CT: Yale University Press.

Dewey, J. (1927). *The public and its problems*. New York, NY: H. Holt and Company.

De Vreese, C. H., & Boomgaarden, H. (2006). News, political knowledge and participation: The differential effects of news media exposure on political knowledge and participation. *Acta Politica*, 41(4), 317–341.

Elvestad, E. (2006). Lokal, kosmopolitt eller frakoblet? En analyse av stedstilknytning og bruk av lokalaviser [Local, cosmopolitan or disconnected? An analysis of local belonging and local newspaper reading]. *Tidsskrift for samfunnsforskning*, 47(4), 545–573.

Elvestad, E. (2007). Ressurs eller flukt? Unge norsk-vietnameseres bruk av "hjemlandsmedier" [How do young Norwegians with parents from Vietnam use "homeland" media?]. *Norsk medietidsskrift*, 14(1), 4–26.

Elvestad, E. (2009). Introverted locals or world citizens? A quantitative study of interest in local and foreign news in traditional media and on the internet. *Nordicom Review*, 30(2), 105–124.

Elvestad, E. (2015). *Barn av informasjonsrike medieomgivelser* [Children of information-rich environments]. Skriftserien fra Høgskolen i Buskerud og Vestfold [Report from University College of Buskerud and Vestfold], nr. 23, 2015. Retrieved January 20, 2016 from https://brage.bibsys.no/xmlui/handle/11250/2368736

Elvestad, E., Phillips, A., & Feuerstein, M. (2017). Can trust in traditional news media explain cross-national differences in news exposure of young people online? *Digital Journalism* (Published online June 16, 2017). doi:10.1080/21670811.2017.1332484

Elvestad, E., & Shaker, L. (2017). Media choice proliferation and shifting orientations towards news in the United States and Norway, 1995–2012. *Nordicom Review*, 38(1), 1–17. doi:10.1515/nor-2016–0390

Enders Analysis (2017, June). UK General Election online – news and advertising. Retrieved June 30, 2017 from www.endersanalysis.com/publications?date[value]&&&title=&page=1

Eveland Jr, W. P., & Scheufele, D. A. (2000). Connecting news media use with gaps in knowledge and participation. *Political Communication*, 17(3), 215–237.

Fenton, N., Metykova, M., Schlosberg, J., & Freedman, D. (2010). *Meeting the news needs of local communities*. Executive report for Mediatrust.

Fine, G. A. (1979). Small groups and culture creation: The ideoculture of little league baseball teams. *American Sociological Review*, 44(October), 733–745.

Fiske, J. (1987). *Television culture*. London, England; New York, NY: Methuen.

Giddens, A. (1991). *Modernity and self-identity: Self and society in the late modern age*. Cambridge, England: Polity Press.

Glasser, T. L. (2000). Play and the power of news. *Journalism*, 1(26), 23–29.

Gottfried, J. A., Hardy, B. W., Holbert, R. L., Winneg, K. M., & Jamieson, K. H. (2017). The changing nature of political debate consumption: Social media, multitasking, and knowledge acquisition. *Political Communication*, 34(2), 172–199. doi:10.1080/10584609.2016.1154120

Habermas, J. (1989). *The structural transformation of the public sphere: An inquiry into a category of bourgeois society*. Cambridge, MA: MIT Press.

Hannerz, U. (1996). Cosmopolitans and locals in world culture. In U. Hannerz (Ed.), *Transnational connections: Culture, people, places* (pp. 102–111). Florence, KY: Routledge.

Hoffman, L. H., & Eveland, W. P. (2010). Assessing causality in the relationship between community attachment and local news media use. *Mass Communication and Society*, 13(2), 174–195. doi:10.1080/15205430903012144

Holt, D. B. (1998). Does cultural capital structure American consumption? *Journal of Consumer Research*, 25(June), 1–25.

Holt, K., Shehata, A., Strömbäck, J., & Ljungberg, E. (2013). Age and the effects of news media attention and social media use on political interest and participation: Do social media function as leveller? *European Journal of Communication*, 28(1), 19–34. doi:10.1177/0267323112465369

Høst, S. (2017). *Avisåret 2016*. [Newspapers in Norway 2016]. (Volda University College report 84/2017). Retrieved April 4, 2017 from http://medienorge.uib.no/files/Eksterne_pub/Avisaret_2016.pdf

Howells, R. (2015). *Journey to the centre of a news black hole: Examining the democratic deficit in a town with no newspaper* (Unpublished doctoral dissertation). Cardiff School of Journalism, Cardiff University, Cardiff, Wales.

Hunter, A. (2015). When sharing is not sharing. In H. Crawford, A. Hunter, & D. Filipovic (Eds.), *All your friends like this: How social networks took over the news* (pp. 116–158). Sydney, Australia: HarperCollins.

Jang, S. M., Lee, H., & Park, Y. J. (2014). The more friends, the less political talk? Predictors of Facebook discussions among college students. *Cyberpsychology, Behavior, and Social Networking*, 17(5), 271–275.

Janowitz, M. (1952). *The community press in an urban setting*. Glencoe, IL: Free Press.

Jenkins, H. (2008). *Convergence culture: Where old and new media collide*. New York, NY: New York University Press.

Jenkins, H. (2016). Youth voice, and political engagement: Introducing the core concepts. In H. Jenkins, S. Shresthova, L. Gamber-Thompson, N. Kligler-Vilenchik, & A. M. Zimmerman (Eds.), *By any media necessary: The new youth activism* (pp. 1–60). New York, NY: New York University Press.

Jenkins, H., Shresthova, S., Gamber-Thompson, L., Kligler-Vilenchik, N., & Zimmerman, A. M. (2016). *By any media necessary: The new youth activism*. New York, NY: New York University Press.

Kaminska, M., Gallacher, J. D., Kollany, B., Yasseri, T., & Howard, P. N. (2017). *Social media and news sources during the 2017 UK General Election*. COMPRO Data Memo 2017.6, Oxford. Retrieved June 7, 2017 from http://comprop.oii.ox.ac.uk/wp-content/uploads/sites/89/2017/06/Social-Media-and-News-Sources-during-the-2017-UK-General-Election.pdf

Karlsen, R. (2017). Mediebruk i lokalvalgkampen 2015: informasjon om politikk og kandidater [Media use in the local election 2015: Information about politics and candidates]. In D. A. Christensen & J. Saglie (Eds.), *Lokalvalget 2015: Et valg i kommunereformens tegn?* [The local election in 2015: An election in a time with regional reforms] (pp. 125–146). Oslo, Norway: Abstrakt.

Karlsen, R., & Aalberg, T. (2015). Selektiv eksponering av medievalgkampen [Selective exposure in the media election campaign]. In B. Aardal (Ed.), *Valg og velgere. Stortingsvalget 2013* [Elections and voters. Parliamentary elections 2013] (pp. 111–134). Oslo, Norway: Universitetsforlaget.

Kim, Y. C., & Ball-Rokeach, S. J. (2006). Community storytelling network, neighborhood context, and civic engagement: A multilevel approach. *Human Communication Research*, 32(4), 411–439.

Lee, A. M. (2013). News audiences revisited: Theorizing the link between audience motivations and news consumption. *Journal of Broadcasting & Electronic Media*, 57(3), 300–317. doi:10.1080/08838151.2013.816712

Livingstone, S. M., & Sefton-Green, J. (2016). *The class: Living and learning in the digital age*. New York, NY: New York University Press.

Lizardo, O. (2006). How cultural taste shape personal networks. *American Sociological Review*, 71(October), 778–807.

Macedo, S., & Karpowitz, C. F. (2006). The local roots of American inequality. *PS: Political Science & Politics*, 39, 59–64.

Marchi, R. (2012). With Facebook, blogs and fake news, teens reject journalistic "objectivity". *Journal of Communication Inquiry*, 36(3), 246–262. doi:10.1177/0968859912458700

Media Reform Coalition. (2014). *The elephant in the room: A survey of media ownership and plurality in the United Kingdom*. Retrieved February 16, 2017 from www.mediareform.org.uk/wp-content/uploads/2015/11/The_Elephant_in_the_Room-A_Survey_of_Media_Ownership_and_Plurality_in_the_UK.pdf

Merton, R. K. (1949). Patterns of influence: A study of interpersonal influence and of communications behavior in a local community. In P. Lazarsfeld & F. Stanton (Eds.), *Communication research 1948–1949* (pp. 180–219). New York, NY: Harper and Brothers.

Miller, D., Costa, E., Haynes, N., Tom, M., Nicolescu, R., Sinanan, J., … Wang, X. (2016). *How the world changed social media*. London, England: UCL Press.

Morley, D. (1980). *The nationwide audience: Structure and decoding* (British Film Institute Television Monograph No. 11). London, England: British Film Institute.

Nielsen, R. K. (2015a). Local newspapers as keystone media: The increased importance of diminished newspapers for local political information environments. In R. K. Nielsen (Ed.), *Local journalism: The decline of newspapers and the rise of digital media* (pp. 51–72). London, England; New York, NY: I.B. Tauris.

Nielsen, R. K. (2015b). Introduction: The uncertain future of local journalism. In R. K. Nielsen (Ed.), *Local journalism: The decline of newspapers and the rise of digital media* (pp. 1–25). London, England; New York, NY: I.B. Tauris.

Park, R. E. (1929). Urbanization as measured by newspaper circulation. *The American Journal of Sociology*, 35(1), 60–79.

Peterson, R. A., & Kern, R. M. (1996). Changing highbrow taste: From snob to omnivore. *American Sociological Review*, 61(5), 900–907.

Poindexter, P. M., Heider, D., & McCombs, M. (2006). Watchdog or good neighbor? The public's expectations of local news. *The Harvard International Journal of Press/Politics*, 11(1), 77–88. doi:10.1177/1081180X05283795

Prior, M. (2007). *Post-broadcast democracy: How media choice increases inequality in political involvement and polarizes elections.* New York, NY: Cambridge University Press.

Putnam, R. D. (2000). *Bowling alone.* New York, NY: Simon & Schuster Paperbacks.

Ramsay, G., & Moore, M. (2016). *Monopolising local news: Is there an emerging democratic deficit in the UK due to the decline of local newspapers?* London: Kings College London, Centre for the Study of Media, Communication and Power.

Sampedro, V. (1998). Grounding the displaced: Local media reception in a transnational context. *Journal of Communication*, 48(2), 125–143.

Schaffer, J. (2007). *Citizen media: Fad or the future of news? The rise and prospects of hyperlocal journalism.* College Park, MI: J-Lab – The Institute for Interactive Journalism.

Shaker, L. (2014). Dead newspapers and citizens' civic engagement. *Political Communication*, 31(1), 131–148. doi:10.1080/10584609.2012.762817

Simmel, G. (1949). The sociology of sociability (transl.). *The American Journal of Sociology*, 55(3), 254–261.

Soroka, S., Andrew, B., Aalberg, T., Iyengar, S., Curran, J., Coen, S., ... Tiffen, R. (2013). Auntie knows best? Public broadcasters and current affairs knowledge. *British Journal of Political Science*, 43(4), 719–739. doi:10.1017/S0007123412000555

Stamm, K. R. (1985). *Newspaper use and community ties: Toward a dynamic theory.* Norwood, NJ: Ablex.

Strömbäck, J., & Shehata, A. (2010). Media malaise or a virtuous circle? Exploring the causal relationships between news media exposure, political news attention and political interest. *European Journal of Political Research*, 49(5), 575–597. doi:10.1111/j.1475-6765.2009.01913.x

Strömbäck, J., Djerf-Pierre, M., & Shehata, A. (2013). The dynamics of political interest and news media consumption: A longitudinal perspective. *International Journal of Public Opinion Research*, 25(4). doi:10.1093/ijpor/edso18

Sunstein, C. R. (2009). *Republic.com 2.0.* Princeton, NJ: Princeton University Press.

Turkle, S. (2011). *Alone together: Why we expect more from technology and less from each other.* New York, NY: Basic Books.

Turkle, S. (2012, April 21). The flight from conversation. *The New York Times.* Retrieved January 7, 2017 from www.nytimes.com/2012/04/22/opinion/sunday/the-flight-from-conversation.html

Turkle, S. (2015). *Reclaiming conversation: The power of talk in a digital age.* New York, NY: Penguin Press.

Vaage, O. F. (2017). *Norsk mediebarometer 2016* [Media use in Norway 2016]. Oslo-Kongsvinger, Norway: Statistisk sentralbyrå.

Van Aelst, P., Strömbäck, J., Aalberg, T., Esser, F., De Vreese, C., Matthes, J., ... Stanyer, J. (2017). Political communication in a high-choice media environment: A challenge for democracy? *Annals of the International Communication Association, 2017,* 41(1), 3–27.

Wadbring, I., & Bergström, A. (2015). A print crisis or a local crisis? *Journalism Studies,* Online. doi:10.1080/1461670X.2015.1042988

Wadbring, I., Weibull, L., & Facht, U. (2016). Nyhetsvanor i ett förändrat medielandskap [News habits in changed media environments]. In SOU 2016:30 (Ed.), *Människorna, medierna & marknaden* [People, media & market]. Stockholm, Sweden: Statens Offentliga Utredningar.

Weber, M. (1924/2009). *Towards a sociology of the press: An early proposal for content analysis.* Speech delivered at the first Congress of Sociologists, meeting in Frankfurt, 1910. Translated by Klaus Krippendorff. In K. Krippendorff & M. A. Bock (Eds.), *The content analysis reader* (pp. 9–11). London, England: Sage Publications.

Williams, A., & Harte, D. (2016). Hyperlocal news. In T. Witschge, C. W. Anderson, & D. Domingo (Eds.), *SAGE handbook of digital journalism* (pp. 280–294). Los Angeles, CA: Sage Publications.

Woodstock, L. (2014). The news-democracy narrative and the unexpected benefits of limited news consumption: The case of news resisters. *Journalism*, 15(7), 834–849. doi:10.1177/1464884913504260

Zaller, J. (2003). A new standard of news quality: Burglar alarms for the monitorial citizen. *Political Communication*, 20(2), 109–130. doi:10.1080/10584600390211136

7

THE END OF TRUST IN MAINSTREAM MEDIA

Myth: the Internet and social media have replaced edited news

For decades, social scientists have been discussing how trust is important for our society. Niklas Luhmann claims that "a complete absence of trust would prevent (one) even getting up in the morning" (Luhmann, 1979, p. 4) because, as Putnam proposes, honesty and trust lubricate the inevitable frictions of social life (Putnam, 2000, p. 135). Mass media produce both trust and uncertainty (Luhmann, 2000), and several researchers have investigated the linkage between news media use and political distrust (cf. Cappella & Jamieson, 1997; Robinson, 1976; Strömbäck, Djerf-Pierre, & Shehata, 2016). Trust in news media affects individuals' attention to news media (Chaffe & McLeod, 1973), and the changing media environment has been claimed to affect trust in society in general (Putnam, 2000).

In a society with abundant information from different media online and offline, Onora O'Neill (2002) claims that placing trust is as demanding as it was in Athens; she is concerned that we are now living in a "culture of suspicion" (p. 79). The more information news audiences are exposed to, the more they have to exercise their critical faculties. When there are more news sources, there may also be more contradictions in the reports of the same story.[1] New technology and social media also increase the ability for propagandists and hoaxers to spread inaccurate and invented information, and populist politicians have counter-claimed that mainstream news organisations are presenting "fake news". These claims challenge trust in established bridging news media such as the BBC, CNN, *The New York Times* and other national news sources which people have trusted to deliver information that is checked and reliable. Several studies across the USA and Europe have shown a decrease in people's trust in their traditional news media (Newman, Fletcher, Levy, & Nielsen, 2016; Swift, 2016).

This leads us to the sixth hypothesis we want to discuss in this book: "We have lost trust in mainstream media". We start this chapter with a discussion of media's potential for influencing both trust and distrust among individuals in society, and its consequences for democracy. Secondly, we show how different media systems can explain the variation in trust in media. Thirdly, we show how trust in media has a potential for both increasing and decreasing over time, and is not therefore something we can expect to be stable. Finally, we suggest that the new media environment does not necessarily imply the end of trust in mainstream media nor does it imply increased trust in non-mainstream news.

Trust, facts and "truthiness"

The effects of exposure to news media, on trust in a country's political institutions and its leaders, is a key element in the legitimacy of government and its political institutions (Aarts, Fladmoe, & Strömbäck, 2012; O'Neill, 2002). According to Coleman (2012), trust is "the foundation of the social relationship that we call citizenship" (p. 36). The theory of the news media as a creator of "imagined communities" (Anderson, 1983) or their function as a "social glue" (Strömbäck, 2015) highlights how citizens may feel connected and trust each other because they share the same news media experiences.

Media exposure also relates to certain kinds of trust and social capital. Putnam (2000) distinguishes between "thick trust" and "thin trust".

> While thick trust is trust embedded in personal relations that are strong, frequent, and nested in wider networks, thin trust is a kind of trust in people we do not know personally, which rests implicitly on some background of shared social networks and expectations of reciprocity.
>
> *(Gambetta, 1988, as cited in Putnam, 2000, p. 137)*

While thick trust is a precondition for "bonding" social capital, thin trust is part of a "bridging" social capital: "...bridging social capital can generate broader identities and reciprocity, whereas bonding social capital bolsters our narrower selves" (Putnam, 2000, p. 23). Thin trust is important for creating and maintaining the trust we need to maintain social cohesion and the rule of law.

To achieve trust in people we do not know personally, mainstream media can play an important role. Indeed, Roger Silverstone goes as far as to suggest that journalists have a particular responsibility in this regard (Silverstone, 2006). Exposure to bridging media can also help citizens to agree on facts (Lynch, 2012) or achieve a "common currency" for political debates in society (Hampton, 1989). Coleman (2012) argues that "unless we can trust the news media to deliver common knowledge, the idea of the public – a collective entity possessing shared concerns – starts to fall apart" (p. 36). That common currency or common knowledge is produced via a largely unspoken and unacknowledged process of selection or "framing", which journalists use in order to organise material and, to an important degree, audiences also use to interpret the material that they see or read (Entman, 1993). These organisational frames shape news narratives to conform to the editorial positioning of the news organisation in relation to the ruling elite, political priorities or geo-political positioning as well as audience preferences (Gitlin, 1980, p. 7).

While critiques of the mass media emphasise the way in which framing favours an elite view of society, such critiques are themselves predicated on the assumption that there is a general standard of fact-checking and responsibility against which journalists and the media in a democracy can be measured and held to account. Without a common narrative, even if we disagree with the particulars, we have no way of making sense of the world or understanding one another (Schudsen, 2009, as cited in Zelizer, 2009, pp. 104–114).

Of course, people don't only consume news because they want to be informed citizens, and they often consume news they do not trust (Tsfati & Cappella, 2005). When an individual's exposure to news is just a way of getting support for their perceptions and opinions about the world, this challenges the role of mainstream media as a source for "common currency" or "glue" in a society. The impact of personalisation (see Chapter 2) makes it easier for people to insulate themselves from views that they disagree with, and in recent years some researchers have noted a gradual erosion of trust in factual reporting, and a growing reliance on material that feels emotionally true even when it is demonstrably factually incorrect.

The term "truthiness" has been coined to describe this tendency. In an essay called "Believable Fictions", Jeffrey T. Jones (2009) discusses the way in which some politicians make statements that are patently untrue and yet maintain support from their followers. He concludes that "truthiness is the product of a political culture in which citizens are full participants in [such] a will to believe" (Jones, 2009, p. 136). In 2016, the very concept of fact-based reporting came under sustained attack. So much so that the *Oxford English Dictionary* picked "post-truth" as their word of the year, an adjective defined as: "relating to or denoting circumstances in which objective facts are less influential in shaping public opinion than appeals to emotion and personal belief".

While the Internet has provided the tools with which "believable fictions" can be very easily circulated, at the same time trust in journalism and news media has been attacked by powerful populists in Europe, the USA, and also from authoritarian and new-authoritarian regimes in Eastern Europe, the Middle East and Asia. In the contemporary world it is easy for authoritarian organisations and regimes to use the Internet to spread dis-information beyond their borders as a means of destabilising countries considered unfriendly or to undermine internal progressive movements (Morozov, 2011).

Even in the high-trust Nordic countries, populist politicians are now using the "post-fact strategy" to deny rather than to argue against the facts or arguments presented in the news. By saying, "this is fake news", some politicians try to convince the audience to distrust journalists and media in order to win the discussion and strengthen their own power. The strategy of denouncing unwelcome news reports as "Fake" has been used by a number of politicians. While these politicians may have legitimate reasons to criticise the news media for unfair coverage, and the differing interests of nation states often result in sharply contrasting versions of world events, there is a price to be paid for deliberately undermining trust in journalism.

On an individual level, it is those citizens least likely to engage with mainstream, bridging news, who are most vulnerable to propaganda messages served via social media networks because they have little background knowledge that would help them to contextualise or verify what they are receiving. News avoiders are most likely to be those who have low levels of education and low levels of social and political capital (Blekesaune, Elvestad, & Aalberg, 2012). The wholesale onslaught against mainstream, bridging news by President Trump in the USA has arguably increased the likelihood that these groups will avoid mainstream news and has therefore left them vulnerable to manipulation by forces happy to circulate entirely invented material as news.

According to Michael P. Lynch, "post-truth" journalism and the lack of trust in bridging media is problematic because "without a common background of standards against which we measure what counts as a reliable source of information, or a reliable method of inquiry and what doesn't, we won't be able to agree on the facts, let alone values" (Lynch, 2012, p. 9). He also refers to Jean Hampton (1989, p. 809), who claims that:

> No matter what religion, moral beliefs, or metaphysical commitments, if we are to work together in one system of cooperation, we have to have a 'common currency' for debating and setting disputes or our society will be in ruins.

To measure trust in media is troublesome

In surveys across the world, citizens are very often asked about their trust in the press or media in general. However, people seldom trust the press, media or journalists "in general"; they find some news media and some journalists more reliable than others. So when people are asked about trust in media, it is not usually obvious what the question is actually measuring (Fisher, 2016). For instance, do people trust a news organisation because it offers a balanced frame of reference for the issue, or do they trust it because it favours their point of view? If individuals answer that they have little trust in media or journalists in general, it is not necessarily the case that they find all news media and journalists to be untrustworthy.

Comparative media credibility research has found that people evaluate some media to be more credible than others. Across Europe, radio and television is a more credible medium than newspapers and social media has less credibility than newspapers in most countries (EBU, 2016a). Trust in the Internet decreased by eight points between 2011 and 2016, and online social networks are only trusted as a news source in Albania (EBU, 2016a). The provider of the information is also important for credibility. Trust in a provider or a media organisation is based on journalistic reputation that is anchored in the brand name (Blöbaum, 2014).

For example, in 2014, Norwegian researchers published some results indicating that Norwegians have very low trust in media and in journalists (Staksrud et al.,

2014), while in the same period other researchers found that when people were asked about their trust in the news of their public broadcaster, NRK, 93 per cent agreed that NRK was doing a very good or good job in producing trustworthy news, information and documentaries (TNS Gallup, 2016). The high trust in NRK was confirmed in a sample of Norwegian students in 2014 (Elvestad, 2015). This shows how individuals distinguish between trust in different news media (TV, radio, newspapers, Internet and social media), different types of news provider (public service broadcasting, commercial broadcasting, broadsheet and tabloid press), different news brands (BBC, CNN, *The New York Times, The Guardian*, Al Jazeera, Russia Today, etc.), or informal sources found online or in social media.

Trust is also based on personal preference, and some media are considered more believable and trustworthy than others. In most countries, newspapers have historically been linked with political parties (Seymour-Ure, 1974), so much so that parties established newspapers (or newspapers established political parties[2]), and parties subsidised newspapers and harnessed them to mobilise sympathetic voters. In the era of the party press in Europe and the USA, editors and journalists became political activists (Baldasty, 1992). Facts were perceived through the prism of party loyalty, and neutrality was the worst sin of all (Perloff, 2016). Under these circumstances general trust in the news media would not have been expected. People trusted only their own party paper. Increasing commercialisation and consolidation of the press in many countries has led to the gradual replacement of the party press by "independent" news organisations. This started in the USA, where newspaper editors developed what has been referred to as "the strategic ritual" of objectivity (Tuchman, 1972), as a means of protecting their position and influence in an increasingly concentrated, and highly commercial, media environment. This approach meant that most newspapers maintained a relatively neutral, or centrist, role in American politics in relation to the two major parties even while broadcast news became partisan.

However, outside the USA, many newspapers (and their websites) are still influenced by historic loyalties; for instance in Norway where, according to Allern (2007), most newspapers still pay tribute to their political roots in the form of statutes defining their editorial platform in ideological terms like conservative, liberal or social democratic. In the UK, newspapers profess their independence but the majority support the Conservative Party and partisanship is the norm. In the Southern European countries, journalism is not strongly differentiated from political activism, and the autonomy of journalism is often limited (Hallin & Mancini, 2004); indeed, the populist Italian Five Star movement grew from the blog of its leader.[3]

Broadcasting, first radio and later television, was in a different situation from newspapers. Established in the first half of the twentieth century, broadcasting was seen as a ready weapon for totalitarianism and steps were taken to ensure that such power could be regulated and channelled. In Europe, unlike the USA, the discussion of political balance in the media is closely linked to the establishment of the electronic broadcasting media.[4] While the press was not expected to be politically balanced (Hopmann et al., 2011, p. 242), broadcasters both in the USA and Europe were required to balance news coverage (Cushion & Lewis, 2009; Starkey, 2007). Public service broadcasting started with the BBC in the UK in the 1920s, and several countries copied these normative ideals for broadcasting as a public good, with balanced news coverage catering for all citizens (Syvertsen, 1999). With only one or two channels per country, news was produced for a large audience that was not confined by distinct party-political preferences.

While newspaper readers may have trust in their newspaper because they agree with the political or ideological platform of this particular newspaper, the trust in radio and television channels in Europe rests on the ability to be recognised as a relatively neutral or impartial news source. Similar regulation for "fairness" was initially imposed on the broadcast media oligopoly of the United States but, when the Fairness Doctrine was repealed by president Ronald Reagan in 1987, less balanced approaches were proven to be commercially successful and now, in the USA, news exposure is more selective and partisan than in Europe (see Stroud, 2011). When the Fox News president, Roger Ailes, in 2010 said "I want to elect the next president,"[5] it was probably fine with the Fox News viewers, but it would have been a scandal if a leader of a public service broadcaster in Europe said the same.

From the 1990s, the Internet opened up for alternative news sources, but also for a new platform for mainstream media to offer news. Curran et al. (2013) found that the leading conglomerates had extended their hegemony across technologies so that traditional news brands also dominate content online and on social media. A Reuters news report from 2016 shows that the BBC was the most used brand online and offline and the *Daily Mail* was the second largest circulation newspaper, as well as the largest circulation newspaper brand online (Newman et al., 2016). An Israeli study with a representative sample of the Jewish population also showed that the audiences who trust traditional news brands offline transfer this trust to the same media brands online (Tsfati, 2010). So in spite of concern expressed about the decline in trust in traditional news media, traditional mainstream news brands are still seen as trustworthy online. In our own studies of UK and Norwegian students, we found that young people develop a repertoire of ways of establishing the veracity of the news they read. One key factor was longevity. Sources that have been available for a long time have developed a reputation that can be evaluated. Jacob, a 21-year-old UK male, expressed it like this: "I guess it's because like they're just there, because they've been running for a long time now, so, I sort of put my trust in them".

Both the UK and Norwegian students show higher trust in their mainstream media, in particular their public service broadcasters, BBC and NRK, than in news sources on social media. In the Norwegian sample, several of the students stressed that NRK is more neutral because it is publicly owned. Dina (female, Norwegian, 20 years) shows how the ownership of the NRK is something she and many of the Norwegian students are aware of, but they were not so knowledgeable about the ownership of other news media: "I do think about it, I think of NRK as very trustworthy, because in a way it is the Public[6] and it should behave properly so in a way I feel I can trust them, but otherwise I don't think so much about it (the ownership of news media)…" Similarly, the statements about the BBC expressed in the UK sample also indicate that the BBC is most trusted because it is expected to be a more neutral news source. Yolanda (UK, female, 22 years) expressed it this way: "The fact that it's [the BBC] funded by everybody gives it a certain truth in a way because, there is no really … there is no one certain set people that is trying to bring out their ideologies in terms".

In our interviews with students, we also found that the public service broadcasters were considered to be more trustworthy than newspapers. For the UK students, newspapers are associated with political affiliation, scandals and untrustworthiness. For the Norwegian students, newspapers have a much higher credibility, and the young people were not very concerned about the newspaper ownership. They are aware that there are some ideologically framed newspapers (for instance *Klasse-kampen*, a socialist/left-wing national newspaper), but most of them do not think of newspapers in general as politically framed. Frida, a 22-year-old female Norwegian student, put it like this:

> I feel like some newspapers are very politically framed, but in general I don't think there is very much differences between right-wing and left-wing news-papers. So I think that most of them are neutral, but I try to think critically about what I read, also if I read a very left-wing newspaper, or it matters if it is a serious big newspaper, or whether I have never heard about the news source before, of course that matters.

These students are developing skills that help them navigate in a more fragmented news media landscape. While they are open to exploring alternative news sources and platforms, many of them still use public service or mainstream media as a touchstone for checking factual information. This was sometimes the case even when, in the case of the more sceptical UK students, they had expressed doubts about the reliability of mainstream media. In a confusing world some sources of information are, relatively, more trustworthy than others. As news exposure becomes more fragmented, it becomes even more challenging to measure whether trust in mainstream media in particular is decreasing or not.

How trust varies across countries and time

Trust in media is highly related to the national context. While 62 per cent of the respondents in Finland agreed that you can trust the news most of the time, less than a quarter of respondents did so in Greece and South Korea (Newman, Fletcher, Kalogeropoulos, & Nielsen, 2017). Trust in news media varies greatly according to national media systems (Strömbäck et al., 2016; Tsfati & Ariely, 2014). For instance, trust and media exposure varies a lot between Nordic and Northern European countries with a strong public service media, citizens in the USA with a market-oriented public sphere, or citizens in authoritarian regimes such as Russia. Müller (2013) argues that while a market-oriented public sphere does not lead to higher trust, interventions by the state to ensure plurality, in the form of public service media, do lead to higher trust in the news media. Surveys from the EU countries confirm this (EBU, 2016a, 2016b).

Müller (2013) also found that authoritarian regimes have high trust in the press. In this case, trust seems to be artificially produced by high levels of state control over the media and the marginalisation of discordant messages. Elena Vartanova (2011) argues that after the election of Vladimir Putin in 2000, "the presidential administration reinforced control over political programmes on national (federal) TV channels, and mass-circulation newspapers" (Vartanova, 2011, p. 127). Further she argues that "Russian media, especially nationally distributed TV channels, have been increasingly used by the state as tools to support the vertical power system, create a unified national identity, and minimize politically incorrect debates" (Vartanova, 2011, p. 134). The Chinese state also maintains control over media and enjoys high levels of public trust (Desilver, 2013; Hyun & Kim, 2015; Orlik, 2012).

In general, in non-authoritarian countries where the public service media is independent and has a high market share, the trust in radio and TV is higher than in countries where the PBS has a lower market share (EBU, 2016a, 2016b).[7] In the democratic-corporatist media systems of Belgium, the Netherlands, Norway and Sweden, a recent study shows a positive relationship between using newspapers and public service broadcasting and levels of political trust. In the UK that relationship holds only for BBC News, not for reading newspapers (Aarts et al., 2012).[8] The Nordic countries are among the countries with the highest trust in television, radio and newspapers and the lowest trust in social media. The UK, however, is on the other side of the trust scale: they have the lowest level of trust in newspapers among the EU countries and they are lower on trust in radio and TV than other countries with public service broadcasters. This is in spite of the fact that the BBC is still the most trusted source by a very long margin (Schifferes, 2012). There is also low trust in social media as a source of news (EBU, 2016a).[9]

Greece is the exception to this pattern. In Greece, there are low levels of trust in the media in spite of the existence of a public broadcaster. This, according to media analyst Petros Iosifidis (2016), is because the public broadcaster is seen by many as a state broadcaster. The service was launched while Greece was ruled by a dictatorship, has been historically poorly funded, and has never achieved full independence from state control. The service was abolished in 2013 at the height of the Greek economic crisis and, although it has been relaunched, it is still seen by many as too close to the government. The economic crisis in Greece undermined any residual trust in mainstream media and many Greeks put their faith in online sites, blogs and social media instead (Newman et al., 2016, p. 28). In their 36-country study, the Reuters Institute found that Greece is the only country where the people trust social media more than mainstream news media (Newman et al., 2017).

In countries with high trust in institutions and in people they do not know, national media such as radio and television are more likely to play an integrative function, which again maintains the general trust among citizens in the society.

The EBU also found evidence for a strong positive correlation between strong, well-funded public service media in the EU countries and several indications of greater democracy and less corruption. In the countries with strong public service media, there is a high degree of press freedom and higher voter turnout than in other countries with weaker public service media. Further, there are also lower levels of right-wing extremism and better control of corruption in countries with a strong public service media (EBU, 2016b). The correlations are significant, but it is not obvious what the direction of causality is. Is high trust in society a precondition for a well-functioning public service media or do the public service media contribute to a higher level of trust in society? We will argue that this is a reciprocal process, which means that a public service media of high quality is not enough.

The historical development of mainstream media tells us that trust in media fluctuates. It depends on the media technology available, media regulations and national context. The World Values Survey (www.worldvaluessurvey.org) is a global network of social scientists studying changing values and their impact on social and political life, which started collecting survey data in 1981. One of the questions in the survey is "how much confidence do you have in the press?". Figure 7.1 shows how answers to this question have changed in Japan, India, Mexico, Sweden, Spain, Poland, the USA and Russia from 1981 until 2014.

Figure 7.1 shows that trust in the press is not stable over time and it changes across countries. Trust in the press has not been stable in any of these eight countries, and they have changed differently. While the USA has the biggest decrease in trust, Japan has had the biggest increase. Spain, Poland and Mexico show a downward trend in the period, while in Sweden and Russia trust in the press increased or stabilised over the last ten years up until 2014. And finally, India has experienced an increase in trust since the mid 1990s. Trust in mainstream news started to drop away in the USA after the repeal of the Fairness Doctrine in the 1980s (Hayes & Zechowski, 2014; Young, 2016), which had ensured that news on broadcast media was balanced. The rise of ideological radio in the 1980s with highly opinionated radio "shock jocks", and Fox television in the 1990s with its relentless attacks on the so-called liberal press, seems to have undermined trust in all forms of news reporting.[10]

In Sweden, the lowest trust was in the period with a strong party press, and since then there has been a small increase in trust.[11] This is confirmed by a more recent EU study which found that Swedes (like most Europeans) have become more sceptical towards the Internet and online social networks; however, there has been a slight positive increase of trust in television, radio and newspapers in the period from 2011–15 among the Swedes (EBU, 2016a).[12] In Greece, citizens have also recovered some trust in radio as a news source over the last five years, but from very low levels (EBU, 2016a). In Spain, the trend of decrease in trust shown in Figure 7.1 could be temporary. In the recent Reuters Report, they found that trust in news continued to increase after it hit its lowest level in 2015 (Newman et al., 2017, p. 93).

Historically, Japanese news brands have been highly trusted, and Figure 7.1 shows that the Japanese have the highest trust in the press among the countries

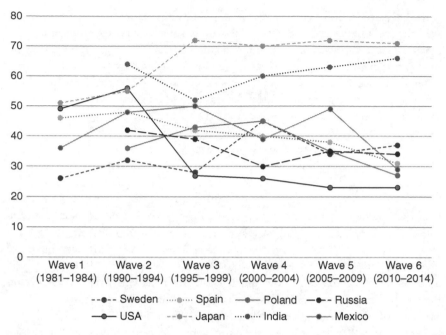

FIGURE 7.1 Confidence in the press. Percentage share of the population who answered "A great deal" or "Quite a lot"
(Source: World Value Survey)

presented in this chart, but this might change. During the nuclear disaster in 2011, the mainstream media was accused of failing to report the truth (to protect the government) and more recently a number of respected journalists have stepped down or did not get their contracts renewed following pressure from the conservative government. In a Reuters 2017 survey (Newman et. al., 2017), the Japanese are not at the top of the list of countries with high trust as only 43 per cent said they trust news media most of the time. We also expect that trust in media will change in Russia, Poland, Mexico and India as the national situation changes. Trust in the press or trust in other media increases or decreases differently across countries and political systems over time. This shows that news media cannot take trust and recognition from their audience for granted, but it also shows that trust in media can be re-established.

Distrust in mainstream media, the hostile media effect and alternative news sources

Trust is an important factor that influences people's relationship with news media, and distrust in mainstream media can be a motivation for use of alternative news sources, for differing views and attempts to validate the credibility of the news (Elvestad, Phillips, & Feuerstein, 2017; Fletcher & Park, 2017). Based on a study of 11 countries, Fletcher and Park (2017) show that those with low levels of trust tend to prefer non-mainstream news sources like social media, blogs, and digital-born providers, and are more likely to engage in various forms of online news participation. In their study, these associations tend to be strongest in Northern European countries, but are weaker elsewhere. Others have argued that "obtaining accurate and objective information about the world is just one motivation for watching the news. When other motivations are present, trust in the media becomes less relevant" (Tsfati & Cappella, 2005, p. 254).

The Australian edition of Reuters Digital News Report showed that:

> people predominantly using online media were not necessarily motivated by a specific intention to become informed via the news media they trusted, instead their use of online news media was a consequence or by-product, rather than a purposeful goal, of their daily online use.
>
> *(Fisher, 2016, p. 460)*

Further, personal beliefs are important for the way in which individuals evaluate the news. Through an analysis of three focus group interviews among students in the USA, Dochterman and Stamp (2010) found that 12 categories emerged as factors of Web credibility (authority, page layout, site motive, URL, cross-checkability, user motive, content, date, professionalism, site familiarity, process, and personal beliefs). This study highlights how both motivations and personal beliefs are of importance for news exposure and credibility. More literate, sceptical news users, who use alternative news sources for comparing information, learning different angles and questioning the content, show a healthy distrust of news media (Fisher, 2016). It is more problematic if the distrust in mainstream media leads to more unilateral perspectives of society.

People's personal beliefs affect both news exposure and how they view and accept different messages. They tend to trust news frames that they agree with, more than news that they see as biased against their side. Those people with a strong pre-existing attitude on an issue tend to perceive *any* media coverage as biased against their side and in favour of the point of view of their antagonists (Gunther & Chia, 2001; Perloff, 2015; Vallone, Ross, & Lepper, 1985). In 1985, Vallone et al. discovered that both pro-Israeli and pro-Arab partisans rated television coverage of the Beirut massacre as being biased against their side, a phenomenon that has been called *the hostile media effect*. Going through recent research, Perloff (2015) found that group loyalty affects the way in which people understand news. If they feel that their group is being attacked in the media in a way that undermines its legitimacy in the larger society, they manage their feelings by "derogating media coverage, viewing it as hostilely biased. In this way, they reduce the symbolic threat and restore valued social self-esteem" (p. 708).

The Reuters Institute report from 2017 shows a strong connection between distrust in the media and perceived political bias, and this is particularly true in countries with high levels of political polarisation (Newman et al., 2017). Studies in Denmark, the Netherlands, Norway, Sweden or the USA have shown that this mistrust of mainstream news media seems to be most present among citizens on the political right. A recent Swedish study (Strömbäck & Karlsson, 2017) showed an increase in trust in mainstream media in the population, but not among the supporters of the right-wing party ("Sverigedemokraterna"). A Norwegian study showed that citizens who are more negative towards immigrants also have less trust in the media (Staksrud et al., 2014). Individuals on the right in the USA are more likely to avoid news because they find it less reliable than do people on the left. 62 per cent of news avoiders on the right cited this as a reason, while only 18 per cent of people on the left did so (Kalogeropoulos, 2017). A study of trust in the USA, between 1974 and 2010, found that trust in the reporting of science has also declined among those who identify as conservative or are frequent church attendants. Among all other groups, trust in science has remained stable (Gauchat, 2012). There is a debate in these countries about the so-called "liberal media bias" supposedly caused by left-leaning journalists (Albæk, Hopmann, & De Vreese, 2010; Alterman, 2003; Van Praag & Brants, 2005, as cited in Hopmann et al., 2011).

However, the bias is not always perceived to lean to the left. In the UK it is those on the left of politics who are least likely to trust the news media (Newman et al., 2016). This is likely to be because the majority of national newspapers have a conservative rather than a liberal bias. Television is the most trusted source[13] and still dominates news consumption in the UK, but research suggests that the right-leaning newspapers maintain an agenda-setting role (Cushion & Sambrook, 2015). Citizens who find the mainstream media to be hostilely biased may find alternative sources more relevant. For example, those Americans who believed that media coverage of 9/11 and the ground war in Iraq was too sympathetic to Muslims connected to blogs in order to avoid perceived liberal media bias (Kaye & Johnson, 2004, 2011; Reynolds, 2004).

In the USA and Australia, researchers have also suggested that, where people turn away from regular news sources, entertainment news and satirical news productions can serve as important alternative sources for political information and contribute to civic engagement, especially among young people (Marchi, 2012; Turner, 2005). In her US study, Marchi maintains that adolescents who use entertainment news shows get a clearer understanding of current events and see what is at stake regarding a given event or policy. She refers to US studies that have shown that viewers of talk shows, such as *The Daily Show*, are better informed about national and international affairs than those who rely exclusively on official news. Young adults who watched *The Daily Show* scored higher on campaign knowledge tests than those who watched network news or read newspapers (NAES, 2004). Turner (2005) is also positive about satirical productions in Australia, and argues that they offer audiences a taste of what current events news could be like, stripped of dependence on the authority of the presenter, focusing instead on the quality of political arguments.

We would argue, on the contrary, that satirical productions are even more dependent on the authority of a presenter to frame news – without Jon Stewart *The Daily Show* has struggled. Moreover, people have difficulties with evaluating what is real from what is fake and satirical news is often taken to be real when it is circulated online without its context. The information overload on the Internet creates difficulties for citizens who navigate and evaluate different news sources. The flood of information and misinformation provides little but confusion unless it can be sorted and assessed (O'Neill, 2002, pp. 72–73).

In a recent study, Stanford education scholars found that many US students have trouble judging the credibility of online news. Their study of middle school, high school and college students in the USA showed that "digital natives" may be able to flit between Facebook and Twitter while simultaneously uploading a selfie to Instagram and texting a friend, but when it comes to evaluating information that flows through social media channels, they are easily duped (SHEG, 2016).[14] Similarly, a study from the British broadcaster Channel 4 showed that British people are very bad at spotting misinformation or fake news. Channel 4 and YouGov surveyed 1,700 people, showing them six individual story headlines. Of these, three were true, and three were fake. Half (49 per cent) said they are confident that they can tell the difference between a fake news story and a real news story, even though only 4 per cent identified them correctly from the headline alone.[15] Further, Young (2016) found in his study that the majority of Americans could not recall a specific experience with a news source that made them trust it less. In all, only 4 in 10 recalled a specific bad experience they had with a news source that they said had caused them to lose trust in an organisation.

The Internet also changes the way we relate to facts and news. Lynch (2016) argues that we have changed from saying, "seeing is believing", to "Googling is believing". He says that when we Google-know, we no longer take responsibility for our own beliefs, and we lack the capacity to see how bits of facts fit into a larger whole. We can always Google for facts, but as Lynch points out, what you see when you Google is a function of, among other things, your language, your location, and your personal Web history. If we ask Google what is happening in Ukraine or how the country's immigrant policy is working, browsers will not get the same answers (Lynch, 2016). Today, robots are also writing news articles. In an experiment with German participants, Graefe, Haim, Haarmann, and Brosius (2016) tested how audiences give credit to news written by robots or computers compared with news written by journalists. They found that "computer-written news tended to be rated higher than human-written news in terms of credibility" (Graefe et al., 2016, p. 10). We will argue that computer-written news is not neutral or necessarily closer to the truth, and agree with Graefe et al. (2016) in their call for ethical guidelines in relation to robot or computer-written news.

Moreover, when people share news on social media they do not necessarily check whether what they are sharing is trustworthy news or not. According to a survey by Pew Research, 23 per cent of Americans say that they have shared a made-up news story, either knowingly or not (Barthel, Mitchell, & Holcomb, 2016). Research on how we react to news shared by friends on social media shows that, "If others think it is a good story, then I should think so too" (Sundar, 2008, p. 83). This tells us that the new media environment can add to fragmentation rather than creating a common currency, and create uncertainty rather than trust. The new media environment is challenging the way in which we relate to facts, and challenging the role of mainstream bridging media in providing a "common currency".

Media, trust and democracy

Consumers of news media are not necessarily motivated by a civic duty to be informed (Fisher, 2016), and mainstream media exposure may not always contribute to politically engaged citizens (Cappella & Jamieson, 1997; Robinson, 1976). Some researchers suggest that media (especially television) actually has the opposite effect. The *media malaise hypothesis* posits that news media, because of its focus on conflicts, violence and other negative aspects of politics, results in political cynicism and apathy (Robinson, 1976). According to Cappella and Jamieson (1997), *media malaise* also relates to the way in which media frame politics, which has direct effects on the public's cynicism about politics, government, policy debates and campaigns. A more recent Swedish study supports this hypothesis. The researchers found that, when serious news media frame politics as though it were a game or a sport, people are less likely to trust what they are told (Hopmann, Sheheta & Strömbäck, 2015). This effect could be seen in the coverage of the British European Union referendum when people complained that they did not feel that the news media were informing them about the issues at stake (Galpin & Trenz, 2017).

The linkage between media and political distrust is not alike for all media or all countries. International studies find that, while general TV viewing is associated with greater political distrust, newspaper reading and public service broadcast news is generally associated with greater political trust (Aarts et al., 2012; Norris, 2000; Strömbäck et al., 2016). In the USA, where the media malaise theory was developed, several researchers have claimed that distrust in mainstream news media does not have to be negative. Schudson (1998, p. 301) points out that "because of distrust, we have checks and balances: because of distrust, we are enjoined as citizens to be watchful". Further, Bennett (2008) argues that for the younger generations with lower trust in traditional bridging news media, the "Actualizing citizen", who expresses political engagement, has replaced the "Dutiful citizen" model. However, those who argued that mistrust of the media might imply a healthy scepticism (e.g. Marchi, 2012; Schudson, 1998) get no support from Tsfati and Ariely's (2014) study of 44 countries that shows it is not the mistrusting audiences who are involved in politics, but those who have high trust in mainstream media.

Research in Europe has also shown how news exposure, trust and social capital are related. In the USA, the trend of decreasing trust in other people has been running in parallel with decreasing media trust since the end of the 1980s. Moreover, in countries where citizens have a high degree of trust in each other, such as Sweden, the trust in mainstream, bridging media is significantly higher (World Values Survey, 2016). In countries with a high level of general trust, fewer citizens avoid news (Blekesaune et al., 2012). This suggests that there is a positive relationship between trust in news media and trust in democratic institutions. Norris (2000) argues that there is a virtuous circle at work (the virtuous circle hypothesis) in which people who consume more news develop a more positive orientation towards the political system (though it is also plausible that those with higher political trust are using more news). Curran et al. (2014, p. 829) argue that it is the quality of information that counts: "Public service television, we have found in line with others, is more effective than commercial television in fostering a democratic culture."

Mainstream media and trustworthiness

From a deliberative democratic perspective, it is important for mainstream media to search for ways to curb hostile media effects (Perloff, 2015) and to increase trust. Mainstream media also play an important role for citizens who navigate in a flood of information and misinformation. Concerned by the proliferation of fake news online, some news organisations are attempting to bolster trust in their own products and increase audiences, with a number of interventions. The French newspaper, *Le Monde*, has released a suite of products (Decodex) designed to throttle the spread of fake news online. *Le Monde*'s database of unreliable sites includes some that are not just false sites but sites which manipulate truth by aggregating extremist stories from other sources in single places on their sites. Readers will also be able to ask the Les Décodeurs team whether a story is a conspiracy theory or not (Davies, 2017). In the UK, the BBC is also establishing a team with the intention of revealing fake news. In Sweden, "Viralgranskaren", a webpage produced by the free newspaper *Metro*, has been doing this for several years. Facebook and Google have also developed tools to help people check the source of stories. However, those who already distrust the mainstream media are unlikely to make use of corrections provided by them and may well dismiss them as attempts to shore-up the authority of the elite (Nyhan & Reifler, 2010).

We would argue, with Müller (2013), that well-funded, responsible, independent, news journalism and public service media is the best antidote to fake news. Research suggests that in countries with strong public service media and high exposure to ethical news journalism, the fake news industry will be less damaging for democracy. For example, before the 2016 US elections 33.5 per cent of Tweets sharing relevant news, in the state of Michigan, were classified as "junk". In France before the 2017 elections, between 5.1 and 7.6 per cent were classified as "junk" (Kaminska, Gallacher, Kollany, Yasseri, & Howard, 2017). Where public service news media are available, trust levels are typically higher than in societies that depend on either the market, or state-sponsored news, and overall the traditional mainstream media are still the most trusted source for information online (EBU, 2016a). The importance of a strong public service broadcaster (also available online) is shown in several studies (see for instance EBU, 2016b).

People living in countries where the population has most trust in the press are also more willing to pay for online news. Payment levels are far higher in countries like Finland, Sweden, Norway and South Korea[16] where there is a powerful national broadcaster (Newman et al., 2016). However, in the USA, the willingness to pay for news sources online increased from 9 per cent in 2016 to 16 per cent in 2017, and this willingness to pay for news has increased most among young people and those on the political left (Newman et al., 2017). *The New York Times* had a net increase of 41,000 paid subscriptions to its news products, both print and digital, seven days after the election of Donald Trump in 2016. Mark Thompson, the president and CEO of The New York Times Company says, "…this is clear evidence of how much public demand there is for high quality, deeply reported, independent journalism…" (Press release, *The New York Times*, November 17, 2016).[17] It gives some hope for the future of quality news media as more news users seek out specific news sources they trust – and are willing to pay for them.

To sum up, we found that the hypothesis "We have lost trust in mainstream media" was not confirmed. Mainstream media do still have the potential to work as a "common currency" (Hampton, 1989), and the evidence suggests that citizens are still making use of traditional, bridging, news media, even if they only do so as a means of checking material from other sources. In some countries, such as the USA, the trust in all news media is low and lower than it used to be 30 years ago, but to what degree people trust their mainstream media varies strongly across countries and media systems. Trust in the national public service broadcasters in many European countries is much higher than other news media brands. Mainstream news media can also serve as a "fact check" service for citizens in the new media environment where it is harder to navigate between news that is "fake or real, pleasantly fake or too fake, pleasantly real or too real, detached or involved, warm or cold, one-sided or multivoiced" (Costera Meijer, 2007, p. 103). Our findings also show that trust in media is not something stable; it can increase, decrease and be resurrected as consequence of changes in media and society.

Notes

1 However, there is also a tendency towards more homogeneity in mainstream media (c.f. Allern, 2001).
2 In Norway several political parties were established with a background in newspapers (Bastiansen, 2015).
3 Beppe Grillo, a comedian, was encouraged to start a blog by IT executive Gianroberto Casaleggio. The blog became the means of organizing the Five Star Movement.
4 For a discussion about the US see Grabe and Bucy (2009, p. 190).
5 http://blog.seattlepi.com/seattlepolitics/2014/01/09/fox-news-boss-i-want-to-elect-the-next-president/
6 The Norwegian students used the word "State".
7 Trust in radio and TV is highest in Nordic countries and Estonia, while it is low in Southeast Europe (EBU, 2016a).
8 This may be linked to the fact that British citizens tend to read many more tabloid newspapers than citizens in the other European countries (Aarts et al., 2012, p. 114).
9 Sweden: 42 per cent tend not to trust the press, 21 per cent tend not to trust television, 11 per cent tend not to trust radio and 77 per cent tend not to trust online social networks. UK: 73 per cent tend not to trust the press, 46 per cent tend not to trust television, 39 per cent tend not to trust radio and 68 per cent tend not to trust online social networks (Eurobarometer, 2015).

10 In 2016, 33 per cent of Americans trust news most of the time (Newman et al., 2016, p.32).
11 In 2016, 40 per cent of Swedes trust news most of the time (Newman et al., 2016, p. 50).
12 A national study in Sweden also confirms this increase in trust trend (Strömbäck & Karlsson, 2017).
13 Kantar Media produces a regular trust and impartiality report for the BBC: www.bbc.co.uk/aboutthebbc/insidethebbc/howwework/reports/trust_and_impartiality_2015
14 For example, the Stanford researchers hoped that middle school students could distinguish an ad from a news story. By high school, they hoped that students reading about gun laws would notice that a chart came from a gun owners' political action committee. And, in 2016, they hoped that college students, who spend hours each day online, would look beyond a .org URL and ask who's behind a site that presents only one side of a contentious issue. But in every case and at every level they were taken aback by students' lack of preparation (SHEG, 2016).
15 http://digiday.com/publishers/demographic-divides-global-state-fake-news-5-charts/
16 In South Korea the public service broadcaster is heavily politically controlled, which is not the case in the Nordic countries.
17 http://investors.nytco.com/press/press-releases/press-release-details/2016/The-New-York-Times-Adds-41000-New-Subscriptions-Since-Election-Day/default.aspx

References

Aarts, K., Fladmoe, A., & Strömbäck, J. (2012). Media, political trust, and political knowledge. In T. Aalberg & J. Curran (Eds.), *How media inform democracy: A comparative approach* (pp. 98–118). London, England: Routledge.

Albæk, E., Hopmann, D. N., & De Vreese, C. H. (2010). *Kunsten at holde balancen. Dækningen af folketingsvalgkampe i tv-nyhederne på DR1 og TV2: 1994–2007* [The art of balancing. Television news coverage of Folketing elections on DR1 and TV2, 1994–2007]. Odense, Denmark: University Press of Southern Denmark.

Allern, S. (2001). *Flokkdyr på Løvebakken: Søkelys på Stortingets presselosje og politikkens medierammer* [Political journalists and how the media frames political issues]. Oslo, Norway: Pax.

Allern, S. (2007). From party press to independent observers?: An analysis of election campaign coverage prior to the general elections of 1981 and 2005 in two Norwegian newspapers. *Nordicom Review, 28*(Jubilee Issue 2007), 63–79.

Alterman, E. (2003) *What liberal media? The truth about bias and the news.* New York, NY: Basic Books.

Anderson, B. (1983). *Imagined communities: Reflections on the origin and spread of nationalism.* London, England: Verso.

Baldasty, G. J. (1992). *The commercialization of news in the nineteenth century.* Madison, WI: University of Wisconsin Press.

Barthel, M., Mitchell, A., & Holcomb, J. (2016). Many Americans believe fake news is sowing confusion. *Pew Research Center: Journalism & Media.* Retrieved June 10, 2017 from www.journalism.org/2016/12/15/many-americans-believe-fake-news-is-sowing-confusion/

Bastiansen, H. G. (2015). Partipressen: En introduksjon [Party press: An introduction]. In Ø. Ihlen, E. Skogerbø, & S. Allern (Eds.), *Makt, medier og Politikk. Norsk politisk kommunikasjon* [Power, media and politics: Norwegian political communication] (pp. 159–170). Oslo, Norway: Universitetsforlaget.

Bennett, W. L. (2008). Changing citizenship in the digital age. Civic Life Online: Learning how digital media can engage youth. In W. L. Bennett (Ed.), *The John D. and Catherine T. MacArthur foundation series on digital media and learning* (pp. 1–24). Cambridge, MA: MIT Press.

Blekesaune, A., Elvestad, E., & Aalberg, T. (2012). Tuning out the world of news and current affairs: An empirical study of Europe's disconnected citizens. *European Sociological Review*, 28(1), 110–126. doi:10.1093/esr/jcq051

Blöbaum, B. (2014). *Trust and journalism in a digital environment*. Working paper. Oxford, England: Reuters Institute for the Study of Journalism, University of Oxford.

Cappella, J. N., & Jamieson, K. H. (1997). *Spiral of cynicism: The press and the public good.* New York, NY: Oxford University Press.

Chaffe, S. H., & McLeod, J. M. (1973). Individual vs. social predictors of information seeking. *Journalism Quarterly*, 50(2), 237–245.

Coleman, S. (2012). Believing the news: From sinking trust to atrophied efficacy. *European Journal of Communication*, 27(1), 35–45. doi:10.1177/0267323112438806

Costera Meijer, I. (2007). The paradox of popularity: How young people experience the news. *Journalism Studies*, 8(1), 96–116. doi:10.1080/14616700601056874

Curran, J., Coen, S., Aalberg, T., Hayashi, K., Jones, P. K., Splendore, S., ... Tiffen, R. (2013). Internet revolution revisited: A comparative study of online news. *Media, Culture & Society*, 35(7), 880–897. doi:10.1177/0163443713499393

Curran, J., Coen, S., Soroka, S., Aalberg, T., Hayashi, K., Hichy, Z., Iyengar, S., Jones, P., Mazzoleni, G. & Papathanassopoulos, S. (2014). Reconsidering 'virtuous circle'and 'media malaise' theories of the media: An 11-nation study. *Journalism*, 15(7), 815–833. doi: 10.1177/1464884913520198

Cushion, S., & Lewis, J. (2009). Towards a 'Foxification' of 24-hour news channels in Britain? *Journalism*, 10(2), 131–153. doi:10.1177/1464884908100598

Cushion, S., & Sambrook, R. (2015). The 'horse-race' contest dominated TV news election coverage. In D. Jackson & E. Thorsen (Eds.), *UK election analysis 2015: Media, voters and the campaign*. Project Report. Poole, England: The Centre for the Study of Journalism, Culture and Community, Bournemouth University.

Davies, J. (2017). Le Monde identifies 600 unreliable websites in fake-news crackdown. *Digiday UK*. Retrieved February 3, 2017 from http://digiday.com/publishers/le-m onde-identifies-600-unreliable-websites-fake-news-crackdown/

Desilver, D. (2013). Confidence in government falls in much of the developed world. *Pew Research Center*. Retrieved May 31, 2017 from www.pewresearch.org/fact-tank/2013/11/ 21/confidence-in-government-falls-in-much-of-the-developed-world/

Dochterman, M. A., & Stamp, G. H. (2010). Part 1: The determination of web credibility: A thematic analysis of web user's judgements. *Qualitative Research Reports in Communication*, 11(1), 37–43. doi:10.1080/17459430903514791

EBU. (2016a). Trust in media 2016. *The European Broadcasting Union Media Intelligence Service*. Retrieved December 18, 2016 from www.ebu.ch/publications/trust-in-media-2016

EBU. (2016b). PSM correlation links between public service media and societal well-being. *The European Broadcasting Union Media Intelligence Service*. Retrieved December 18, 2016 from www.ebu.ch/news/2016/08/ebu-research-shows-strong-public-service-media-con-tributes-to-a-healthy-democracy

Elvestad, E. (2015). *Barn av informasjonsrike medieomgivelser* [Children of information-rich environments]. Skriftserien fra Høgskolen i Buskerud og Vestfold, nr. 23, 2015. Retrieved from https://brage.bibsys.no/xmlui/handle/11250/2368736

Elvestad, E., Phillips, A., & Feuerstein, M. (2017). Can trust in traditional news media explain cross-national differences in news exposure of young people online? *Digital Journalism* (Published online June 16, 2017). doi:10.1080/21670811.2017.1332484

Entman, R. M. (1993). Framing: Toward clarification of a fractured paradigm. *Journal of Communication*, 43(4), 51–58. doi:10.1111/j.1460-2466.1993.tb01304

Eurobarometer. (2015). Media use in the European Union. *Standard Eurobarometer*, 84, Autumn 2015. Retrieved March 18, 2017 from http://ec.europa.eu/commfrontoffice/publicopinion/archives/eb/eb83/eb83_first_en.pdf

Fisher, C. (2016). The trouble with 'trust' in news media. *Communication Research and Practice*, 2(4), 451–465. doi:10.1080/22041451.2016.1261251

Fletcher, R., & Park, S. (2017). The impact of trust in the news media on online news consumption and participation. *Digital Journalism* (Published online February 2, 2017). Retrieved March 29, 2017 from www.tandfonline.com/doi/abs/10.1080/21670811.2017.1279979

Galpin, C., & Trenz, H. J. (2017). The spiral of euroscepticism: Media negativity, framing and opposition to the EU. In M. Caiani & S. Guerra (Eds.), *Euroscepticism, democracy and the media* (pp. 49–72). London, England: Palgrave Macmillan UK. https://link.springer.com/book/10.1057/978-1-137-59643-7

Gauchat, G. (2012). Politicization of science in the public sphere. *American Sociological Review*, 77(2), 167–187. doi:10.1177/0003122412438225

Gitlin, T. (1980). *The whole world is watching: Mass media in the making & unmaking of the New Left*. Berkeley, CA: University of California Press.

Grabe, M. E., & Bucy, E. P. (2009). *Image bite politics – News and the visual framing of elections*. Oxford, England: Oxford University Press.

Graefe, A., Haim, M., Haarmann, B., & Brosius, H. B. (2016). Readers' perception of computer-generated news: Credibility, expertise, and readability. *Journalism*, Online first. doi:10.1177/1464884916641269

Gunther, A. C., & Chia, S. C. Y. (2001). Predicting pluralistic ignorance: The hostile media perception and its consequences. *Journalism & Mass Communication Quarterly*, 78(4), 688–701.

Hallin, D. C., & Mancini, P. (2004). *Comparing media systems: Three models of media and politics*. Cambridge, England: Cambridge University Press.

Hampton, J. (1989). Should political philosophy be done without metaphysics? *Ethics*, 99(4), 791–814.

Hayes, J. E., & Zechowski, S. (2014). Shock jocks and their legacy: Introduction. *Journal of Radio & Audio Media*, 21(2), 199–201. doi:10.1080/19376529.2014.950142

Hopmann, D. N., Van Aelst, P., & Legnante, G. (2011). Political balance in the news: A review of concepts, operationalizations and key findings. *Journalism*, 13(2), 240–257. doi:10.1177/1464884911427804

Hopmann, D. N., Shehata, A., & Strömbäck, J. (2015). Contagious media effects: How media use and exposure to game-framed news influence media trust. *Mass Communication and Society*, 18(6), 776–798. doi:10.1080/15205436.2015.1022190

Hyun, K. D., & Kim, J. (2015). The role of new media in sustaining the status quo: Online political expression, nationalism, and system support in China. *Information, Communication & Society*, 18(7), 766–781. doi:10.1080/1369118X.2014.994543

Iosifidis, P. (2016, December 15). The Greek broadcaster ERT: A state or public service broadcaster? [*LSE Media Policy Project Blog*]. Retrieved February 4, 2017 from http://blogs.lse.ac.uk/mediapolicyproject/2016/12/15/the-greek-broadcaster-ert-a-state-or-public-service-broadcaster/

Jones, J. P. (2009). Believable fictions: Redactional culture and the will to truthness. In B. Zelizer (Ed.), *The changing faces of journalism: Tabloidization, technology and truthiness* (pp. 127–143). London, England: Routledge.

Kalogeropoulos, A. (2017). News avoidance. In *Digital News Report*. Oxford, England: Reuters Institute, University of Oxford. Retrieved August 3, 2017 from www.digitalnewsreport.org/survey/2017/news-avoidance-2017/

Kaminska, M., Gallacher, J. D., Kollany, B., Yasseri, T., & Howard, P. N. (2017). Social media and news sources during the 2017 UK General Election. *COMPRO Data Memo 2017.6*, Oxford. Retrieved June 7, 2017 from http://comprop.oii.ox.ac.uk/wp-content/uploads/sites/89/2017/06/Social-Media-and-News-Sources-during-the-2017-UK-General-Election.pdf

Kaye, B. K., & Johnson, T. J. (2004). Weblogs as a source of information about the 2003 Iraq War. In R. D. Berenger (Ed.), *Global media goes to war: Role of news and entertainment media during the 2003 Iraq War* (pp. 291–301). Spokane, WA: Marquette.

Kaye, B. K., & Johnson, T. J. (2011). Hot diggity blog: A cluster analysis examining motivations and other factors for why people judge different types of blogs as credible. *Mass Communication and Society*, 14(2), 236–263. doi:10.1080/15205431003687280

Luhmann, N. (1979). *Trust and power*. Avon, England: John Wiley & Sons Ltd.

Luhmann, N. (2000). *The reality of the mass media*. Stanford, CA: Stanford University Press.

Lynch, M. P. (2012). *In praise of reason: Why rationality matters for democracy*. London, England: MIT Press.

Lynch, M. P. (2016). *The internet of us: Knowing more and understanding less in the age of big data*. New York, NY: Liveright Publishing.

Marchi, R. (2012). With Facebook, blogs and fake news, teens reject journalistic "objectivity". *Journal of Communication Inquiry*, 36(3), 246–262. doi:10.1177/0968859912458700

Morozov, E. (2011). *The net delusion: The dark side of internet freedom* (1st ed.). New York, NY: Public Affairs.

Müller, J. (2013). *Mechanisms of trust: News media in democratic and authoritarian regimes*. Frankfurt, Germany; New York, NY: Campus Verlag.

NAES (National Annenberg Election Survey). (2004). *Daily Show viewers knowledgeable about presidential campaign*. Retrieved April 4, 2017 from http://cdn.annenbergpublicpolicy center.org/wp-content/uploads/2004_03_late-night-knowledge-2_9-21_pr2.pdf

Newman, N., Fletcher, R., Levy, D. A. L., & Nielsen, R. K. (2016). *Reuters Institute digital news report 2016*. Retrieved December 3, 2016 from http://reutersinstitute.politics.ox.ac.uk/sites/default/files/research/files/Digital%2520News%2520Report%25202016.pdf

Newman, N., Fletcher, R., Kalogeropoulos, D., & Nielsen, R. K. (2017). *Reuters Institute digital news report 2017*. Retrieved July 3, 2017 from https://reutersinstitute.politics.ox.ac.uk/sites/default/files/Digital%20News%20Report%202017%20web_0.pdf?utm_source=digitalnewsreport.org&utm_medium=referral

Norris, P. (2000). *A virtuous circle: Political communications in postindustrial societies*. Cambridge, England: Cambridge University Press.

Nyhan, B., & Reifler, J. (2010). When corrections fail: The persistence of political misperceptions. *Political Behavior*, 32(2), 303–330. doi:10.1007/s11109-010-9112-2

O'Neill, O. (2002). *A question of trust*. Cambridge, England: Cambridge University Press.

Orlik, T. (2012, September 19). In China we trust, for now. *The Wall Street Journal*. Retrieved April 11, 2017 from www.wsj.com/news/articles/SB10000872396390444 620104578005610344417502

Perloff, R. M. (2015). A three-decade retrospective on the hostile media effect. *Mass Communication and Society*, 18(5), 701–729. doi:10.1080/15205436.2015.1051234

Perloff, R. M. (2016). What the moon hoax story and other fake news of the past can teach us today. *Cleveland.com*. Retrieved May 28, 2017 from www.cleveland.com/opinion/index.ssf/2016/12/what_the_moon_hoax_story_and_o.html

Putnam, R. D. (2000). *Bowling alone*. New York, NY: Simon & Schuster Paperbacks.

Reynolds, G. H. (2004). The blogs of war. *National Interest*, 75(Spring), 59–64.

Robinson, M. J. (1976). Public affairs television and the growth of political malaise: The case of 'The selling of Pentagon'. *American Political Science Review*, 70(2), 409–432.

Schifferes, S. (2012). Trust-meltdown for business journalism. *British Journalism Review*, 23(2), 55–59.

Schudson, M. (1998). *The good citizen: A history of American civic life*. New York, NY: Free Press.

Seymour-Ure, C. (1974). *The political impact of mass media*. Beverly Hills, CA: Sage Publications.

SHEG (Stanford history education group). (2016). *Evaluating information: The cornerstone of civic online reasoning*. Retrieved January 17, 2017 from https://sheg.stanford.edu/upload/V3LessonPlans/Executive%20Summary%2011.21.16.pdf

Silverstone, R. (2006). *Media and morality: on the rise of the mediapolis*. Cambridge, England: Polity Press.

Staksrud, E., Steen-Johnsen, K., Enjolras, B., Gustafsson, M. H., Ihlebæk, K. A., Midtbøen, A. H., … Utheim, M. (2014). *Status for ytringsfriheten i Norge. Resultater fra befolkningsundersøkelsen 2014* [Status of freedom of expression in Norway: Results from a population survey 2014].(I. Fritt Ord, IMK, FAFO Ed.). Oslo, Norway: Fritt Ord, ISF, IMK, FAFO.

Starkey, G. (2007). *Balance and bias in journalism: Representation, regulation and democracy*. Basingstoke, England; New York, NY: Palgrave Macmillan.

Strömbäck, J. (2015). Social sammanhållning och medianvänding [Social cohesion and media use]. In A. Bergström, B. Johansson, H. Oscarsson, & M. Oskarson (Eds.), *Fragment* (pp. 63–79). Göteborg, Sweden: SOM-institutet.

Strömbäck, J., Djerf-Pierre, M., & Shehata, A. (2016). A question of time? A longitudinal analysis of the relationship between news media consumption and political trust. *International Journal of Press/Politics*, 21(1), 88–110. doi:10.1177/1940161215613059

Strömbäck, J., & Karlsson, M. (2017). Sjunkande förtroende för svenska medier? En analys av hur medborgarnas medieförtroende och betydelsen av partisympati har förändrats mellan 2014 och 2016 [Decreasing confidence in Swedish media? An analysis of how citizens' trust in media and the importance of party preferences have changed between 2014 and 2016]. In L. Truedeson (Ed.), *Misstron mot medier* [Media distrust] (pp. 84–99). Stockholm, Sweden: Institutt for mediestudier.

Stroud, N. J. (2011). *Niche news: The politics of news choice*. Oxford, England: Oxford University Press.

Sundar, S. S. (2008). The MAIN model: A heuristic approach to understanding technology effects on credibility. In A. J. Flanagin & M. J. Metzger (Eds.), *Digital media, youth, and credibility* (pp. 73–100). Cambridge, MA: MIT Press.

Swift, A. (2016). Americans' trust in mass media sinks to new low. *Gallup*. Retrieved May 28, 2017 from www.gallup.com/poll/195542/americans-trust-mass-media-sinks-new-low.aspx

Syvertsen, T. (1999). The many uses of the "public service" concept. *Nordicom Review*, 20(1), 5–12.

TNS Gallup. (2016). *NRKs Profilundersøkelse 2016* [NRK's (public broadcaster in Norway) profile survey 2016].

Tsfati, Y. (2010). Online news exposure and trust in the mainstream media: Exploring possible association. *American Behavioral Scientist*, 54(1), 22–42. doi:10.1177/0002764210376309

Tsfati, Y., & Ariely, G. (2014). Individual and contextual correlates of trust in media across 44 countries. *Communication Research*, 41(6), 760–782. doi:10.1177/0093650213485972

Tsfati, Y., & Cappella, J. N. (2005). Why do people watch news they do not trust? The need for cognition as a moderator in the association between news media skepticism and exposure. *Media Psychology*, 7(3), 251–271. doi:10.1207/S1532785XMEP0703_2

Tuchman, G. (1972). Objectivity as strategic ritual: An examination of newsmen's notions of objectivity. *American Journal of Sociology*, 77(4), 660–679. doi:10.1086/225193

Turner, G. (2005). *Ending the affair: The decline of television current affairs in Australia.* Sydney, Australia: University of New South Wales Press.

Vallone, R. P., Ross, L., & Lepper, M. R. (1985). The hostile media phenomenon: Biased perception and perceptions of media bias in coverage of the Beirut massacre. *Journal of Personality and Social Psychology,* 49(3), 577–585. doi:10.1037=0022–3514.49.3.577

Vartanova, E. (2011). The Russian media model in the context of post-Soviet dynamics. In D. C. Hallin & P. Mancini (Eds.), *Comparing media systems beyond the Western world* (pp. 119–142). New York, NY: Cambridge University Press.

World Values Survey. (2016). Data retrieved December 13, 2016 from: www.worldvalues survey.org/wvs.jsp

Young, E. (2016). *Anew understanding: What makes people trust and rely on news.* American Press Institute. Retrieved June 1, 2017 from www.americanpressinstitute.org/wp-content/uploads/2016/04/What-Makes-People-Trust-and-Rely-on-News-Media-Insight-Project.pdf

Zelizer, B. (2009). *The changing faces of journalism: Tabloidization, technology and truthiness.* London, England: Routledge.

8

THE NET GENERATION WILL REVOLUTIONISE THE WAY WE RELATE TO NEWS

Myth: there is a digital generation with an innate understanding of digital communication

A major reason for conducting studies on how young people relate to news seems to be the assumption that they are the closest we can get to saying something about the future of news exposure, and the studies very often treat their sample of young people as representatives of a new generation of news audience. Concepts like the "net generation" (Tapscott, 1998, 2009), "digital natives" (Prensky, 2001) and the "Internet generation" (Edmunds & Turner, 2005) are used to describe the way in which technology is apparently changing young people's behaviour and creating a new generation of news audiences. These concepts offer a perspective on digital technology, as not solely something that will change the way people that search for and disseminate information, but as something that will produce a new type of mind and intelligence, especially for those who were born into it (Vittadini, Siibak, Reifova, & Bilandzic, 2014).

According to Tapscott (2009), the net generation (born between 1982 and 1991), growing up with the Internet and social media, are also changing the world as we know it. He claims that the net generation is the first generation in history where youth are the authorities on something really important.

> The second half of the twentieth century was dominated by a generation – the baby boomers. During that period, strong models of mass media, enterprise, work, commerce, family, play, and social life were established. The new Web and the new generation are beginning to shatter these old ways – and our evidence points to a better world, if we permit them to succeed. This massive wave of youth has rights, growing aspirations, truly awesome capabilities, and nascent demands that are far-reaching.
>
> *(Tapscott, 2009, p. 310)*

Tapscott describes how the net generation use their massive demographic muscle and unconstrained minds in creating a new world, and how they are using the

Web and their social networks to discover and collaborate, debate and take action in new ways. According to Tapscott, the net generation is also implementing new and radical ideas about the process of democratic governance. He talks about this new generation as a more unified generation, unlike any other, one that is more politically engaged and will seek to share the wealth they create.

Lance W. Bennett (2008, 2009) has similar ideas. He claims there has been a profound shift in citizenship style that seems to be occurring to varying degrees in most post-industrial democracies (Bennett, 2008). He argues that there is a broad, cross-national generational shift in the post-industrial democracies from a "dutiful citizen" model (still adhered to by older generations and many young people who are positioned in more traditional social settings) to an "actualising citizen" model, favouring loosely networked activism to address issues that reflect personal values. While the "dutiful citizen" becomes informed about issues and government by following the mainstream media (mass media), he describes the net generation as "actualising citizens" who mistrust the mainstream media and politicians and receive information from interactive information technology (Bennett, Wells, & Allison, 2009).

However, news consumption is a habit that develops with age. Generations of research into news consumption has found that young people are "just not that into news" (Buckingham, 2000; Marchi, 2012). With each new wave of research, the same concerns are raised: youth are disengaged and things are not what they used to be. So what part of the current wave of change is cyclical and what is genuinely transformative and a consequence of generation differences? In this chapter, we will discuss the myth of young people as a homogeneous net generation of empowered actualising citizens who will receive the news they need and do not have to rely on boring mainstream media to be informed about what is important in society. We will argue that this kind of digital native rhetoric can be dangerous.

Age and generation in news media research

In media research, age is often used as a background variable in the construction of different audience segments and profiles. Age is seldom analysed in its own right, as a research problem in itself (Bolin & Skogerbø, 2013). Many studies of news exposure are based on empirical samples of adolescents, students or young adults, while others compare young and older groups within representative population samples. Recent studies show that news usage is less frequent among young people compared to senior citizens (cf. Elvestad & Blekesaune, 2008; Shehata & Wadbring, 2012), and that younger people use online media and social media for news more often than traditional media such as TV, newspapers and radio (Newman, Fletcher, Levy, & Nielsen, 2016; Pew, 2016). In the European Union, the share of Internet users who participated in social networking was 88% for 16–24 year olds, compared to 66% for 25–54 year olds and 38% for 55–74 year olds (Eurostat, 2016). Similarly, a Pew study revealed that in 2016 the share of Americans who use at least one social media site was 86% for 18–29 years old,

80% for 30–49 years old, 64% for 50–64 years old and 34% for those aged 65 years and older (Pew, 2017).

These studies very seldom have data that allow researchers to make conclusions about a generation. If one uses a concept of generation as age cohorts of people who were born at the same time and also share experiences of similar formative events and collective memories (Eyerman & Turner, 1998; Vittadini et al., 2014), then a media generation refers to cohorts who grew up with a particular media technology and who experience the same media events at the same time in their life. To be part of the same age cohort does not have to mean that you are part of the same generation, and differences between different age groups in a study don't have to be a consequence of generation gaps.

Karl Mannheim's work, *The Sociological Problem of Generations*, from 1952 is a major contribution to the understanding of generations and social change. He distinguishes between generations as solely biological age cohorts and a cultural approach which understands generations on the basis of experiences of formative events. Mannheim (1952, pp. 290–291) claims we must first of all try to understand the generation as a particular type of "social location", and not solely as the biological rhythm of birth and death. He claims that social consciousness and the perspective of youth reaching maturity in a particular time and place is significantly influenced by the major historical events of that era (thus becoming a "generation" in actuality).

> The fact that people are born at the same time, or that their youth, adulthood, and old age coincide, does not in itself involve similarity of location; what does create a similar location is that they are in a position to experience the same events and data etc., and especially that these experiences impinge upon a similarly 'stratified' consciousness. It is not difficult to see why mere chronological contemporaneity cannot itself produce a common generation location.
>
> *(Mannheim, 1952, p. 297)*

So,

> 'age', which in its simplest definitions may refer to an unquestionable personal characteristic, takes on a number of different meanings depending on the perspective applied. 'Generation' refers to a collective that may be defined in relation to many different aspects, e.g. age, experiences, memories, lifestyle, media use, etc.
>
> *(Bolin & Skogerbø, 2013, p. 4)*

Vittadini et al. (2014) argue that the cultural concept of a media generation creates a bridge between demographic absolutism on the one hand and technological absolutism on the other hand. It is neither solely age nor available technology that determines how individuals consume news.

Further, global news media help to give each generation similar collective memories across countries. The experience of evolving historical events, like the Second World War, the fall of the Berlin Wall or the 9/11 attack are transmitted across national boundaries by a small number of news agencies and global news networks and have left their mark on people all over the world. In addition, new media technology has been claimed to be formative for those who were young when this technology was introduced. In a cross-national study, Volkmer and her team (2006) studied how different national media users in three specific generations[1] related to media technologies on the one hand, and on the other, to international media events or news stories such as the first moon landing, the Second World War, the Vietnam War, the assassination of John F. Kennedy, the Prague Spring, Woodstock, the death of Princess Diana etc. Volkmer and the other researchers found that events of the past century are not only historical "facts" but have become substantial elements of a new global collective memory that has been integrated into generational identity worldwide.

The cross-national comparison in this study encourages the idea that the world is an interconnected whole, but it also shows how different perceptions of global and local news emerge from various cultural angles and geographical regions (Volkmer, 2006). These findings show how young people experiencing the same concrete historical media events or the same media technological innovations are part of what Mannheim describes as the same "actual generation", but within the same actual generation different groups of young people will create different experiences and interpretations, which constitutes what Mannheim has defined as separate "generation units" (Mannheim, 1952).

The above discussion of generation highlights how describing an age cohort as a generation, such as the net generation, which assumes similar news experiences and behaviour, is problematic. According to Tapscott (2009), eight characteristics, or norms, describe the net generation and differentiate them from their "boomer" parents (pp. 6–7). They prize freedom and freedom of choice. They want to customise things, make them their own. They're natural collaborators, who enjoy a conversation, not a lecture. They'll scrutinise you and your organisation. They insist on integrity. They want to have fun, even at school. Speed is normal. Innovation is part of life (Tapscott, 2009, pp. 6–7). He drew his conclusion about the net generation from interviews with 5,935 individuals aged between 16 and 29 years old in 12 countries in 2007.

However, research on young people has found that "members of different generations pass through individual life courses, and emphasise that they do so at different historical locations in relation to both society and its media system" (Bolin & Skogerbø, 2013, p. 6). Research data is not always comparable. There are differences in research method and samples. In some studies, young people are children from the age of nine, while in other studies young people are college or university students, including individuals at the age of 30. There is a huge difference between children, adolescents and people in their late twenties when it comes to news exposure. Their news exposure is neither stable nor unchangeable. Even among those identified as the digital natives or the net generation, the way they receive, search for and use the news and engage in political activities will change over their life cycle. We tend to forget that, even among the older generations, news exposure is changing. We agree with Bolin and Skogerbø (2013) who showed how a simple categorisation of media use in different age groups may camouflage other cultural and social aspects of media consumption. The individuals who were born in years defined as years of the digital natives, or the net generation, are not born with the necessary skills for information searching and actively participating in democratic processes in society. School, social background, including their parents and mainstream media, are still important.

Data for studies of young people's news exposure, similar to the majority of media studies, are very often collected in a US context. Despite the global network structure of social media, and the fact that young people across the world are heavy users of social media, there are huge national differences in the way they relate to news. For instance, while less than 20 per cent of the young people in the USA read a newspaper daily (Pew Research Center, 2016), the majority of young people in Norway were still reading their local and national newspapers (mainly online) on a daily basis in 2015 (Vaage, 2016).[2] These variations in political knowledge suggest that there are also variations in the ability of young people to engage effectively in civic or political action in different countries. (cf. Moeller, de Vreese, Esser, & Kunz, 2014).

News exposure is not stable over the life cycle

It is a common perception that people have to be introduced to news at an early stage in life to become news users (Prior, 2007). According to Prior (2007):

> Young people's first experiences with the news are bound to be very important for the formation of their content preferences. After preferences have formed, news content may have little additional impact on them, at least in the short run. This is true among entertainment fans in particular. If your first experiences have taught you that entertainment programming can reliably offer you greater enjoyment than news programming, you have little reason to try news programming again.
>
> *(Prior, 2007, pp. 287–288)*

Similarly, he argues of political interest: "you either get it or you don't" before you are in your early twenties (Prior, 2010). There is little doubt that the early formative years at school and living with parents are of importance for the political socialisation which news exposure is a part of, but there is little evidence that news consumption stabilises permanently at such an early life stage.

Several critics have warned against making assumptions about young people as a global homogenous net generation differing totally from older generations in the ways in which they are exposed to and think about news in society. Recent empirical findings in fact show evidence that the media lives of the "young" are marked by much heterogeneity (Westlund & Bjur, 2014). The reading of quality printed papers is less frequent among the young than among the elderly in all generations (Westlund & Weibull, 2013). Several studies have shown that younger people are more likely than older people to consume news online (Newman et al., 2016; Vaage, 2016) but studies also point out how news exposure changes over the life cycle. For instance, newspaper reading and subscribing are something that increases when individuals settle down, start to work and have children. There is also a danger in focusing only on the effects of digital media use on young people (Holt, Shehata, Strömbäck, & Ljungberg, 2013), and in the oversimplified perception of older age groups (Selwyn, 2004).

The assumption of widespread digital skills among the generation of young people has not been supported by empirical evidence either (Bennett, Maton, & Kervin, 2008; Hargittai, 2010). Studies of the media use of pensioners show that digital skills can be acquired and developed late in life (Riley, 2013). In his study of retired people's Internet use in the UK, Riley argues that "as the Internet has become more pervasive, the distinction made between 'digital natives' and 'digital immigrants' and the concepts of a 'digital' or a 'net' generation appear outmoded" (Riley, 2013, p. 65). Like for other age groups, Riley (2013) found a diversity of knowledge, use and activity within his group of retired Internet users. This also shows how individuals in older generations are not a homogeneous group either, without potential for changing their news exposure. This challenges stereotypical images of the young as "digital natives" and the old as "sporadics" (Brandtzæg, 2012).

Raban and Brynin (2006) argue that: "aging is not a one-dimensional process [and] it would be wrong to assume that only the young have learning curves, even if they move along these curves faster" (p. 43). In Norway in 2016, 58 per cent of the individuals in the age group 67–79 years used the Internet on an average day (Vaage, 2017). Studies of how the younger generation use news media must take into account the fact that older generations may also change their news habits, as several studies have shown (Bakker & de Vreese, 2011; Dimitrova, Shehata, Strömbäck, & Nord, 2011; Holt et al., 2013; Lee, Shah, & McLeod, 2013).

Westlund and Weibull (2013) note that much of the research into generational use is hampered because, typically, in studies of young individuals as a new generation: "there is no longitudinal approach, no cross-generational comparison, no historical reflections on the relations between media and society, and sociology of generations is typically absent in their theoretical frameworks" (Westlund & Weibull, 2013, p. 149). In their own research, they built on unique data,[3] which allows them to investigate how news media exposure varies across generations and life cycle. In their study of the news usage among "dutifuls", "baby boomers", "generation X" and "dotnets" in five media eras[4] in Sweden from 1986 to 2011, they found that generations and life courses are intertwined (Westlund & Weibull, 2013), which implies that there are both generational and age effects. To conclude that the net generation is very different from older generations without taking into account that the young have not stabilised their news habits is more than problematic. The lack of interest in mainstream news about politics and current affairs is part of being a child or an adolescent, and not necessarily a permanent generational position.

Just not that into news

It is not something new that the youngest generation in a society finds the mainstream news media less interesting or less fun than the older generations. Research repeatedly finds that young people express a low level of interest in media coverage of political affairs (Buckingham, 1998; Costera Meijer, 2007) and mainstream news (Westlund & Weibull, 2013). In 1993, J. Katz argued that young people in the UK have a different orientation to news and information, and prefer the more "informal" and "ironic" style of news media to the "monotonously reassuring voice" of conventional news journalism. A few years later, Buckingham (1998, 2000) argued that to avoid what he saw as the "crisis" in young people's relationship with politics and with news journalism, more popular and relevant forms of news journalism for young people were needed (Buckingham, 2000). In his study of 11–17 year old students from the UK and the USA, he found that these young people found news "boring", and he suggested that "the avoidance of 'entertainment' in favour of a narrow insistence on seriousness and formality which characterises dominant forms of news production systematically alienates and excludes substantial sectors of the audience" (Buckingham, 1998, p. 180).

Costera Meijer's study of young people in the Netherlands also highlights the demand for another news format. Her interviews with young people between 15 and 25 in the Netherlands show how young people watch and enjoy light ("stupid", "junk") news on television because it is entertaining (Costera Meijer, 2007). She argues that if news media are to cater to the imagination of young people, they need to be prepared to move beyond the conventional contradiction between quality and popularity, private and public sphere, emotions and reason, autonomy and situatedness (Costera Meijer, 2007, p. 113). In a more recent study of high school students in the USA, Marchi (2012) found that these young people prefer Facebook postings, YouTube videos, blogs, opinionated talk shows and fake news because they find traditional news to be boring and "the same". Further, these high school students argued that news on social media and satirical news programmes provided background information and perspectives that enabled them to understand the larger meanings of political events and develop their own opinions. For them, this was a more truthful and authentic rendition of news (Marchi, 2012, p. 255).

However, the fact that young people prefer to be entertained is not new and neither are the many attempts to engage children and adolescents as avid news consumers. For decades the international newspaper organisation, World Association and Newspapers (WAN), has had young readers as a priority, and has distributed information and stimulus packages with ideas of how to reach a young audience (Elvestad & Fogt, 2010). In Sweden, Ebba Sundin (2004) found newspaper content for children as early as the 1920s, and Elvestad and Fogt (2010) found an increase in the number of newspaper pages designed for children since the 1970s in Norway. Entertainment and "light" news have always been the recipe. Similar strategies have been seen on television. News programmes for children and adolescents are common, particularly on public service channels. Bolin and Skogerbø (2013) show how age groups make up cultural groups, which in turn form niche markets for cultural production (children, teenagers, young adults, mature adults, elderly), but they also stress how media products are designed according to social and background characteristics within an age group. Production of news for young people "the way young people want it" is not easy because young people differ according to social and background characteristics, and they cannot be treated as one homogenous group who want news in one particular way.

According to Marchi (2012), distrust in mainstream media is part of the reason why the high school students she interviewed preferred alternatives, but the net generation do not have a lower level of trust in mainstream media than the older generations. The young people's relative lack of engagement with or awareness of different news sources is not based on some sort of deep-seated mistrust of the news media. A Pew Research study shows that, of the sources they are familiar with, the net generation or Millennials[5] from the USA are no less trusting than older generations (Mitchell, Gottfried & Matsa, 2015). Costera Meijer's (2007) study of young people in the Netherlands also shows how the traditional journalism ideals of independence, factuality and trustworthiness seem to be more important than ever. In 2016, a Norwegian survey showed that 94 per cent of the young people between 15 and 29 years (93 per cent in the total sample) found the public service broadcaster (NRK) to be very good or quite good in fulfilling their goal as a producer of trustworthy news, information and documentary programmes (TNS Gallup, 2016). The same study also showed that 80 per cent of this age group said that the NRK was unbiased (82 per cent in the total sample).

Having a mobile device continuously within arm's reach, young people have changed their media use, but also their news consumption. They now have access to several news sources, both mainstream news and digital native on their mobile phone. Although new online-only providers have some relevance to mobile Internet users, traditional journalism's content dominates the mobile information repertoire (Wolf & Schnauber, 2014). The 2016 digital news report from Reuters also concluded that, although aggregators and social media are important gateways to news, most of the content consumed still comes from newspaper groups, broadcasters, or digital-born brands that have invested in original content (Newman et al., 2016). The decrease in the number of young people who read local morning papers in Sweden does not have to imply that they have lost interest in local news (Wadbring & Bergström, 2015). The local broadcast media retained a stable share over time in this study, and young people may well be consuming local news online or via social media.

Research from the Reuters Institute has also shown that young people are more comfortable when algorithms rather than editors choose their news (Newman et al., 2016). While this might tell us something about young people's attitudes to perceived authority, it does not imply that these young people have the skills or critical understanding necessary to make judgements about the information that they receive this way. In our own research into the news-seeking behaviour of young people in the UK and Norway, we found that, even when they used algorithmic selection through social media, they tended to rely on legacy media for verification and there are far lower levels of trust in social media as a form of news delivery than in, for example, public service media, across all age groups (Elvestad, Phillips, & Feuerstein, 2017). But research also shows that young people are becoming more willing to pay for news. In the USA, the proportion of people aged 18–24 paying for online news rose from 4 per cent in 2016 to 18 per cent in 2017 (Newman, Fletcher, Kalogeropoulos, & Nielsen, 2017). There was an increase in all age groups between 2016 and 2017, but the increase was significantly higher in the youngest age group. This could show a growing awareness that the quality of news is important.

News exposure and political socialisation

According to Tapscott (2009) and Bennett (2008), the net generation are changing the traditional role of mainstream media in democracies but does this mean that young people do not need the traditional news media in their political socialisation? For the last 60 years, there has been a focus on the determinants and mechanisms leading to the development of political efficacy (Beaumont, 2010). Political efficacy is at the core of the beliefs and values needed to participate in a democratic society. Niemi, Craig, and Mattei (1991) distinguish between external efficacy (a belief that governmental authorities and institutions will respond to citizens' demands) and internal efficacy (beliefs about one's own skills or competence to understand and participate in politics). Kaid, McKinney, and Tedesco (2007) use information efficacy as a dimension expressing citizen voters' confidence in their own political knowledge, which is similar to internal efficacy. The traditional media have been found to play a central role in the development of political efficacy among young citizens (Chaffee & Kanihan, 1997; Delli Carpini, 2000; Shah, McLeod, & Lee, 2009) and internal political efficacy is a key driver for turnout in elections for young people (Moeller et al., 2014). In their study in the Netherlands, on a sample of adolescents between 15 and 18 years old, Moeller et al. (2014) tested their internal efficacy in relation to differential media use by using a three-wave panel survey. They found that civic messaging online (participating in differential forms of political online communication)[6] is of importance, but also that newspaper reading online or offline is still the most effective information source with regard to the development of internal political efficacy (Moeller et al., 2014).

Other studies have also shown how traditional media, and newspapers in particular, are of high importance for political interest, political knowledge and civic engagement (for further details, see Chapter 6). In her study of how US youth consume news online, Boulianne (2016) found that online mainstream news increases civic awareness, which indirectly affects civic and political engagement. In a study from South Korea, Lee and Yang (2014) investigated how different news behaviour correlates with political knowledge. "Traditional seekers", who heavily consume news from older media including network television, pay television, newspapers, and radio (and tend to be older and male),[7] outperformed "emerging seekers" who mainly used newer media such as the Internet, mobile, and SNSs for news consumption (and were slightly younger than the other groups)[8] in the acquisition of political knowledge. The news avoiders, which were the largest group in the sample, showed a lower level of political knowledge than both the traditional seekers and the emerging seekers (Lee & Yang, 2014). This study shows that newer media sources do not, on this assessment, seem to replace the informational value of traditional news media and in particular the newspapers (online or offline).

Others argue that the Internet and social media have become the new arena for political information and political socialisation (Bennett, 2008; Tedesco, 2007). Some research (Palfrey & Gasser, 2008) suggests a positive effect on political participation for those who use social media. A Swedish study by Holt and colleagues (2013) shows how frequent social media use among young citizens can function as a leveller in terms of motivating political participation. Based on their study of young people between 16 and 29 years old in the USA, UK and Australia, Xenos, Vromen, and Loader (2014) also argue that there is reason to be optimistic. Their study suggests a strong positive relationship between social media use (time spent on nine popular social media platforms) and political engagement among young people across the three countries. However, this study did not distinguish between various social media platforms and political participation, which makes it impossible to conclude whether social media in general, or particular social media, have greater potential for developing engagement than others. Nor does the researcher include traditional news media exposure (online or offline), so we do not know if heavy social media users are also spending more time on traditional news sources online or not. Other studies indicate that most news on social media comes from mainstream sources (Newman, 2011).

Moeller et al.'s study (2014) also found that digital natives can indeed be well informed and assume an active role in the communication process: "The effect [on internal political efficacy] is stronger than the effects of usage of any of the more passive form of news, including newspapers" (p. 8). However, only 15 per cent of the sample were actively engaged in "civic messaging". Bakker and de Vreese (2011) found that different forms of political participation (offline and online) among 16–24 year olds in the Netherlands are related to the type of media they use. Adolescents with a variety of Internet use (Internet news use, services, e-mail, forums and social networking) are more often politically active both offline and online. This study also shows how young people who prefer, and spend more time on, entertainment programmes, are less politically active (both offline and online). This and other studies (Blekesaune, Elvestad, & Aalberg, 2012; Prior, 2007) have also found that the share of all news avoiders in the population is increasing, especially among the youngest, and in particular among those who choose entertainment rather than news programmes (Aalberg, Blekesaune, & Elvestad, 2013; Bakker & de Vreese, 2011). This highlights the concern that a majority of Tapscott's net generation may not be politically engaged in spite of growing up in an information-rich media environment including the Internet and social media.

Young people are not a homogenous group

Bolin and Skogerbø (2013) show how a simple categorisation of media use in different age groups may camouflage other cultural and social aspects of media consumption. For instance, differences in social background also vary across youth in the net generation. Even in Marchi's study of high school students in the USA there are differences among the adolescents in her sample. For instance, she reported that all those who reported reading a paper daily had parents who subscribed to daily papers (Marchi, 2012, p. 249). Similarly, Xenos et al. (2014) found a positive correlation between parents' education, political talk at home and political engagement, which also indicates that parents who use mainstream media are important for the net generation's political efficacy, knowledge and engagement. Young people want to be entertained and are both idealistic and rebellious, but their parents and other trusted adults are still important for the net generation. Those who read papers daily in Marchi's study (2012) were urged by their teachers, parents, grandparents and older siblings to pay attention to news. In our own studies in the UK and Norway, we have also found that young university students' news exposure is coloured by their parents' news preferences. Anders, a male Norwegian student (26 years) expressed it this way:

> I've got a rather enlightened family, and there are definitely some underlying expectations there that you ought to pay attention to the news, be updated, because that is normally what we discuss in my family, when I'm at home. And I feel a little embarrassed when I haven't paid attention.

Many of Marchi's adolescents also listed these adults as their main sources of news (Marchi, 2012). Conversations with trusted adults are more important now than ever. In a world of "information overload", where youth report feeling overwhelmed by information (Nordenson, 2008), trusted adults can serve as news "filters" and "translators" for young people, pointing out important issues and explaining their relevance. Even Tapscott (2009) claims that older generations' wisdom might be of importance to help the net generation to manage the dark side of the Internet and social media. However, as Anders, the student mentioned above, points out, parents' educational level, political skills, economic status, news media consumption and expectations, matter, and it may vary between young people. Hargittai's (2010) study of a first-year college class of an urban public research university in the USA shows that Internet know-how is not randomly distributed among the population; rather, higher levels of parental education, being male, and being white or Asian American, are associated with higher levels of Web-use skill (Hargittai, 2010).

Regarding parental educational background, her findings suggest that "even when respondents' education level is constant – all respondents in the sample are in their first year of college – parental education nonetheless matters in explaining variation in user skill" (Hargittai, 2010, p. 10).

This generational transference is likely to be impacted both by class and by national political system. OECD studies have shown that parental education is a far less important variable in the literacy levels of children in Sweden than it is in the USA. In the context of the USA, Hargittai (2010, p. 110) argues that the more privileged stand to benefit more from the numerous opportunities on the Internet than those in less advantageous positions, raising concerns about possibly increased rather than decreased inequality resulting from the spread of Internet use across the population. In the Nordic countries, news exposure has been high across different social groups, but in recent years there has been a decline in news consumption, newspaper reading in particular (SOU, 2016; Vaage, 2016), and the information gaps in the parent generation is increasing. This will also affect their children.

This shows how the net generation is not a homogenous group of young people, and how social background interacts with news exposure and its consequences. An early study of types of activities online by user background found that while people with high levels of education are more likely to search for news, people with lower levels of education are more likely to engage in such activities as browsing just for fun, playing a game or gambling online (Howard, Rainie, & Jones, 2001). Further, the need to be watching news out of a sense of duty – to stay informed, be able to join conversations and not be embarrassed ("dutiful citizens" model) was expressed by a small well-educated group in Costera Meijer's (2007) study of youngsters from the Netherlands. These same considerations apply less to others; they feel they will learn about news anyway (Costera Meijer, 2007, p. 104). There are also some cross-national differences. A comparative study showed that while the UK sample is sceptical of institutions and news from traditional news sources, and more politically engaged online (closer to the "actualising citizens" model of Bennett, 2008), the young Norwegians are more in line with the classic "dutiful citizen" (Putnam, 2000) as they trust institutions and follow their traditional news media closely (Elvestad & Phillips, 2017).

There are also gender differences. Women and men follow different types of news stories and they go to different places for their news (Pew Research Center, 2008). While boys or men are more likely to express an interest in foreign news and news about politics, business and sports, girls or women are more likely to express an interest in the environment, art and culture, community news and health news (Buckingham, 2000; Elvestad, 2015; Newman et al., 2016; Pew Research Center, 2008). A recent study among more than 21 million Facebook users in 10 countries across Asia, Africa, the Americas and Europe, showed that the gender differences in civic engagement that exist offline to a large degree are replicated and reinforced on Facebook (Brandtzæg, 2016). Women are more often news avoiders than men (Blekesaune et al., 2012; Newman et al., 2017). Traditional platforms such as print (newspapers) and radio appeal more to men, while social media are significantly more important for news for women, who are also less likely to go directly to a news website or app (Newman et al., 2016). A US study also found that women are more likely to use Facebook for news purposes than men are (Glynn, Huge, & Hoffman, 2012).

The media technology has made it easier for generations across the world to experience similar news and to achieve similar memories. However, as Mannheim (1952) points out, the location where you experience the news events is of importance. Further, it is also important to highlight that there are cross-national differences in media access, both according to technology and content. In the Nordic countries, the number of mobile subscriptions exceeds that of the population, and use and adoption is high in all age groups (Bolin & Westlund, 2009; Skogerbø & Syvertsen, 2004 in Bolin & Skogerbø, 2013, p. 6). In many other countries in the world, access to media technology varies much more between different social groups in the population. Further, the news coverage and framing of similar events are still quite different in the USA, Sweden, Russia or China. Despite growing up at a time when social media is their dominant media, young people across the world do not have the same modes of behaviour, feeling and thought. To talk about a net generation or a generation of digital natives with the same memories and ways of interpreting the world is therefore problematic.

There is evidence that young people's news media exposure is something that is both a result of age (what peers do), generation and life cycle, but gender, class and social background might have become even more important explanatory factors in a high-choice environment. A South Korean study (Lee & Yang, 2014) found that a considerable proportion of media users constantly turn their faces away from news under high-choice conditions (almost three-quarters of the respondents in this study were characterised as news-avoiders who seldom consume news regardless of media or platform). In Europe, those who tune out of the news are more likely to be young, but they do also have less education, are more often female and are less interested in news and politics (Blekesaune et al., 2012; Shehata & Wadbring, 2012).

Based on their study of 9–16 year olds in Sweden, Westlund and Bjur (2014) argue that the pronounced heterogeneity in media life limits the soundness of labelling these young as a generation: "Such intra-generational differences instead call for analysing the presence of so-called generation units (Mannheim, 1952) and generational cohorts (Westlund & Färdigh, 2014), which give significance to groups within a generation" (Westlund & Bjur, 2014, p. 36).

A dangerous rhetoric

In 1998, Tapscott talked of the net generation as a generation of youth who have been taught that everything they see and hear may not be true. He argues that the net generation understands the complexity of the world better than older people do: "The growing wisdom of the new youth stands in stark contrast to the utter dumbness of much of the adult world" (Tapscott, 1998, p. 297). However, the assumption of a whole generation of young people skilled with information and communication technology is rarely grounded in empirical evidence (Hargittai, 2010). This net generation or digital native rhetoric may also be dangerous (Boyd, 2014). It allows parents, teachers and politicians to eschew responsibility for helping young people to access important information. Boyd (2014) highlights how focusing on today's youth as a net generation or digital natives "presumes that all we as a society need to do is to be patient and wait for a generation of these digital wunderkinds to grow up" (p. 197). This attitude is more than problematic, as it disguises social inequalities and does nothing to empower young people to be more sophisticated news consumers.

For young people, the opportunities for receiving and sharing mainstream news is greater than ever and for those who use a variety of sources there are more possibilities for "incidental exposure" (Wonneberger & Kim, 2017). However, the younger generation is not a homogeneous group when it comes to news exposure. It consists of both news junkies and news avoiders who disconnect from news about politics and current affairs (Blekesaune et al., 2012; Prior, 2007) and factors such as social inequality, gender, education level and news exposure are important as well as age. Nor can we assume that the kind of news preferred by young people, and their methods of accessing it, will become a blueprint for the future. Like the generations before them, their needs will change as they grow up. They may be more interested in amusing news as teenagers but, as adults, they may become aware of the need for participation in democratic change – and that this might not always be entertaining.

The naive assumption that there is such a thing as the net generation, and that its members are "naturally" able to understand the digital world in a way that is closed to older people, hides the fact that many young people struggle with finding important information. They still find that the mainstream media offers the most trustworthy news and their parents play an important role in their news media socialisation. As we wait for more research on "generation Z" (who were born in the late 1990s), also called "Post-Millennials" and the "iGeneration", we do not expect them to be a homogenous group of young people either. Perhaps the only attribute that we know this generation have in common is that they will grow up and that maturity will add to, rather than subtract from, their knowledge of the world.

Notes

1   The generations studied were born in three cohorts: 1924–1929 (the radio generation), 1954–1959 (the black-and-white TV generation) and 1979–1984 (the Internet generation).
2   In Norway, 73 per cent in the age group 20–24 years and 54 per cent in the age group 16–19 years "read one or more newspapers online/print on an average day" (Vaage, 2016). In the USA, 17 per cent in the age group 25–34 years and 16 per cent in the age group 18–24 years "read any daily newspaper yesterday" (Pew, 2016).
3   They use data nationally representative of Sweden for the period 1986 to 2011, originating from the annually conducted omnibus survey project organised by the SOM-Institute at the University of Gothenburg, as a partnership between the departments of Political

Science and Journalism, Media and Communication (for further details, see Westlund & Weibull, 2013, p. 158).

4   The first era, called the *legacy media* era (1986–1990), was characterised by a strong newspaper culture (especially local and subscribed newspapers) and a broadcasting system governed through public service institutions (SVT, SR and UR or their public fore-runners). The *commercialisation era* (1991–1995) signifies a period in which broadcasting was deregulated and a number of commercial media firms established operations that included national and local news reporting, especially in television and radio (TV3 and TV4). The *digitisation era* (1996–2001) acknowledges digitisation, as well as the invention and diffusion of the Web and online news sites in the 1990s (such as aftonbladet.se in 1994), but also the rise of free dailies such as the *Metro* in 1998. The *cross-media era* (2002–2006) meant that legacy media as well as commercial broadcasters fuelled a rapid growth of online publishing initiatives, in parallel to their existing news delivery. During the 2000s, news media experimented with additional solutions for publishing and distribu-tion, to become accessible anytime and anyplace, and conglomerates of local newspapers started to publish Web-TV. In 2007, a *ubiquitous media era* took off (2007–2011) as the first successful touch-screen mobile device was launched in Sweden, which was rein-forced through the rapid diffusion of laptops and tablets equipped with mobile broadband (Westlund, 2013, as cited in Westlund & Weibull, 2013, pp. 150–151).

5   Born 1981–1996.

6   Forms of participation in differential political online communication in this study: posting a political message or video on a social network site, chatting or (micro)blogging about politics, signing an online petition, participating in an online discussion, starting an online discussion about politics, organising an online petition, joining a political cause on a SNS, forwarding an e-mail with political content and e-mailing a politician (Moeller et al., 2014).

7   17.7 per cent of the sample.

8   10 per cent of the sample.

References

Aalberg, T., Blekesaune, A., & Elvestad, E. (2013). Media choice and informed democracy. *The International Journal of Press/Politics*, 18(3), 281–303. doi:10.1177/1940161213485990

Bakker, T. P., & de Vreese, C. H. (2011). Good news for the future? Young people, internet use, and political participation. *Communication Research*, 38(4), 451–470. doi:10.1177/0093650210381738

Beaumont, E. (2010). Political agency and empowerment: Pathways for developing a sense of political efficacy in young adults. In L. R. Sherrod, J. Torney-Purta, & C. A. Flanang (Eds.), *Handbook of research on civic engagement in youth* (pp. 525–558). Hoboken, NJ: Wiley.

Bennett, S., Maton, K., & Kervin, L. (2008). The 'digital natives' debate: A critical review of the evidence. *British Journal of Educational Technology*, 39(5), 775–786. doi:10.1111/j.1467-8535.2007.00793.x

Bennett, W. L. (2008). Changing citizenship in the digital age. Civic life online: Learning how digital media can engage youth. In W. L. Bennett (Ed.), *The John D. and Catherine T. MacArthur Foundation Series on Digital Media and Learning* (pp. 1–24). Cambridge, MA: MIT Press.

Bennett, W. L., Wells, C., & Allison, R. (2009). Young citizens and civic learning: Two paradigms of citizenship in the digital age. *Citizenship Studies*, 13(2), 105–120. doi:10.1080/13621020902731116

Blekesaune, A., Elvestad, E., & Aalberg, T. (2012). Tuning out the world of news and current affairs: An empirical study of Europe's disconnected citizens. *European Sociological Review*, 28(1), 110–126. doi:10.1093/esr/jcq051

Bolin, G., & Skogerbø, E. (2013). Age, generation and the media. *Northern Lights*, 11(1), 3–14. doi:10.1386/nl.11.3_2

Bolin, G., & Westlund, O. (2009). Mobile generations: The role of the mobile in the shaping of Swedish media generations. *International Journal of Communication*, 3, 108–124.

Boulianne, S. (2016). Online news, civic awareness, and engagement in civic and political life. *New Media & Society*, 18(9), 1840–1856. doi:10.1177/1461444815616222

Boyd, D. (2014). *It's complicated: The social lives of networked teens*. New Haven, CN: Yale University Press.

Brandtzæg, P. B. (2012). *Social implications of the Internet and social networking sites: A user typology approach* (Unpublished doctoral dissertation). Department of Media and Communication, Faculty of Humanities, University of Oslo, Oslo.

Brandtzæg, P. B. (2016). Facebook is no "Great equalizer": A big data approach to gender differences in civic engagement across countries. *Social Science Computer Review*, Online first. doi:10.1177/0894439315605806

Buckingham, D. (1998). Young people, politics and news media: Beyond political socialisation. *Oxford Review of Education*, 25(1–2), 171–184.

Buckingham, D. (2000). *Making of citizens: Young people, news and politics*. London, England: Routledge.

Chaffee, S. H., & Kanihan, S. F. (1997). Learning about politics from the mass media. *Political Communication*, 14(4), 421–430. doi:10.1080/105846097199218

Costera Meijer, I. (2007). The paradox of popularity: How young people experience the news. *Journalism Studies*, 8(1), 96–116. doi:10.1080/14616700601056874

Delli Carpini, M. X. (2000). Gen.com: Youth, civic engagement, and the new information environment. *Political Communication*, 17(4), 341–349. doi:10.1080/10584600050178942

Dimitrova, D. V., Shehata, A., Strömbäck, J., & Nord, L. W. (2011). The effects of digital media on political knowledge and participation in election campaigns: Evidence from panel data. *Communication Research*, November 2.

Edmunds, J., & Turner, B. S. (2005). Global generations: Social change in the twentieth century. *The British Journal of Sociology*, 56(4), 559–577.

Elvestad, E. (2015). *Barn av informasjonsrike medieomgivelser* [Children of information-rich environments]. Skriftserien fra Høgskolen iBuskerud og Vestfold [Report from University College of Buskerud and Vestfold], nr. 23, 2015. Retrieved January 20, 2016 from https://brage.bibsys.no/xmlui/handle/11250/2368736

Elvestad, E., & Blekesaune, A. (2008). Newspaper readers in Europe: A multilevel study of individual and national differences. *European Journal of Communication*, 23(4). doi:10.1177/0267323108096993

Elvestad, E., & Fogt, A. (2010). *Hva skal vi med aviser når vi har Facebook? Barn og unges forhold til aviser under omstilling* [Do we need newspapers when we have Facebook? Children and young people's relation to newspapers]. Kristiansand, Norway: IJ-forlaget.

Elvestad, E., & Phillips, A. (2017). *The role of news media in high trust and low trust societies*. Paper presented at the European Sociological Association, August 29 to September 1, 2017, Athens, Greece.

Elvestad, E., Phillips, A., & Feuerstein, M. (2017). Can trust in traditional news media explain cross-national differences in news exposure of young people online? *Digital Journalism* (Published online June 16, 2017). doi:10.1080/21670811.2017.1332484

Eurostat. (2016). Statistics from the European Union. Retrieved May 21, 2017 from http://ec.europa.eu/eurostat/web/main/home

Eyerman, R., & Turner, B. S. (1998). Outline of a theory of generations. *European Journal of Social Theory*, 1(1), 91–106. doi:10.1177/136843198001001007

Glynn, C. J., Huge, M. E., & Hoffman, L. H. (2012). All the news that's fit to post: A profile of news use on social networking sites. *Computers in Human Behavior*, 28(1), 113–119.

Hargittai, E. (2010). Digital na(t)ives? Variation in internet skills and uses among members of the "net generation". *Sociological Inquiry*, 80(1), 92–113. doi:10.1111/j.1475-682X.2009.00317.x

Holt, K., Shehata, A., Strömbäck, J., & Ljungberg, E. (2013). Age and the effects of news media attention and social media use on political interest and participation: Do social media function as leveller? *European Journal of Communication*, 28(1), 19–34. doi:10.1177/0267323112465369

Howard, P. E. N., Rainie, L. E. E., & Jones, S. (2001). Days and nights on the internet. *American Behavioral Scientist*, 45(3), 383–404. doi:10.1177/0002764201045003003

Kaid, L. L., McKinney, M. S., & Tedesco, J. C. (2007). Introduction: Political information efficacy and young voters. *American Behavioral Scientist*, 50(9), 1093–1111. doi:10.1177/0002764207300040

Katz, J. (1993). The media's war on kids. *Rolling Stone*, 25(November), 47–49.

Lee, N. J., Shah, D. V., & McLeod, J. M. (2013). Processes of political socialization. *Communication Research*, 40(5), 669–697. doi:10.1177/0093650212436712

Lee, H., & Yang, J. (2014). Political knowledge gaps among news consumers with different news media repertoires across multiple platforms. *International Journal of Communication*, 8(1), 597–617.

Mannheim, K. (1952/2000). The problem of generation. In P. Kecskemeti (Ed.), *Essays on the sociology of knowledge* (pp. 276–321). London, England: Routledge & Kegan Paul.

Marchi, R. (2012). With Facebook, blogs and fake news, teens reject journalistic "objectivity". *Journal of Communication Inquiry*, 36(3), 246–262. doi:10.1177/0196859912458700

Mitchell, A., Gottfried, J., & Matsa, K. E. (2015). Millennials and political news: Social media—the local TV for the next generation?*Pew Research Center: Journalism & Media*. Retrieved December 21, 2016 from www.pewresearch.org/fact-tank/2015/06/01/political-news-habits-by-generation/

Moeller, J., de Vreese, C., Esser, F., & Kunz, R. (2014). Pathway to Political Participation: The Influence of Online and Offline News Media on Internal Efficacy and Turnout of First-Time Voters. *American Behavioral Scientist*, 58(5), 689–700. doi:10.1177/0002764213515220

Newman, N. (2011). *Mainstream media and the distribution of news in the age of social discovery*. Oxford, England: Reuters Institute for the Study of Journalism, University of Oxford.

Newman, N., Fletcher, R., Levy, D. A. L., & Nielsen, R. K. (2016). *Reuters Institute digital news report 2016*. Retrieved December 3, 2016 from http://reutersinstitute.politics.ox.ac.uk/sites/default/files/research/files/Digital%2520News%2520Report%25202016.pdf

Newman, N., Fletcher, R., Kalogeropoulos, D., & Nielsen, R. K. (2017). *Reuters Institute digital news report 2017*. Retrieved July 3, 2017 from https://reutersinstitute.politics.ox.ac.uk/sites/default/files/Digital%20News%20Report%202017%20web_0.pdf?utm_source=digitalnewsreport.org&utm_medium=referral

Niemi, R. G., Craig, S. C., & Mattei, F. (1991). Measuring internal political efficacy in the 1988 National Election Study. *The American Political Science Review*, 85(4), 1407–1413.

Nordenson, B. (2008). Overload! Journalism battle for relevance in an age of too much information. *Columbia Journalism Review*, 47(4), 30–42.

Palfrey, J., & Gasser, U. (2008). *Born digital: Understanding the first generation of digital natives*. New York, NY: Basic Books.

Pew Research Center. (2008). Where men and women differ in following the news. Retrieved May 3, 2017 from www.pewresearch.org/2008/02/06/where-men-and-women-differ-in-following-the-news/

Pew Research Center. (2016). Newspapers: Daily readership by age. Retrieved May 28, 2017 from www.journalism.org/media-indicators/newspapers-daily-readership-by age/

Pew Research Center. (2017). Social media fact sheet. Retrieved May 12, 2017 from www. pewinternet.org/fact-sheet/social-media/

Prensky, M. (2001). *Digital games-based learning.* New York, NY: McGraw-Hill.

Prior, M. (2007). *Post-broadcast democracy: How media choice increases inequality in political involvement and polarizes elections.* New York, NY: Cambridge University Press.

Prior, M. (2010). You've either got it or you don't? The stability of political interest over the life cycle. *The Journal of Politics,* 72(3), 747–766. doi:10.1017/S0022381610000149

Putnam, R. D. (2000). *Bowling alone.* New York, NY: Simon & Schuster Paperbacks.

Raban, Y., & Brynin, M. (2006). Older people and new technologies. In R. Kraut, M. Brynin, & S. Kiesler (Eds.), *Computers, phones, and the Internet: Domesticating information technology* (pp. 43–50), New York, NY: Oxford University Press.

Riley, T. (2013). Self-initiated (re)education of digital technology in retired content creators. *Northern Lights,* 11, 51–69. doi:10.1386/nl.11.51_1

Selwyn, N. (2004). The information aged: A qualitative study of older adults' use of information and communications technology. *Journal of Aging Studies,* 18(4), 369–384. doi:10.1016/j.jaging.2004.06.008

Shah, D. V., McLeod, J. M., & Lee, N. J. (2009). Communication competence as a foundation for civic competence: Processes of socialization into citizenship. *Political Communication,* 26(1), 102–117. doi:10.1080/10584600802710384

Shehata, A., & Wadbring, I. (2012). Allt fler står utanför nyhetsvärlden [More people stand outside the world of news]. In L. Weibull, H. Oscarsson, & A. Bergström (Eds.), *I framtidens skugga* [In the future shadow] (pp. 373–386). Göteborg, Sweden: SOM-institutet.

SOU. (2016). *Människorna, medierna & marknaden* [People, media & market]. Stockholm, Sweden: Statens offentliga utredningar.

Sundin, E. (2004). *Seriegubbar och terrorkrig: barn och dagstidningar i ett förändrat medielandskap* [Cartoon characters and terror war: Children and newspapers in a changed media landscape]. Göteborg, Sweden: Institutionen för journalistik och masskommunikation.

Tapscott, D. (1998). *Growing up digital: The rise of the net generation.* New York, NY: McGraw-Hill.

Tapscott, D. (2009). *Grown up digital: How the net generation is changing your world.* New York, NY: McGraw-Hill.

Tedesco, J. C. (2007). Examining Internet interactivity effects on young adult political information efficacy. *American Behavioral Scientist,* 50(9), 1183–1194. doi:10.1177/0002764207300041

TNS Gallup. (2016). *Profilundersøkelsen for NRK* (Survey data). Survey measuring Norwegians' attitudes toward their national public broadcaster (NRK).

Vaage, O. F. (2016). *Norsk mediebarometer 2015* [Media use in Norway 2015]. Oslo-Kongsvinger, Norway: Statistisk sentralbyrå.

Vaage, O. F. (2017). *Norsk mediebarometer 2016* [Media use in Norway 2016]. Oslo-Kongsvinger, Norway: Statistisk sentralbyrå.

Vittadini, N., Siibak, A., Reifova, I., & Bilandzic, H. (2014). Generations and media: The social construction of generational identity and differences. In N. Carpentier, L. Hallett, & K. C. Schrøder (Eds.), *Audience transformations: Shifting audience positions in late modernity* (pp. 65–81). New York, NY: Routledge.

Volkmer, I. (2006). *News in public memory: An international study of media memories across generations.* New York, NY: Peter Lang.

Wadbring, I., & Bergström, A. (2015). A print crisis or a local crisis? *Journalism Studies,* Online. doi:10.1080/1461670X.2015.1042988

Westlund, O., & Bjur, J. (2014). Media life of the young. *Young,* 22(1), 21–41. doi:10.1177/1103308813512934

Westlund, O., & Färdigh, M. A. (2014). Accessing the news in an age of mobile media: Tracing displacing and complementary effects of mobile news on newspapers and online news. *Mobile Media & Communication*, 3(1), 53–74.

Westlund, O., & Weibull, L. (2013). Generation, life course and news media use in Sweden 1986–2011. *Northern Lights*, 11(1), doi:147–173. doi:10.1386/nl.11.147_1

Wolf, C., & Schnauber, A. (2014). News consumption in the mobile era: The role of mobile devices and traditional journalism's content within the user's information repertoire. *Digital Journalism*, 3(5), 759–776. Published online August 14, 2014. www.tandfonline.com/doi/full/10.1080/21670811.2014.942497

Wonneberger, A., & Kim, S. J. (2017). TV news exposure of young people in changing viewing environments: A longitudinal, cross-national comparison using people-meter data. *International Journal of Communication*, 11, 72–93.

Xenos, M., Vromen, A., & Loader, B. D. (2014). The great equalizer? Patterns of social media use and youth political engagement in three advanced democracies. *Information, Communication & Society*, 17(2), 151–167. doi:10.1080/1369118x.2013.871318

9

CONCLUSION

We started out to write a book that would examine the myths that have built up around the Internet. On the one hand, these myths suggested that human agency would be powerless to control this transformational force, but on the other hand it would open up democratic processes; enfranchise the marginalised; usher in a new era of bottom-up news in which audiences would become participants in the processes of news-making; make us all global citizens; and deprive old media of its legitimacy. Over the final months of writing, it has been an effort to sidestep a new wave of myth-making, with almost daily news updates on stolen elections, oligarchs of the Internet with secret plans to manipulate data, and moral panics about fake news.

We have concerns about all of these things but our object has not been to add to a new set of myths, but to drill down into a growing body of audience and media research and look for deeper patterns and shifts that will stand the test of time and help us to understand how the news landscape is changing, the forces that are changing it and how they differ, according to the national and international regulatory landscape and varying media systems. The evidence we have found, from international news audience research, challenges these myths. It tells us that we are not helpless in the face of technology, nor are we liberated by it. As with previous major technical shifts, we are in the process of adapting it to our needs and that process varies according to who we are and where we live. Much of the available audience research comes from the USA. We have used it cautiously and critically, wherever possible finding studies from elsewhere that challenge or question its assumptions.

One thing we can be sure of is that human behaviour is not fixed; we learn and adapt, so that everything we have discovered is subject to change. We have no way, for example, of being able to tell how the "discovery" of fake news by the mainstream news media will impact on the way in which news is consumed in the future. However, as we complete this book, we are already aware of what appears to be a related event: the rise in the number of people who have taken out sub-scriptions to *The New York Times* and the similar rise in the numbers of people becoming supporters of the UK-based *Guardian*. This is a timely reminder of the reflexivity of audiences and the ability of individuals to evaluate events and adjust their own behaviour in the face of threats. So, although our conclusion may be pessimistic about the democratic performance of the Internet, we remain opti-mistic about the ability of human beings to act collectively in order to safeguard democratic gains.

The impact of personalisation

Both the promise and the threat of the World Wide Web lie in the ability to personalise data (Chapter 2). The algorithms that power Google, Facebook and other online platforms allow us instant access to each other and to the most up-to-date data on any subject. But unless we know how to use search tools and are sufficiently aware of how data is produced to be able to evaluate what we read, the World Wide Web has become largely a means by which personal data is manipulated by com-mercial or political interests, for ends that have little to do with personal enlight-enment. This shift from the "Daily Me" (Negroponte, 1995), a conception of communication in which each individual devises their own information network, to what Joseph Turow (2011) calls the "Daily You", in which our attention is a com-modity bought and sold by others, is powered by the desire for Net entrepreneurs to make money out of our engagement online. As we discuss in Chapter 4, ("The Wisdom of Crowds?"), for those who consume their news via any form of online aggregator, this means that attention is being focused not on what might be useful to us democratically, but on news items that are most likely to be shared.

This looks like the ultimate audience-powered news-machine and indeed in some ways it is, but there are serious drawbacks for society about a system of news distribution based entirely on personal preferences. The myth of democratisation rested on the hope that easy access to a wealth of varied information would expose us all to a wider variety of differing views online than is usually available via mainstream news. Research evidence indicates that those exposed to more varied information are more tolerant of the views of other people (Yardi & Boyd, 2010). Conversely, the more people are exposed to a single, narrow viewpoint, the less tolerant they become of alternatives and the more likely it is that contradictory information will serve to confirm their prejudice rather than challenging it (Stroud, 2010). However, as we discuss in Chapter 2, computerised, personalised selection is far less likely to include "cross-cutting" information than selections made by indi-viduals themselves (Beam, 2014; Zuiderveen Borgesius et al., 2016) and, with the advent of social media, computerised selection is becoming the norm.

Algorithmic news selection, based on audience preferences, focuses on news that is popular and will spread virally, rather than news that is important but may not be passed on. This popular news is spread when people respond emotionally. Those who post rarely consider the source of what they pass on, or its veracity (Barthel, Mitchell, & Holcomb, 2016); they are responding emotionally to heuristic cues, which resonate with their own past experience (Crawford, Hunter, & Filipovic, 2015, p. 122). The cumulative effect of people passing on news that causes an emotional reaction to people in their own friendship groups, or with similar views to themselves, tends to narrow news choices and has opened up a greater likelihood of polarisation between those who are informed and those who are not and between those with differing political views (Pariser, 2011; Prior, 2007; Sunstein, 2009). Indeed, the impact of personalisation has been to atomise news so that no two people receive exactly the same daily information and those with different life experiences may have no idea of what others think or feel about events even if they live next door.

Perhaps the clearest evidence of this polarising effect lies in the political shifts of 2016 and 2017. In the UK and the USA, mainstream media found that they had been insulated from the full extent of the rising levels of social discontent circulating online. In spite of the different kinds of media situations in these two countries and the different role of mainstream media, the polarising bubbles of the Internet had worked so effectively that even those whose job it is to find out what is happening in their society had failed to spot the depth of disaffection with the status quo, or the degree to which this attitude had spread from initial bubbles of discontent into the practical politics of voting. There is some evidence that this activity was fostered by political campaigners making use of the ability to personalise messages and focus them on specific groups of people (Chapter 4) but it is the function of the algorithms themselves that makes this messaging so potent.

For those who mainly consume news online via aggregators (on social media or otherwise) and do not access mainstream media directly, algorithms ensure that personal prejudice takes the place of editorial judgement in selecting what appears in our feeds. As we explain in Chapter 4, the need to appeal to audience prejudice is now also leading a shift in news organisations themselves towards emotional, as opposed to reasoned, journalism as they attempt to find new sources of funding online (Wadbring & Ödmark, 2016). Of course, human editors have never been above selecting news for its emotional impact, rather than its political probity. Indeed, the success of Fox News in the USA and the British tabloid press has long been predicated on the desire to give the readers what they want. However, as we find in Chapter 7 on Trust, when news is clearly branded and labelled, audiences are better able to recognise what is trustworthy and what is entertainment (Hopmann, Shehata, & Strömbäck, 2015). In social media, all news looks much the same and it is harder to establish where it comes from. Research suggests that many young people have a hard time working out what is fake and what is fact (Barthel et al., 2016).

News audiences and political action

As we discuss in Chapter 3, when raw information finds its way into the public domain, via social media, it is still largely journalists, not audience members, who put it into a form that can easily be accessed. But journalism is expensive to produce and news organisations are retreating, damaged by the loss of advertising revenue, which is flowing away from news and into the pockets of the Internet tycoons. New online news sources have not taken the place of the traditional mainstream media (particularly at local level) because they have exactly the same difficulty in finding sources of revenue as the news media they seek to displace. While the Internet rewards those producing popular, personalised material, it is less helpful to those who seek to provide a broad diet of news, and the result is that local communities are being left without the information they need for democratic engagement (Chapter 6) (Hoffman & Eveland, 2010).

Those who depend on social media for news updates may be losing out on a broad diet of news information, but political activists have found Internet communications a boon. As we explore in Chapter 6, the ability to instantly share information with like-minded people has allowed people to spread information and organise more easily. This has intensified bonding social capital, but on the other hand, it appears to be having the opposite effect on the creation of bridging capital because it creates divisions between people who may share a locale but have no shared cultural connections. There are similar contradictions in our use of the Internet to make global connections (see Chapter 5). In the early days of the Web it was assumed that the ability to communicate across geographic borders would turn us all into global citizens. Certainly we are now capable of making contact with like-minded people in other countries, but the impact of personalisation, with its narrow focus on personal likes and attributes, makes it unlikely that any of us will stumble across debates in other languages on subjects that are not of the most immediate personal utility. We can certainly find information if we seek it out, but for the majority of people, news has become more national rather than more global.

This tendency for the algorithmic organisation of the Web to favour close bonds over cosmopolitan, bridging connections, has meant that it is particularly helpful for those keen to pull people together along lines of separation. This favours the politics of xenophobia and anger but is less useful for the more nuanced debates needed to build bridges between people who are unfamiliar with one another. Indeed, so toxic has social media become to those who are not politically aligned, that it is now harder to disagree online than it is in real life. People fear being socially ostracised or attacked if they step out of line (Flaxman, Goel, & Rao, 2016; Jang, Lee, & Park, 2014). To be sure the ingenuity of people who believe in connection, rather than division, has led to the practice of "virtue-signalling" in which people are able to wordlessly demonstrate their solidarity with people going through difficult experiences by changing their Facebook profile. But the closed bubbles of the Internet mean that people who disagree with such actions are largely insulated from them until they are picked up by the mainstream media.

Who do we trust?

Surveys on trust are hard to compare because people don't tend to trust news media in general; they trust specific sources – usually those that are most in tune with their own beliefs. Trust levels also fluctuate, rising and falling according to external events and according to an individual's perceived distance from the political consensus. However, in most countries, people say that they trust traditional mainstream media more than alternative forms of news found on social media or served up via aggregators (EBU, 2016; Newman, Fletcher, Levy, & Nielsen, 2016). Trust in mainstream media also tends to be higher in countries that have independent public service media (EBU, 2016; Müller, 2013), and in these countries there is also a greater tendency to be prepared to pay for news than there is in countries with highly commercialised news services that are entirely supported by advertising.

Surveys find that younger people also tend to trust legacy and public service broadcasting (PSB) media more than alternative sources, but they suggest that young people are apt to believe that news edited by computers is more trustworthy than human editors (Newman et al., 2016) and that news written by robots is more reliable than that produced by human journalists (Graefe, Haim, Haarmann, & Brosius, 2016). We have no way of predicting whether they will change their views and news habits as they mature (as generations before them have done), whether they will develop the means and the tools with which to evaluate what they read through social media, or whether they will remain loyal to mainstream news and re-learn the habit of paying for it.

Young people are not a homogeneous group; their news consumption varies according to their social background and nationality, just as that of their parents does (Chapter 8), and they are as dependent as the generations before them on the guidance of older people in forming their news habits. If there is a specific concern to be drawn from research, it is that we should not take it for granted that being born into the "net generation" brings with it the skills to navigate online, any more than being born into the car generation ensured that their parents knew how to drive. Young people learn about news and democratic engagement from those with experience – just as they have always done. If we assume that they have some form of innate knowledge, by virtue of their youth, we are not honouring them; we are failing them.

Today's young people are no more "into news" than their parents were at the same age. However, they are learning their news habits from adults who, far from being drawn into democratic engagement by the increase in choice, are increasingly disengaged from news. News avoidance has been growing in the older democracies (see Chapters 2 and 8) but it is not just a problem of the young; it affects everyone, particularly those living with highly commercialised news media. In countries with high levels of news avoidance, the groups least likely to access news regularly, and least likely to have knowledge of political events, tend to be those with lower levels of education – and to be women rather than men (Aalberg & Curran, 2012). These "news gaps" increase inequality, fuel myths and conspiracy theories and fuel political apathy, and they are of far greater significance in countries that do not have independent, public service news media.

The need for a mediated centre

The Internet is not a neutral space. It is a reflection of offline society, but crucially, without the legal checks and balances that have been agreed to protect democracy. The speed at which algorithmically organised news has developed, and the gap in public understanding of how it works, has allowed changes to take place below the radar of democratic oversight. Although large-scale research in the USA (Prior, 2007) had already foreshadowed the likely impact of increased choice on political polarisation, the introduction of social media, as a vehicle for news dissemination, speeded up change in ways that have outrun the slower pace of democratic deliberation.

It is not the first time that a major technical change has impacted the news landscape. Concerns about the telegraph, radio and television also led to debates about how new media technology should be managed in order to preserve fairness and plurality of political messaging and to prevent influential news media from falling into monopoly control. In the past, the forms of intervention in Europe and the USA have been different. Europe favoured taking the means of media dissemination into public ownership or providing licences for the use of it. In the USA, commercial monopolies were allowed to develop. In the case of broadcasting they were, for a short time, subject to regulation, but thereafter left broadly to the market.

Now the global reach of the Internet, and the location of the largest Internet firms in California, has meant that US free-market policies have found their way inside the more closed European systems as well as the increasingly de-regulated markets of India and elsewhere. The sheer size of the Californian oligopoly, and the degree to which their products have so swiftly been embedded into everyday practices, has left policy makers on the sidelines. At first, the reflexive assumption was to accept them on the basis of their own rhetoric and to treat them as insurgent new businesses, rather than as media companies. They have been allowed to expand without any of the checks and balances that have been built into democratic systems to control the growth of media monopolies and without the regulatory oversight that is intended (rather weakly) to promote plurality of media voices.

The response of news organisations has been to try to accommodate to the disruption by hyper-commercialising and personalising their own products while, at the same time, attacking public service media for having the temerity to compete in the same online space. However, as research now demonstrates, it is in those countries that maintain well-funded, independent public service media that the majority of people have continued to trust their media and to be reasonably well informed during this period of extreme disruption to news services (EBU, 2016; Tsfati & Ariely, 2014). In countries with high levels of trust in mainstream news, PSBs haven't simply provided information, they have also set standards for news production across the sector and, where there are strong PSB services, there tends also to be a generally higher level of news consumption (Aarts, Fladmoe, & Strömbäck, 2012). The UK is the outlier here. Its hyper-commercial, tabloid press enjoys the lowest trust ratings in Europe (EBU, 2016).

The Internet has undoubtedly opened up channels of communication for subaltern voices. These voices have not necessarily been progressive and have often been disruptive, but the ability to collectively demonstrate outrage has forced that anger into the mainstream, where it has crossed over from the insulated bubbles of private complaint and into public consciousness. But without the continuing existence of mainstream media, producing common news narratives available to all, at both local and national level, the Internet will too easily become a place that divides us into factions rather than uniting us into communities. The Internet was designed as a space of dispersed networks but democratic debate requires a central space in which ideas can be both heard and contested. Without a centre, there cannot be a periphery, merely a number of unconnected and deeply divided spheres (Karppinen, 2013).

The research we have analysed tells us that the best way of ensuring that a central space for democratic debate is maintained, and not polluted by accusation and counter-accusation of bias and "fake news", is by investing in public service media that is rigorously independent and funded for the public good. PSBs will never be capable of satisfying all political factions. That is not their role. They need to be protected for the same reason they were invented: as a bulwark against totalitarianism and a means by which people can speak and be heard across bitter divisions. The compromises necessary for communities to live together cannot be made if we are unable to hear one another.

In every study that examines the effectiveness of news media in ensuring that all citizens are equally well informed, the evidence clearly demonstrates that the provision of publically funded, independent media improves outcomes. Those with access to publicly funded media are better informed (Aalberg & Curran, 2012; Esser et al., 2012; Soroka et al., 2013), and more aware of debates across the political spectrum or less polarised (Fletcher, 2017a). There appears also to be some evidence that people are more willing to pay for news media in countries that maintain well-respected and universal public service provision (Fletcher, 2017b).

It may now be time to consider whether it is in the interests of democracy for the major communication platforms to be owned by private companies operating globally. When John Perry Barlow wrote the declaration of the independence of Cyberspace, he said: "Governments derive their just powers from the consent of the governed. You have neither solicited nor received ours" (Barlow, 1996, web page). Well, today we are all citizens of Cyberspace and the mood has changed. There seems little doubt that governments, particularly in Europe, will move towards the regulation of the Internet, almost certainly with a view to curtailing "extremist" political activity. This is a difficult and dangerous moment because moves to limit communication, without at the same time considering ownership structures, will almost certainly hand increased power to global elites and marginalise peripheral voices of all kinds.

The evidence we have gathered here suggests that, while discussion is underway and will continue well into the future, communities will need to ensure that, whatever is being discussed in the closed spaces of the Internet, there is always a parallel debate that happens in the open space of public media. We need to protect both spaces, ensure that they remain accessible to all, and that young people are equipped with the knowledge to navigate online as well as offline.

References

Aalberg, T., & Curran, J. (2012). *How media inform democracy: A comparative approach.* London, England: Routledge.

Aarts, K., Fladmoe, A., & Strömbäck, J. (2012). Media, political trust, and political knowledge. In T. Aalberg & J. Curran (Eds.), *How media inform democracy: A comparative approach* (pp. 98–118). London, England: Routledge.

Barlow, J. P. (1996). Declaration of the Independence of Cyberspace. *The Electronic Frontier Foundation.* Retrieved June 2, 2017 from www.eff.org/cyberspace-independence

Barthel, M., Mitchell, A., & Holcomb, J. (2016). Many Americans believe fake news is sowing confusion. *Pew Research Center: Journalism & Media.* Retrieved June 10, 2017 www.journalism.org/2016/12/15/many-americans-believe-fake-news-is-sowing-confusion/

Beam, M. A. (2014). Automating the news: How personalized news recommender system design choices impact news reception. *Communication Research*, 41(8), 1019–1041.

Crawford, H., Hunter, A., & Filipovic, D. (2015). *All your friends like this: How social networks took over the news.* Sydney, Australia: HarperCollins.

EBU. (2016). Trust in media 2016. *The European Broadcasting Union Media Intelligence Service.* Retrieved December 18, 2016 from www.ebu.ch/publications/trust-in-media-2016

Esser, F., de Vreese, C., Strömbäck, J., van Aelst, P., Aalberg, T., Stanyer, J., ... Reinemann, C. (2012). Political information opportunities in Europe: A longitudinal and comparative study of 13 television systems. *International Journal of Press/Politics*, 17(3), 247–274. doi:10.1177/1940161212442956

Flaxman, S., Goel, S., & Rao, J. M. (2016). Filter bubbles, echo chambers, and online news consumption. *Public Opinion Quarterly*, 80(S1), 298–320. https://doi.org/10.1093/poq/nfw006

Fletcher, R. (2017a). *Polarisation in the news media.* Reuters Institute digital news report. Oxford: University of Oxford. Retrieved August 1, 2017 from www.digitalnewsreport.org/survey/2017/polarisation-in-the-news-media-2017/

Fletcher, R. (2017b). *Paying for news.* Reuters Institute digital news report. Retrieved August 20, 2017 from www.digitalnewsreport.org/survey/2017/paying-for-news-2017/

Graefe, A., Haim, M., Haarmann, B., & Brosius, H. B. (2016). Readers' perception of computer-generated news: Credibility, expertise, and readability. *Journalism*, Online first. doi:10.1177/1464884916641269

Hoffman, L. H., & Eveland, W. P. (2010). Assessing causality in the relationship between community attachment and local news media use. *Mass Communication and Society*, 13(2), 174–195. doi:10.1080/15205430903012144

Hopmann, D. N., Shehata, A., & Strömbäck, J. (2015). Contagious media effects: How media use and exposure to game-framed news influence media trust. *Mass Communication and Society*, 18(6), 776–798. doi:10.1080/15205436.2015.1022190

Jang, S. M., Lee, H., & Park, Y. J. (2014). The more friends, the less political talk? Predictors of Facebook discussions among college students. *Cyberpsychology, Behavior, and Social Networking*, 17(5), 271–275.

Karppinen, K. (2013). *Rethinking media pluralism.* New York, NY: Fordham University Press.

Müller, J. (2013). *Mechanisms of trust: News media in democratic and authoritarian regimes.* Frankfurt, Germany; New York, NY: Campus Verlag.

Negroponte, N. (1995). *Being digital.* London, England: Hodder & Stoughton.

Newman, N., Fletcher, R., Levy, D. A. L., & Nielsen, R. K. (2016). *Reuters Institute digital news report 2016.* Retrieved December 3, 2016 from http://reutersinstitute.politics.ox.ac.uk/sites/default/files/research/files/Digital%2520News%2520Report%25202016.pdf

Pariser, E. (2011). *The filter bubble: What the internet is hiding from you.* London, England: Penguin.

Prior, M. (2007). *Post-broadcast democracy: How media choice increases inequality in political involvement and polarizes elections.* New York, NY: Cambridge University Press.

Soroka, S., Andrew, B., Aalberg, T., Iyengar, S., Curran, J., Coen, S., ... Tiffen, R. (2013). Auntie knows best? Public broadcasters and current affairs knowledge. *British Journal of Political Science*, 43(4), 719–739. doi:10.1017/S0007123412000555

Stroud, N. J. (2010). Polarization and partisan selective exposure. *Journal of Communication*, 60(3), 556–576.

Sunstein, C. R. (2009). *Republic.com 2.0.* Princeton, NJ: Princeton University Press.

Tsfati, Y., & Ariely, G. (2014). Individual and contextual correlates of trust in media across 44 countries. *Communication Research*, 41(6), 760–782. doi:10.1177/0093650213485972

Turow, J. (2011). *The daily you: How the new advertising industry is defining your identity and your worth.* New Haven, CN: Yale University Press.

Wadbring, I., & Ödmark, S. (2016). Going viral: News sharing and shared news in social media. *Observatorio*, 10(4), 132–149. doi:10.15847/obsOBS1042016936

Yardi, S., & Boyd, D. (2010). Dynamic debates: An analysis of group polarization over time on Twitter. *Bulletin of Science, Technology & Society*, 30(5), 316–327.

Zuiderveen Borgesius, F. J., Trilling, D., Moeller, J., Bodó, B., de Vreese, C. H., & Helberger, N. (2016). Should we worry about filter bubbles? *Internet Policy Review*, 5(1). doi:10.14763/2016.1.401

INDEX